Washington Arsenal, 1803-1881

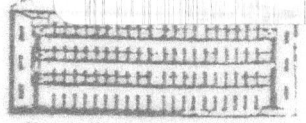
District Penitentiary, 1831-1862

SILENT SENTINEL ON THE POTOMAC
Fort McNair, 1791–1991

Army War College, 1907-1941
National War College 1946
Engineer School, 1901-1919

Industrial College of the Armed Forces, 1962

National Defense University
Academic Operational Center 1992

Phyllis I. McClellan

HERITAGE BOOKS
2012

HERITAGE BOOKS
AN IMPRINT OF HERITAGE BOOKS, INC.

Books, CDs, and more—Worldwide

For our listing of thousands of titles see our website
at
www.HeritageBooks.com

Published 2012 by
HERITAGE BOOKS, INC.
Publishing Division
100 Railroad Ave. #104
Westminster, Maryland 21157

Copyright © 1993 Phyllis I. McClellan

Other Heritage Books by the author:
The Artillerymen of Historic Fort Monroe, Virginia

All rights reserved. No part of this book may be reproduced or transmitted in any form or by any means, electronic or mechanical, including photocopying, recording or by any information storage and retrieval system without written permission from the author, except for the inclusion of brief quotations in a review.

International Standard Book Numbers
Paperbound: 978-1-55613-848-5
Clothbound: 978-0-7884-8997-6

CONTENTS

LIST OF PHOTOGRAPHS v

ACKNOWLEDGMENTS vii

    I.   PROLOGUE 1

    II.   1800-1825, GROWTH OF THE ARSENAL..............................9

    III.   1825-1850, PEACE AND WAR..21

    IV.   1831-1867, THE PENITENTIARY..33

    V.   1850-1875, EXPANSION...47

    VI.   1875-1900, END OF AN ERA..61

    VII.   1901-1919, ENGINEER SCHOOL..73

    VIII.   RECONSTRUCTION, DATE AND COST OF BUILDINGS..........87

    IX.   1904-1941, ARMY WAR COLLEGE......................................131

    X.   1925-1950, OUT OF ONE WAR INTO ANOTHER 147

    XI.   NEW MISSIONS..161
            National War College 163
            Industrial College of the Armed Forces 165
            Inter-American Defense College....................................170
            Old Guard...171
            Military District of Washington 172

    XII.   1950-1975, LIFE ON POST..177

    XIII.   1975-1991, THE LAST QUARTER CENTURY 187
            National Defense University..187
            Life on Post, 1975-1991 189

    XIV.   EPILOGUE 199

ENDNOTES 201

APPENDIX A: POST COMMANDERS, 1791-1991 209

APPENDIX B: OCCUPANTS OF OFFICERS' QUARTERS....................213

GLOSSARY 245

BIBLIOGRAPHY 247

INDEX..259

PHOTOGRAPHS

page

6	1. Military District #5 showing US Arsenal.
14	2. Washington Arsenal Headquarters, 1803-1881.
26	3. Washington Arsenal and Long Bridge over the Potomac.
34	4. District Penitentiary, 1831-1862.
42	5. Quarters #20, east end of Penitentiary built in 1830.
43	6. Lincoln conspirators' trial room in building #20.
45	7. Hanging of Lincoln conspirators, Washington Arsenal.
48	8. Matthew Brady photo: Washington Arsenal and Pendulum Houses.
52	9. On Guard at Model Museum, Washington Arsenal, c.1860s.
54	10. Ramsay family at Washington Arsenal.
56	11. Map of Washington Barracks after penitentiary was razed.
66	12. Dredge creating boat channel and Hains Point, 1890s.
77	13. Model Museum (c. 1838), Engineer Administration Office.
79	14. Engineer floating pile driver, Washington Barracks.
81	15. Engineer masonry students, Company K, 3d Battalion.
86	16. Concrete pilings for officer's quarters.
88	17. Washington Barracks Six-Gun Gate, 1918.
90	18. Latticed rear porches of officer's quarters.
91	19. Officer's quarters completed in 1905 with hospital in rear.
93	20. Old Hospital steward's house (1887-1910); new house #16 (1900).
94	21. Building #17, Engineer Photo Lab with YMCA on left in rear, 1918.
96	22. Layout of Golf Course in 1935-39.
98	23. Engineer Band Barracks showing a boat mast in James Creek.
100	24. Old Quarters 2-B (now #20)
102	25. Major Ord's living room in #21-1 c. 1935.
104	26. Old NCO quarters at Washington Barracks.
105	27. New NCO duplexes built in 1905.
112	28. Historic Bar in NCO Club.
116	29. Unfinished west end of Barracks #52; Present IADC.
118	30. 1880 frame hospital replaced in 1894 by building #54.
119	31. 1894 Army General Hospital, wings added in 1901.
120	32. Army General Hospital tents c. 1898, Washington Barracks.
123	33. Major Walter Reed.
125	34. McNair Room in the Officers' Club was a reading room (1910).

127	35.	LTG L J McNair with artist, Sgt W W Cummings and wife.
132	36.	Placing 20-ton lintel on entrance to Army War College, 1906.
135	37.	Teddy Roosevelt dedicating cornerstone of AWC, 1903.
141	38.	Camp Washington with tents and portable barracks, 1918.
144	39.	1928 photo shows James Creek open; note gardens on banks.
158	40.	Dedication of Fort L J McNair, 14 Jan 1948.
167	41.	NWC, Eisenhower Hall, and ICAF tempo before it burned-1960.
188	42.	Armed Forces Staff College, Norfolk, Virginia.
194	43.	National Defense University Academic Operations Center-1991.

Acknowledgments

The inspiration for this work came from two National Defense University Special Collections Librarians, Susan Lemke and Tina Lavato. They offered me a copy of Julian Raymond's 1951 manuscript which dwelt heavily on the Lincoln Conspiracy Trial. Once they had me hooked on the history of Fort L J McNair, they provided phenomenal sources from their archives which outlined a sequence of events over the past 200 years.

This same dedicated assistance was given by the National Archives, Library of Congress, Office of Military History, and Columbia Historical Society. Some vital notes were lost, so to give credit where it is due I shall have to rely on an untrustworthy memory. John McClellan and Chris Kohler gave me computer advice and assistance. Karen Ackermann of Heritage Books suggested I winnow the wheat from the chaff to condense the text, and Roxanne Carlson expertly edited the result.

Others who helped and inspired me include: Karen McClellan, Rob Alley, Jim Dixon, Joe Owens, Kirk Lewis, Linda Knight, Harold Schram, Brian Cooper, Red Sullivan, Bob Streeter, Jack Webb, Robert Collier, Mike Meiers, Jonathan Heller, Martin Gordon, Kay Keith, Tom Mani, Gayle Osborn, and the 120 former residents who answered my letters. I am also grateful to the National Defense University, the Corps of Engineers' Historical Office, and the Walter Reed Army Medical Facility who reproduced photographs requested.

Pierre L'Enfant's foresight in reserving this vital spit of land to guard the nation's capital has provided a silent sentinel which still fervently serves this country.

Phyllis I. McClellan
1425 4th St SW A-1
Washington DC 20024

CHAPTER I: *Prologue*

The sentinel posted at the confluence of the Anacostia (Eastern Branch) and the Patawomeke (Potomac) Rivers in the District of Columbia was earmarked in 1791 by the visionary French emigre, Pierre L'Enfant, to be Military District #5 at Greenleaf's Point. This installation was established, grew, and has been razed, renamed, remodeled, rebuilt, and renovated. Like any good sentinel, it has dutifully performed each mission assigned. Hold on to that thought, for as you read it may seem that the area now known as Fort Lesley J McNair is not the same piece of real estate as the arsenal, the penitentiary, the Engineer School, the Army War College, or whatever other name it was known by during the past two hundred years.

In the Algonquin language the verbal noun Potomac means "a place where something is brought," or more freely translated, "a trading place."[1] Another interpretation of the word was "a meeting place of the tribes." Either definition aptly fits the river of today's capital city of the United States of America.

There are accounts of Indian tribes holding council meetings at Greenleaf's Point,[2] and of Manahoes, Anacostans, and Potomac Indians setting up wigwams while hunting and fishing in the vicinity.[3] However, some question remains, for a survey done in 1982 by Sorenson & Company stated no prehistoric sites were determined at the marshy isthmus of Fort McNair until the last half of the 19th century.

Captain John Smith passed this way during his explorations and described the "Patawomeke as six or seven myles in breadth...navigable 40 myles, and fed...with many sweet rivers and springs which fall from the bordering hils...with plentie and varieties of fruit...and an abundance of fish."[4] With a small party, Smith went up the Potomac River in June 1608 seeking a passage toward the East India Sea. A few miles above the District of Columbia (DC) boundary, his party met "divers Savages in canoes" and traded trinkets for bear meat and venison. While trading ashore, they found "tinctured spangled scurf [deposit] that made many places seem as gilded" in the rocky riverbed of rushing waters. The surrounding cliffs were liberally sprinkled with "yellow spangles as if it had been pin-dust (or matchqueon)."[5] Since gold was mined in the Great Falls area 200 years later, Captain Smith probably found gold but did not quite believe it.

Following the death of Powhatan in 1618, the tribes began to feud with each other and raids were made on white settlements with an equal number of Indians and colonists falling victim. In 1622, "Captain Madison and 30 men were dispatched to help the king of Potowomek...in the bloody burning of a large Indian settlement that stood at the junction of the Anacostia River with the Potomac."[6] By 1634, Maryland had been settled by Lord Baltimore's Catholic colony, but it was not until 1695 that a body of Scotch and Irish exiles settled in the present limits of the District of Columbia and named their collective farms "New Scotland."[7]

The marshy area where the rivers meet was part of a large land holding owned by James Thompson in 1656. It was first called Turkey Buzzard Point on a 1673 map made by Augustine Herrman, a surveyor, map maker, engineer, fur trader, slave trader, realtor, as well as a public administrator, lawyer, financier and farmer. Born in Prague in 1605, he appeared in Philadelphia in 1633. In 1659 he was commissioned by land holders to map the area between Virginia and Delaware which he surveyed until 1670 before drafting an ornamented 31 x 37.5 inch map printed in 1673.[8]

Thomas Notley, Governor of Maryland from 1676 to 1681, acquired thousands of acres of land, including Turkey Buzzard Point. The title of this property descended to Mrs Benjamin Young, and thence to her son Notley. Much of the land owned by Notley Young was purchased by James Greenleaf who sold some and donated part for L'Enfant's proposed Military District #5.[9]

The Saint James Creek flowed through the middle of Turkey Buzzard Point. The land east of the creek belonged to Daniel Carroll, who plotted a town he hoped would be built there. This area failed to thrive, and Carroll died bankrupt in 1849. The land west of the creek purchased by James Greenleaf extended south of Goose Creek (later named Tiber Creek) bounded by the Potomac River and Saint James Creek, and extending south to the limit set aside for a 28-1/2 acre military reservation given to the government by deed of trust by Notley Young. It was not an attractive plot, a trait shared by many military reservations. George Washington described these "public appropriations bounded on the north by South T Street, on the east by Canal Street, and on the south by the eastern branch of the Anacostia River as 'filth.'"[10]

James Greenleaf was born in Boston in 1765. Little is known of his youth, but he became an attractive, cultured entrepreneur with financial and diplomatic acumen. He married a lady of title and wealth from Holland and was a merchant in Pennsylvania when he heard about the proposed location of the new federal city. He used his contacts to obtain the backing of Amsterdam bankers to purchase 3,000 lots at $66.66 each, with no money down, and payments to be spread over a period of seven years, without interest.[11] With a partner, in 1793 he bought another 6,000 lots at $80 each. General Washington lured speculators by promising that areas not used for streets, parks, and federal buildings could be divided into lots to be sold, with proceeds of each alternate lot to go to build a National Treasury.

Some stately homes were erected near Greenleaf's Point. On 4th and N Streets, SW, were the Wheat Row houses and the Law House built in 1794. The Law House has a plaque reading: "Thomas Law and his wife Elizabeth Parke Custis, granddaughter of Martha Washington, resided here in 1796. Later the home of Richard Bland Lee, who was influential in bringing the capital to the Potomac." The Laws were famous for their parties, but their marriage broke up with the first divorce in the capital in 1804. Elizabeth may have set the precedent for prenuptial agreements when she retook her maiden name along with her fortune. Poor Thomas died insolvent due to risky real estate speculation.

The Wheat Row homes were named for John Wheat who owned the north house. At 468 N Street lived Judge Cranch, and at 470 N lived Captain Duncanson and Doctor Samuel Eliot. The dwellings had attendant coach houses and stables. The Washington Lewis House at 456 N Street, and the houses at 468 and 470 became a community center for neighborhood children called the Barney Neighborhood House. For 50 years, the street would be closed for a May Day party with a Queen and her court dancing around a May Pole as the Marine Band played. When urban renewal razed the southwest section of the city in the 1950s, these stately houses were left standing and again became fashionable residences.[12]

Unfortunately for Greenleaf, the town grew to the north. Sewage from the city not going into the Potomac River and Tiber Creek drained into Saint James Creek making his subdivision smell to high heaven. Earlier purchasers moved, and his dream of an empire crumbled. The site was taken over by squatters and riff-raff, and became the scene of violence and crime. The area from H Street south to the arsenal became known as "Bloodfield." Nevertheless, Greenleaf did leave his mark; his last name was given to the point of land bounded by the rivers, and he himself dropped the "Saint" from James Creek, thus giving that stinking little rivulet his first name.[13]

Although Greenleaf's marriage license gave Washington City as his place of residence, he and "Lady" Greenleaf lived in her mansion in Allentown, Pennsylvania where they moved among the cream of society. She had been clever enough to demand a prenuptial agreement thus protecting her private fortune from her speculator husband. Greenleaf managed to get himself appointed US Consul in Amsterdam from 1793 to 1802, and sold his final Washington holdings to Morris & Nicholson in 1796.

In 1831 Greenleaf built a three-story frame house in Washington at First and C Streets, NE, where he lived alone with a servant -- his wife preferring the provincial lifestyle of Allentown to the roughcut democratic environment. In his last days he wanted to be near a beloved sister. They both died within a day of each other in 1843, and Greenleaf is buried in the Congressional Cemetery overlooking the Anacostia River.

While the Revolutionary War was still being waged, a united military force was established to protect the life and liberty of Americans. In a document entitled *Sentiments on a Peace Establishment*, George Washington outlined a military policy for the new nation which called for (1) a regular standing force, (2) a well-organized militia, (3) military academies, (4) government manufacture of military stores, and (5) national arsenals.[14]

After winning the War for Independence, in 1783 thirteen colonies, federated in statehood, looked for a permanent site for a capital. Between 1776 and 1789, the Continental Congress met in eight cities: Philadelphia, Baltimore, Lancaster, York, Princeton, Annapolis, and Trenton. The Constitution gave Congress the exclusive power to approve a location, not to exceed 100 square miles; the land was to be ceded by the states and be acceptable to Congress.

In Virginia and Maryland, most of the land adjacent to the rivers had been cleared by 1790 and was covered with large plantations of tobacco cultivated by slaves. The owners lived in the same comfort and elegance as English squires. Within the area being considered for the capital were three thriving towns: Alexandria (or Bellhaven) on the Potomac, founded in 1749; Bladensburg, on Eastern Branch; and Georgetown on the Potomac, founded in 1751.

Every state, eager to be the home of the national capital, made generous offers of land and even money for construction of public buildings. Sectional jealousies flared. Speculators schemed to line their pockets. Finally, through compromise and diplomacy, a bill of 16 July 1790 provided for Philadelphia to be the temporary seat of government until 1800, at which time the Federal Government would locate somewhere on the Potomac. It was left to President Washington to select the site and negotiate with individual land owners.

Washington, himself, had surveyed the Potomac River area and knew it well. When he decided in 1791 on an area lying partly in Maryland and partly in Virginia, encompassing the Anacostia River and the navigable Potomac, both states promptly ceded their jurisdiction over the land chosen. Washington's motives for selecting the location of the Federal District could be viewed with suspicion: did he just want to be close to work, or was he the first "double-dipper" in US history selling sandstone from his Mount Vernon quarries to build the Capitol?

The concept of the 100-square-mile area is interesting since the 36-square-mile Virginia portion was retroceded to the State in 1846 as not being needed, and to that date, not utilized. If the original 10-mile square were rotated 45 degrees to the east, it neatly bites off the Virginia portion.[15]

Prologue

A commission of three (Honorable Daniel Carroll, General Thomas Johnson, and Dr David Stuart) was appointed to superintend the building of the national Capitol.

Living in Philadelphia was a middle-aged Frenchman called Major Pierre Charles L'Enfant...educated in the best military schools in France...[who] had hastened to aid the oppressed Americans. He taught them how to build fortifications, and thus attracted the attention of George Washington, who caused him to be appointed major of engineers.[16]

L'Enfant petitioned General Washington for the challenge of laying out the new city. His ideas knew no bounds. This was to be a great capital rivaling any other in the world. Despite the the lay of the land with fields, streams, marshes and rolling hills, he envisioned the Capitol itself to stand atop Jenkins Hill which was like a "pedestal waiting for a superstructure," and the "presidential palace" further west nearer the Potomac and Georgetown.[17] He planned to relieve the dullness of square blocks with diagonal avenues, parks, circles with monuments, leaving broad streets framing stately public buildings. As a military man, remembering Napoleon's campaigns, he could also appreciate what a "whiff of grape" down those broad avenues could do against enemies of state. Breaking up the grids with circles and diagonals would cause an invading force to get lost -- as do today's drivers.

L'Enfant realized that as an independent, neutral power, America must be able to protect her liberties. Without an organized army, navy, and fortified harbors the new country was highly vulnerable. With foresight he set aside fifteen areas encircling the planned city as federal reservations, their purpose to be decided on as needed. The peninsula where the Potomac and Anacostia Rivers met was an obvious, natural military site designated as Military District #5. To utilize these bastions, troops would be needed.

The origin of the US Army can be traced to 14 June 1775 when the Second Continental Congress appointed a committee to draft rules and regulations governing the Army. Sharpshooters of the mid-Atlantic colonies were authorized to serve as light infantry, and George Washington was appointed as the "General and Commander in Chief of the Army of the United Colonies.[18]

The establishment of the US Navy is credited in part to the activities of the *HMS Rose*, a 24-gun frigate built in England in 1756. Because of its illustrious service, the *Rose* was sent to Newport, Rhode Island in 1774 to put an end to smuggling which had become the city's principal industry. The resulting unemployment caused Newport to lose four-fifths of her population. Shortly afterward, a bill was introduced by Steven Hopkins and passed on 13 October 1775 to establish a Navy to deal with ships blockading our shores.[19]

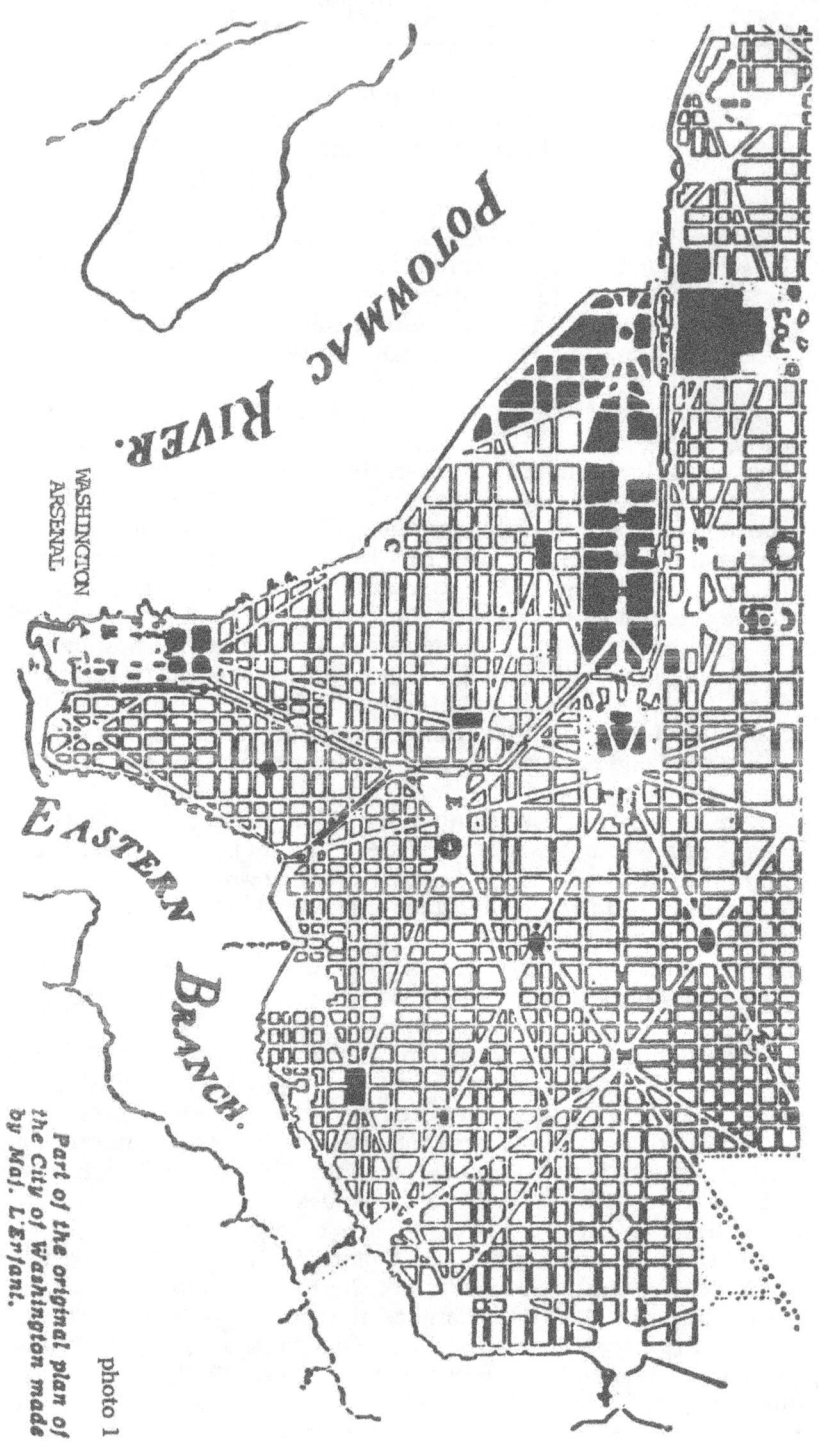

Part of the original plan of the City of Washington made by Maj. L'Enfant.

photo 1

Prologue

In L'Enfant's original plan for the city, submitted to President Washington on 27 August 1791, were detailed plans for the military district on the peninsula. Whereas the President's House and the Capitol building were merely indicated as to site, on the land reserved for an arsenal he drew in seawalls and sketched buildings for shops, magazines, and barracks -- a silent sentinel to guard the heart of the new country. (photo 1)

However, the commissioners took exception to L'Enfant's grandiose scheme. They thought he was crazy to plan such broad avenues where four teams could run abreast, and his use of land for roads, parks, and federal buildings was wildly extravagant. L'Enfant presented other elaborate ideas such as obelisks, fountains, columns, a national church, and even squares set aside for each state to improve as they wished, but the following proposal was the final straw:

> The water of Tiber Creek to be conveyed to the high ground where the Congress House stands, and after watering that part of the city, its overplus to fall from under the base of the edifice, and in a cascade of twenty feet in height and fifty in breadth, into the reservoir below, thence to run in three falls through the gardens in the grand canal.[20]

As a consequence of the serious differences between the fiery, stubborn, opinionated architect and the commissioners, L'Enfant was dismissed. He was later called upon to design Fort Washington across the Potomac from Mount Vernon, but eventually his services were no longer requested, and he died penniless. He was befriended by the Digger family of Prince George's County, Maryland, who cared for him until his death in 1825. They buried him beneath a tree on their property.[21] In 1909 he was disinterred and lay in state in the Capitol rotunda prior to burial with full military honors in Arlington Cemetery.[22]

No specific date has ever been documented for the establishment of the present Fort Lesley J McNair. The year 1791 is the most likely since that is the date the site was proposed for a military installation on the original plans of the city, and was the year the deed of trust for the land was signed. The topography met every requirement for a defensive position, for its capture would require a combined land and waterborne attack. A need existed for military facilities since volunteer militia units were in force even before authorization by the 1792 National Conscription Act.[23]

Fort McNair's first incarnation was as a military arsenal. When Britain prohibited export of arms and ammunition to colonial plantations, on 17 May 1775 Congress appointed a secret committee, under the Board of War, to consider ways to supply the New World with military stores. The position of Commissioner General of Military Stores was created in 1777 authorizing the President to appoint an officer to superintend receipt, safe-keeping, and distribution of military stores. The first Military Storekeeper of Military District #5 was Ezekiel Cheever. An undated item of newsprint states that in 1810 Colonel Henry Burbeck was the Commanding Officer of the District of Columbia, including the arsenal.[24]

A traveler writing of the infant city circa 1794 said:

> "There is a single gun mounted on the point at its southern extremity of the city in charge of a Captain Villiers." This is thought to have been intended for Captain A D Villard, a French officer who for a number of years prior to his death at a very advanced age in 1819 was superintendent of the arsenal.[27]

Congress voted appropriations for construction of two arsenals in 1794, and Secretary of War Pickering announced that Greenleaf's Point in Washington City was to be the site of one, and Whitestone Point near Baltimore the other. On 2 March 1797 Military Reservation #5 was formally transferred to the commissioners of the new federal city by President Washington.[28]

As the turn of the century approached, with the rallying cry "millions for defense, but not one cent for tribute," the way was cleared for strengthening military preparedness. Details only awaited the move of the seat of government from Philadelphia to the District of Columbia in 1800.

FORT LESLEY J. McNAIR

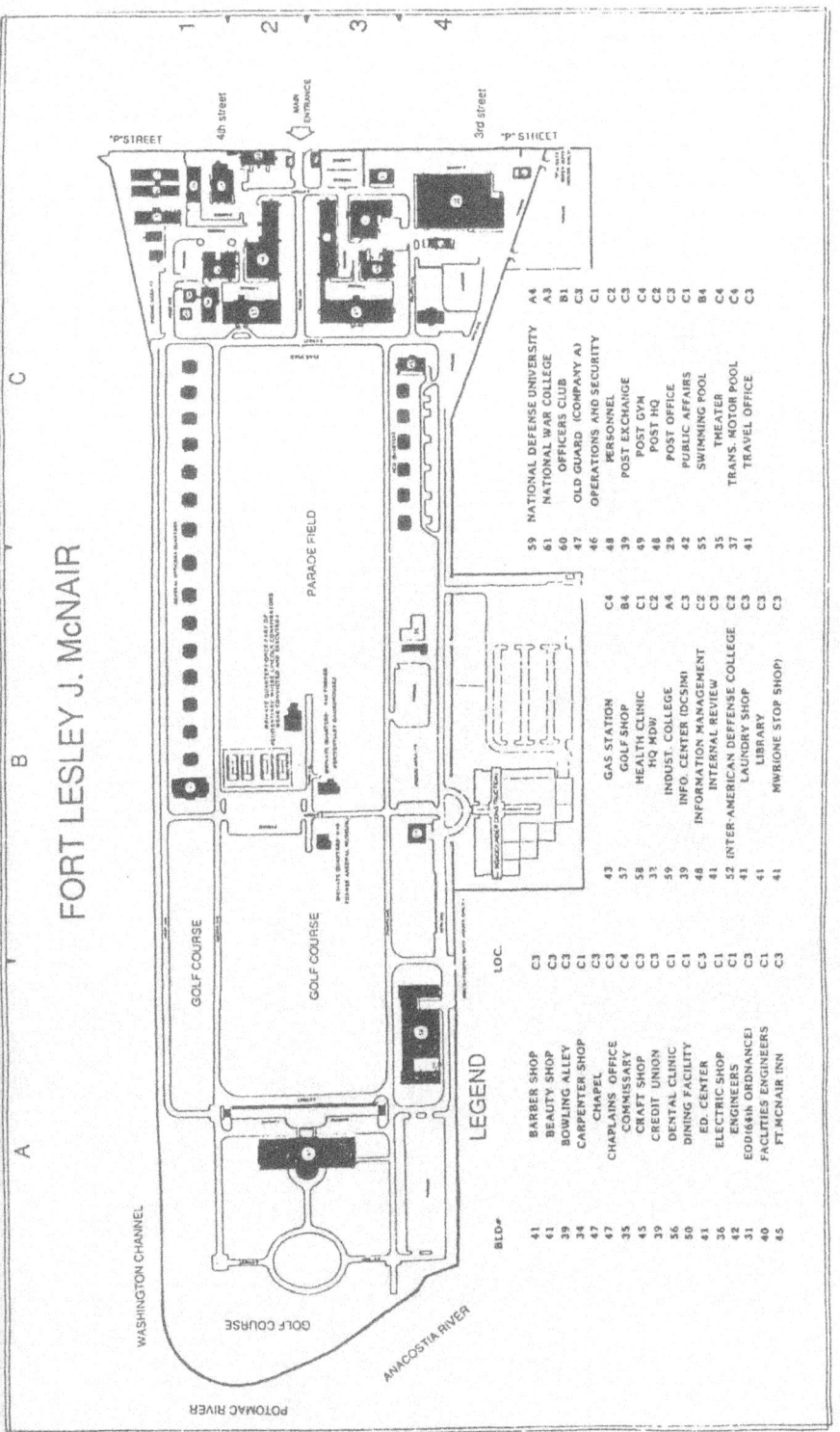

LEGEND

BLD#		LOC.
41	BARBER SHOP	C3
41	BEAUTY SHOP	C3
39	BOWLING ALLEY	C3
34	CARPENTER SHOP	C1
47	CHAPEL	C3
47	CHAPLAINS OFFICE	C3
35	COMMISSARY	C4
45	CRAFT SHOP	C3
39	CREDIT UNION	C3
56	DENTAL CLINIC	C1
50	DINING FACILITY	C1
41	ED. CENTER	C3
36	ELECTRIC SHOP	C1
42	ENGINEERS	C1
31	EOD(66th ORDNANCE)	C3
40	FACILITIES ENGINEERS	C1
45	FT. McNAIR INN	C3

43	GAS STATION	C4
57	GOLF SHOP	B4
58	HEALTH CLINIC	C1
33	HQ MDW	C2
59	INDUST. COLLEGE	A4
39	INFO. CENTER (DCSIM)	C3
48	INFORMATION MANAGEMENT	C2
41	INTERNAL REVIEW	C3
52	INTER-AMERICAN DEFENSE COLLEGE	C2
41	LAUNDRY SHOP	C3
41	LIBRARY	C3
41	MWR(ONE STOP SHOP)	C3

59	NATIONAL DEFENSE UNIVERSITY	A4
61	NATIONAL WAR COLLEGE	A3
60	OFFICERS CLUB	B1
47	OLD GUARD (COMPANY A)	C3
46	OPERATIONS AND SECURITY	C1
	PERSONNEL	C2
48	POST EXCHANGE	C3
39	POST GYM	C4
49	POST HQ	C2
48	POST OFFICE	C3
29	PUBLIC AFFAIRS	C1
42	SWIMMING POOL	B4
55	THEATER	C4
35	TRANS. MOTOR POOL	C4
37	TRAVEL OFFICE	C3

CHAPTER II:
1800-1825, Growth of the Arsenal

The transition of a marshy hayfield to an arsenal was gradual. Although the area was referred to as a fort as early as 1794, there was only an earthen breastwork with a solitary cannon sweeping the approaches up the Potomac. When the seat of government moved to the yet unnamed federal city in 1800, there were only 372 houses, and barely 3,000 inhabitants in the district. The Moore and James map of 1802 shows the outline of the fort with the James Creek canal site marked incomplete.

The first official reference to an arsenal at Greenleaf's Point appears on 11 July 1803 when George Hadfield, a military storekeeper at Albany, was paid $40.00 for drawing plans for an arsenal at Washington City.[1] No known description survives.[2] Other moneys expended for Greenleaf's Point included $700 for buildings, $200/per year plus rations and quarters for the hire of Hezekiah Rogers as storekeeper, and $308.32 was paid George Blagden to erect a building adjoining the barracks.[3]

By 1815 there were 21 enlisted men at the military post commanded by Captain Andrew Villard, the first commanding officer.[5] [There is no evidence the Frenchman was ever granted an official rank with US forces, and in petitions to congress for recognition of military contributions he is referred to as Mr Villiard.] As early as 1806, Andrew Villard was commended by Congress for inventing the disappearing gun carriage and paid $1,000 -- a fortune at that time:

> This carriage, designed for defensive fortifications, could be raised two feet in 15 seconds by the efforts of four men. Raising allowed the gun to be loaded and prepared behind the protection of a breastwork. When the gun was fired, it was merely raised to the top of the rampart, discharged, and lowered again. This new concept not only protected the gun...[it] did not expose the gun crews to enemy fire.[5]

In 1812, 1st Lieutenant Samuel Perkins was commanding officer of the arsenal which stored and distributed government weapons, rifles, and cannon manufactured at arsenals in Harper's Ferry, Virginia, Springfield Missouri, and Foxhall's Columbia Foundry in Georgetown. Workmen cleaned, repaired, and made fittings, and built carriages for the heavier weapons.[6]

Henry Foxhall sent a letter to Congress stating he had inspected Greenleaf's Point "and saw it was good, and the conveniences for its adoption many," but for the government to erect their own cannon manufactory

> will require...a steam engine...foundry, furnaces, [and a] boring mill....I will undertake to build...for the United States to the extent and magnitude determined by you. I will...make all the models in brass or iron...of every kind of Ordnance.[7]

When his proposal went unanswered, Foxhall sent a letter of protest to Secretary of War Dearborn stating he had cast guns for the Army and Navy, and if the arsenal on the Point continued to develop it would put him out of business. He further criticized the operation on Greenleaf's Point saying "your place of desposite [sic] for cannon [could be] much better arranged."[8]

An illuminating letter from storekeeper Hezekiah Rogers was sent to the Department of War on 24 October 1806:

> The public property in this city belonging to the military department...is embraced in the enclosed return. The goods are always landed in Georgetown where a person is instructed by me to forward them immediately to their address....The clothing for the Indian Department has always been distributed and applied by the Secretary of War to the Indians personally, and no receipts taken.[9]

By 1807, the arsenal had a powder magazine, a carpenter's shop, a smithy, and other buildings in various stages of construction, and deserved to be recognized as a full-fledged arsenal by 1810. The strength of the Army had grown from 80 officers and men in 1784, to 3,000 in 1811. A Congressional Act of 15 March 1802 authorized a Corps of Artillerists and Engineers for 32 cadets at the Military Academy in West Point, New York.

The young nation steadily grew unhappy with England's interference with internal matters. It particularly objected to closing European ports to American commerce, and to impressment of American sailors of English birth on the grounds that persons born on English soil are Englishmen. The United States declared that men could give up their inherited citizenship and transfer their allegiance to another country.[11]

On 18 June 1812, President James Madison approved an act declaring war existed between the United Kingdom of Great Britain and Ireland and the dependencies thereof and the United States of America and their territories. The war was most unpopular and might have led to civil war if the Ghent negotiations had not succeeded in December 1814.[11]

In January 1813, First Lieutenant Samuel Perkins, 1st Regiment, US Infantry, was ordered to have Villard send the best mounted six-pounder to York, Pennsylvania to serve as a pattern. In March he was ordered to furnish General Van Ness stands of arms, cartridge boxes, belts and musket cartridges to arm the militia.[12] [Perkins resigned in May 1814 to become a military storekeeper, a more lucrative endeavor.]

In April, Captain Edwin Tyler reported to Greenleaf's Point to oversee the manufacture of musket cartridges and test ammunition for field pieces. He was told to come by stage and bring four or five hands with him as well as a fireman and a turner, and promised he would receive the emoluments of a captain.[13]

In May, 1st Lieutenant Nehemiah Baden was ordered to Greenleaf's Point to assist Captain Tyler who was temporarily detailed to Raleigh, North Carolina to set up a shop to make ammunition. From there he proceeded to New York on 19 August 1814 to prepare a subordinate lab at Albany. [Tyler would resign in 1819.] This left Lieutenant Baden in command when the British marched on Washington, DC. On duty with Baden was Mr A J Villard (in charge of repair of gun carriages), 1st Lieutenant George B Larned (later discharged from the army in 1815), 3d Lieutenant George H Britt (assigned to command the post in June 1815 and died in January 1816), and 2d Lieutenant Thomas T Stephenson, an academy graduate of 1813 (who subsequently would serve periods of temporary command at Washington Arsenal, and die in August 1819).[14]

The War between England and the United States lasted 18 months resulting in 1,877 killed and 3,737 wounded. The capital city was only involved on 24-25 August 1814 when British forces under General Ross and Admiral Cockburn sent a diversionary force up the Potomac and detached a single ship to test the effectiveness of Fort Washington. To their surprise, not a gun was fired! After a minor plundering operation, the British returned down the river.

Expecting the British to renew a water attack, on August 24th, an hastily formed, unarmed regiment of 1,200 infantry and 100 cavalrymen from Alexandria tried unsuccessfully to get weapons from the arsenal. At the arsenal, 1st Lieutenant Baden was ordered to place two travelling guns in front of the Capitol, two more before the President's House, and two at the Post Office. When it became apparent the British were approaching overland toward Bladensburg, Baden was ordered to move his men to the northeastern side of the city.[15]

British General Ross marched 5,000 redcoats overland and soundly defeated the assembled American forces composed of a few hundred regulars and locally organized militia whose handsome regimental uniforms looked dazzling in parades but only served as good targets on the battlefield. Untrained, ineptly led, and hindered by political civilian interference, they broke in battle and fled. About dusk on the 24th, Ross rode into Washington, a city of 28,000, and met no resistance other than one shot which killed his horse.[16]

The invaders used the meager collection of books forming the Library of Congress for kindling to torch the Capitol, President's House, Treasury, Post Office and other public buildings. However, a fortuitous cloudburst doused the fires and saved the rest of the city. At the arsenal, Colonel Decius Wadsworth vouched that wooden sheds were set afire by his order, which ignited Mr Villiard's house and burned it to the ground. Although Villiard saved papers and books of the ordnance office as he marched off to Bladensburg, he undoubtedly suffered grevious personal loss through the destruction of his house.[17]

The following day, 200 British troops and 30 officers were detached by General Ross to capture the magazine at Greenleaf's Point. The sentinels guarding the Potomac were silent for the guns were unmanned! British troops destroyed the barracks and 20,000 stands of small arms. But the most disasterous loss befell the British when gunpowder hidden in a well blew up killing 40 soldiers and maiming 47 others. Their wounds were dressed by Doctors Ewell and Behr in the Carroll Row houses near the present Library of Congress. General Ross paid for their care in gold pieces, and promised continued payment until the invalids returned to England. This promise was voided by Ross' death in Baltimore two weeks later.

Some stories said gunpowder thrown into a dry well near the southeast corner of the arsenal ignited when a British soldier lowered a lantern to inspect the well; another story said a match was carelessly tossed in the well after a pipe was lighted. A Liverpool newspaper credited an American soldier named Callahan with laying a fuse from the dry well to the water's edge, then lighting it when the British gathered by the well. He supposedly escaped by canoe to join his comrades across the Anacostia River at Giesboro Point (the present site of the Bolling Field and the Naval Air Station). If true, Trooper Callahan may be the unsung hero of the War of 1812.

The war ended on 24 December 1814 with the Treaty of Ghent, although the treaty was not signed until 17 February 1815, and was not signed in Belgium but in Washington, DC at the Octagon House on NW New York Avenue. This stately home (which actually only has six sides) was built in 1801 by Colonel John Tayloe, III as his city residence. He offered the home to President and Mrs James Madison until the White House could be restored. It is open to the public where one may see "the circular accounting table on which Madison is believed to have signed the Treaty of Ghent."[18]

After the invasion, the Ordnance Department was ordered to give Congressman R M Johnson's Committee of Inquiry an account of munitions of war on hand in Washington, DC at the time of the British attack. The report was as follows:

1800-1825, Growth of the Arsenal

Mounted on garrison carriages Greenleaf Point:
   8 each 24-pound cannon
   1 each 50-pound Columbiad
   1 each 18-pound Columbiad
In Charge of US arsenal at Greenleaf's Point:
   2 each 18-pound cannon on travelling carriage
   5 each 12-pound   "
   6 each 6-pound   "
   3 each 24-pound Howitzers
Of these:
   2 each 18-pound guns were in front of the Capitol
   2 each 12-pound guns were at the President's House
   2 each 12-pound guns were at the Post Office
In addition:
   12 each 6-pounders were issued to District Artillery
   2 each 12-pounders were loaned to Marine Corps
   4 or 6 each to Brigade in Alexandria
Ordnance stores at the Lab:
     140 bbls (14,000) tons gunpowder
     5 tons lint
   7,180 cannon cartridges (filled & empty)
   8,650 rounds of grape and cannister shot
   2,993 stands of arms
   1,595 cartridge boxes and belts
   2,584 bayonet scabbards
   13,000 flints
  271,000 musket cartridges of various types
Considerable distribution made to regular troops and militia.
     Signed J Morton, US Ord Office.[19]

Through the insistence of Lieutenant Colonel George Bomford, Chief of Ordnance, the arsenal was rebuilt. This letter of 15 July 1816 to Andrew Villard instructed him

> to resume the charge of Superintendant of the Work Shops, and the men employed therein, for the construction of gun carriages, or other work of that nature at the arsenal, Greenleafs Point....You are to consider yourself as under the authority or direction of this Department, and of any officers having charge of the public arsenal, and to the military laws or regulations for the general government of the same.[20]

As reconstruction was underway, Mr Villard was told not to use artificers to erect buildings and workshops -- the Quartermaster General should take care of construction.

photo 2 - Washington Arsenal Headquarters flanked by officer quarters, 1803-1881

A news account described the "restoration of the government works on Greenleaf's Point, destroyed by the British in 1814...now known as the arsenal" thusly:

> The [Federal brick] buildings in that portion of the grounds known as the quadrangle, which in the early days constituted the arsenal proper, were erected during the years 1816 and 1817 at a cost of some $30,000....They are eight in number, two stories in height, and were at first occupied by the officers and enlisted men for quarters and as shops, the latter being in the two warehouses on the north and south sides of the square. They formed an inclosure about the size of a city square, in which prior to 1820 ample room was found for all the purposes of an arsenal. (photo 2)
>
> The magazine for the powder was built at a safe distance from the city, a mile or two above Georgetown, about the same time.
>
> From government documents on file it would appear that Lieutenant Colonel Bomford took a personal interest in the establishment, and that from December 1817 when Brevet Major Joseph S Nelson was placed in command, the charge of it was in the hands of a civilian superintendent, Captain A D Villard.
>
> ...There were 30 enlisted men under Major Nelson, and about the same number of civilian employees prior to 1820, and the old work of building gun carriages and cleaning and repairing arms were the principal industries. Thomas Given and ten men were engaged on gun carriages; Edben Ward and twelve others on arms; and there were a few blacksmiths under Nehemiah Griffin. The wages then were from $1.25 to $2 per day, the time running "from sun to sun," and but little was thought of distance...[workmen] residing not far from the present site of *The Star* office.
>
> The government papers also show that there was a liberal allowance of liquor made the men, for the anti-canteen people had not then commenced their crusade. The grandchildren of some who lived then say their grandfathers on entering the arsenal shops would find two buckets, one of whisky and one of water, with a tin cup between them...and before quitting time each day the liquor bucket would be dry....
>
> Some of the workmen...lived in Carrollsburg on the east side of James Creek, but a few lived on the point....It was one of the finest neighborhoods of the city. Such men as Richard Bland Lee, Judge of the Orphans' Court; Mr Bullfinch, architect; Thomas Dougherty, clerk of the House of Represen-

tatives; Commodore John Rodgers of the navy and John Wheat [had] their homes here....

Major Nelson remained in command to April 1821, and before he left there was improvement beyond the quadrangle or fort. Buildings for shops were erected east of the square, and guns and shot stored north of it, while some lumber sheds were erected about the site of the present barrack building, and the title Washington Arsenal was given the place. [Nelson was commissioned a 1st Lieutenant of Infantry from Maryland in 1813, unusual at a time when all officers were graduates of the military academy. He transferred to Ordnance, became a major, and died in 1843.]

Captain William Wade of the 4th Artillery succeeded Major Nelson in April 1821....Two-thirds of the reservation (that portion between T Street and the building portion)...[was] being cultivated, and the small guard house at T and 4-1/2 Streets was seemingly occupied for the protection of the crops.[21]

Lieutenant Colonel George Bomford, United States Military Academy (USMA) graduate of a three-member class of 1805, headed the Artillery Corps for many years and was Chief of Ordnance for 16 years -- from 1832 to 1848. By 1811 he had designed a large caliber artillery piece (referred to as a Columbiad) that saw much service in the War of 1812. Fairfax Downey's book states the name was derived from Joel Barlow's 12-canto epic on Columbus "which created quite a stir in its day and has seldom been read since." With improvements made by Captain Thomas Jackson Rodman, this became the standard piece of seacoast artillery by 1860.[22] Washingtonians recall the socially elite Bomfords who entertained at their Kalorama estate in NW Washington. In late life Bomford made some unfortunate investments and died impoverished.

Captain Nelson was ordered to send flights of rockets over Tiber creek to entertain dinner guests at the President's House. Rockets were used by the Chinese in wars against Mongol tribes, in India against the British, and by Wellington when he burned Copenhagen. They were most effectively used by General Ross in the Battle of Bladensburg where Sir William Congreve's invention was described in *Sound of the Guns* as "a thing which soared above spitting sparks and trailing a blazing tail....Upon landing, it sputtered, smoked, and writhed through the grass like a serpent. Then a time fuse burst its black powder charge with a sharp report and a spurt of acrid smoke."[23] Rockets had a range of about two miles and were launched much the same as fireworks are today.

The other lethal weapon used at Bladensburg was a projectile developed in 1784 by Lieutenant Henry Shrapnel of the Royal Artillery. It was a spherical case loaded with balls. Designed so a time-fuse would burst overhead raining iron on all below, it was more devastating than grape or canister.[24]

In July 1818, Nelson was ordered to collect guns and ordnance on Mount Vernon Estate, as well as cannon still standing before the President's House and the Post Office, and to pick up 20 stands of muskets cluttering the Ordnance office. Three 32-pound guns on truck carriages about to fall in the water were reported at the mouth of a creek opposite Greenleaf's Point, and three more were at the Virginia end of the Potomac bridge.[25]

War materiel was scattered about for years. Military Storekeeper J Laval at Greenleaf's Point wrote to Commissary General Franklin D Callender in Philadelphia asking what he should do with excess clothing and equipment: "I propose to auction caps for 25 cents, knapsacks for 12 cents, and cap plates for 06 cents. As for 90 infantrymen's coats, it would be prudent to sell them since the moths are after them." Five months later, he wrote again regarding 500 wool blankets destroyed by moths. He reported he was not "gratified" by the report of the Board of Officers sent to inspect: "Those gentlemen came upon me as a hawk upon a sparrow. I have been forty years in this country, and in government employ for the last thirteen years. I deplore being let out of the Army and despair of finding employment to provide for my family."[26]

By 1818 the President's House was ready for reoccupancy. From that time on, it was known as the White House because of the coat of white paint applied to cover the scars of war. Congress adopted a flag with 13 stripes and decreed the number of stars would be increased for each state added to the union.

In 1819, Mr Villard was told to hire someone to transport cannon by scow from the wharf in Georgetown, and asked to build a block carriage for transport of heavy cannon. Not many roads were adequate for hauling such heavy loads which limited the British to one 6-pounder and two 3-pounders at the Bladensburg battlefield. Captain Nelson was ordered to pick up 600 stands of arms at Port Tobacco for overhaul, and to search the arsenal and return to the State of Virginia any arms manufactured at the Richmond Armory.

In October 1820, the Ordnance office asked Nelson to explain what happened to two 32-pound iron guns, nine 24-pounders, five 18-pounders, one 6-pounder, three-18 pound Columbiads, plus miscellaneous items shipped to the arsenal from Fort Washington. A chagrined Captain Nelson replied:

> On the night of 2 December 1819, sometime after tattoo beat, a Sergeant reported the arrival of a scow from Fort Washington loaded with damaged ordnance for this post. The Sergeant who had charge of the scow was directed to make fast the scow to the wharf until morning when assistance would be given his crew to raise the guns, etc. from the

scow to the wharf. The Sergeant stated he had received orders to return to Fort Washington by 4 o'clock the next morning. That he was instructed to throw the ordnance overboard anywhere in the neighborhood of this arsenal and return to Fort Washington without delay. Lieut Buckley, who delivered to the Sergeant my instructions, told the Sergeant that unless the guns were delivered on the wharf, no notice could or would be taken of them. The Sergeant replied no blame can be attached to me, having received the order to return to Fort Washington by a certain hour, I must at all hazards obey it. He then ordered the crew to throw the ordnance from the scow into the river, where I presume they are now.[27]

When the Chief of Ordnance followed up, Nelson replied: "... as I have never considered myself responsible for those stores, I have not adopted any measures for their removal from the river."[28] A letter from 1st Lieutenant W E Williams on duty at the arsenal to Chief of Ordnance Lieutenant Colonel Bomford dated 11 August 1823 was the last heard of this story:

I enclose the receipt of General Mason for the old cannon and castings raised by him from the river and transported to the Columbia Foundry - which were delivered in obedience to your orders of the 14th ultimo.
I wish to be instructed whether they are now to be entered and accounted for as usual with property issued.[29]

First Lieutenant Simonson, who commanded the arsenal from May 1821 to April 1823, was told that since no gun carriages were ordered last year he should "discontinue this task and dismiss workers; the limited budget only permits preservation of public property....Ten men should be sufficient."[30]

When 1st Lieutenant W E Williams took command in September 1823, he was instructed to evaluate muskets made by Rogers, Wickham & Evans, Whitney, Pomeroy and Watkins; rifles by Derringer and Johnson; pistols by North, and cavalry sabers and swords by Stan. He was told if three houses were needed for personnel, he could buy another, but not spend over $100. At this time, someone must have remembered the old cannon about to fall into the water, for he was told to deliver them to General Mason at Columbia foundry. At the end of 1823 he was ordered to give the Maryland militia 5,000 rifles, 165 pistols, 88 artillery swords, 8 noncommissioned officer's (NCO) swords.

He was also told to put on a firing and rocket display for a deputation of Indians accompanied by Governor Clark, and to present them with any swords, pistols, or rifles they selected. This was a ploy adopted by the government to convince chiefs of powerful tribes of the generosity of the Nation; afterwards they would meet the President, be shown battleships, forts, and masses of arms to impress them with the folly of initiating prolonged wars.[31]

As the first quarter of the 19th century closed, Brevet Major Wade again assumed command of the arsenal. Wade was to face a new challenge brought on by construction of a prison for convicted criminals of District Courts.[32] This institution would separate the arsenal from the city -- on the face of it, not only an impractical idea, but also a potentially dangerous one. Before long, the number of prisoners would be greater than personnel manning the arsenal.

CHAPTER III: 1825-1850, Peace and War

Perley's Reminiscences describes the new federal city guarded by the arsenal at Greenleaf's Point. By 1826 there were 24 states in the Union, and the United States was a free, thriving, and growing country. There were now 60,000 inhabitants in the capital and 24 churches. The unpaved streets were dark except on moonlit nights, and conveyances were often stuck in mudholes on principal thoroughfares. There were no public schools for white children, and it was forbidden by law to teach colored children. However, L'Enfant's dream of an unparalleled capital city was slowly materializing as parks were planted with shrubs and flowers, and numerous statues of heroes and statesmen began to be installed.[1]

Major Wade was transferred from the arsenal in July 1826, and 2d Lieutenant William H Bell filled in from July until December when 1st Lieutenant John Symington arrived to take command. The sheds and workshops at the arsenal were completed as well as a seawall shoring up the western banks of the Potomac thereby reclaiming land with earthfill. The installation continued to serve as a storage and distribution point for ordnance and other military stores.

Much of the commanding officer's time was taken up by command visits of inspection to nearby arsenals at Bellona, West Point, Georgetown, Harper's Ferry, Springfield, and Petersburg. Trips were made to the Dupont Powder factory in Wilmington and to General Mason's foundry near Georgetown.

Test firing of eprouvettes was carried on, and balls forged for different size cannon. (An eprouvette was sort of a "shooting gallery duck" apparatus to determine the initial velocity of projectiles fired from cannon or muskets.)[2]

In October 1827, Symington received an urgent order to make forty 6-pounder iron gun carriages with all accompanying equipment for artillery, not to exceed a cost of $300 each, to be issued to several states.

Symington was next ordered to report to New York Harbor and inspect the old 32- and 42-pounders there. In March 1828, he was directed to mark an 8" iron mortar, a trophy of the late war, as "Captured, Fort George, NC, 27 May 1813. Served in the Defense of Plattsburg, 11 September 1814."[3]

The Lieutenant received approval to purchase and plant 200 trees for shade and ornamentation. He was not to pay more than 30 cents per tree.

Equipment was updated with the acquisition of a michronometer for measuring time in very small segments. This item had been made for the Ordnance Department by Mr W Montandon. A steam engine from Mr F Pratt of Pittsburg was promised by the end of the year. Mr W Copeland was hired as Master Machinist at $3 a day to oversee installation of the steam engine for which a building was to be erected immediately.[4] A sum of $2,188 was set aside for the engine house which was to be made primarily of bricks from the building burned in 1814.[5]

While most of the work was with heavy ordnance, the arsenal also conducted experiments with small arms. A rifle invented by Mr Shuttock of Ohio with six charges loaded at the breach was sent for testing. A pistol with a percussion cap and self-priming magazine lock was tested for strength and safety. The idea of a percussion cap was known as early as 1814, but it was a separate item, not incorporated into cartridges and projectiles until later.[6]

As work progressed on the new penitentiary, coordination with the arsenal was needed. A wall to join that enclosing the arsenal was proposed, thereby making a double gateway at the southwest corner. Also, an eight foot wall was needed along the bank to protect the road to T Street.[7]

At the beginning of 1830, there was another cutback in work at arsenals, and commanders were advised to hold auctions and pare down inventories. Old muskets, rifles, swords, and spare parts for Hall's rifles were to be sent to Frankford, Pennsylvania. Items for sale included scrap iron, gunstocks, harness, and timber. Old castings were ordered to be sold for $20 per ton; six-pound carriages with iron cannon and equipment for $400; brass cannon and equipment for $600; and muskets for $13.

On 5 April 1830, Lieutenant Symington was asked to sketch plans for three buildings to be placed on a line north of and perpendicular to the gunhouse. Each building was to be one-story high, 20 feet square, with brick walls and hipped slate roofs. One building was to be used for a magazine; one for filling cartridges, dusting, and separating powder; and the other for cutting paper and flannel, making of fire and rocket cases, musket cartridges, etc. Approval was also given for another small, detached building for driving rockets, fuses, portfires, and items deemed necessary. The cost of all buildings was limited to $3,000.[8]

New orders received at the arsenal were to: check Enoch Hidden's improved percussion lock for cannon; hire a competent clerk for $1.50 per day since the arsenal commander is often away on inspections; pay Calvin Post $75 for the right to use his patented hoopbender; pay blacksmith, filer, and machinist $1.65 per day; and consider Watervliet New York) Arsenal's system of paying by piecework rather than per diem (e.g., $41.00 for the woodwork for each gun carriage).

Poor pay caused dissension, and in September 1831 the workmen struck for higher wages, thus bringing all work to a standstill. The Ordnance office declared that they could not judge a fair wage, and left it up to Symington to do whatever he thought best. His solution was not recorded. Privates were paid from $6 to $10 per month, depending on length of service. Officers despaired of ever becoming a captain and morale was low.

At the end of the year the arsenal received a new fire engine which could shoot a stream of water 65 feet high and 95 feet horizontally. In April 1832, the commanding officer was authorized to construct a gunhouse, erect a board fence along James Creek, build a new gateway, and effect repairs on officers' quarters. There were ten enlisted men and 31 civilian workers, but only a small amount of work was being done -- just minimum maintenance, and care of tools and stores. Tests were completed on Mr Henwood's discovery of a process for melting iron and steel, casting of wrought iron, and providing safer furnaces for workshops.

In December, the arsenal was informed that soon they would be manned with two lieutenants and 25 enlisted men. Symington was told to estimate how many armorers, carriage makers, blacksmiths, artificers, and laborers would be needed.[9]

Since the early 1800s, the arsenal's powder magazine had been located near Great Falls. It was considered to be as close as necessary, yet far enough away to ensure the safety of the city. In 1832 it was discovered the magazine and the caretaker's house had been erected on right-of-way property belonging to a railroad company who planned to exercise their option. It was necessary to find a new place that could hold 1500 barrels of powder. The problem was a long time in finding a solution, but eventually a new magazine was located across the Eastern Branch in Anacostia.

Symington was promoted to captain and reassigned to command the St Louis Arsenal. He was replaced by Captain Alfred Mordecai from April to October 1833 when Mordecai was sent to Paris with $500 to buy anything useful and of interest to the Artillery service. Also, he was to determine the weight of guns for steamships, kinds of projectiles used, mode of mounting, and how they worked. He was to report on the number and caliber of weapons on each ship of specific dimensions (length, breadth, depth, and draught), rate of power, and the number and characteristics of engines and boilers on sailing ships. He was to observe any new approaches for protection from enemy projectiles, and to report on any new weapons for land or sea. In August 1834, Mordecai spent $700 on ordnance items to bring back.[10]

Alfred Mordecai was born in 1804 in North Carolina and graduated number one in his Military Academy class of 1823. In addition to Engineer assignments, he prepared *A Digest of Military Laws* in 1833, experimented with ballistic pendulums, and prepared the *Ordnance Manual of 1841*. He was sent to observe the Crimean War (1855-57), and helped revise the "Programme of Instruction at the Military Academy." Unable to draw his sword against the South, he resigned his commission in 1861 and became a mathematics teacher in Philadelphia. Subsequently he served on various boards until his death in 1887.

Captain Richard Bache took command in October 1833 and started making new block-tail gun carriages. The arsenal was to complete one per month, and to devise a method of preconstruction of component parts. He was also given $2,800 to construct new soldiers' barracks by dismantling the wall of the old magazine at Little Falls, and to cancel the plan for piazzas on the tenement barracks since it darkened the rooms. In June he was instructed to furnish members of Congress with a carbine, bullet mold, and priming box upon request, requiring only their signature. Congressional "perks" existed even then.

In August, Bache was given $400 to repair the wharf, and ordered to postpone the procurement of a crane until the next year. He was directed to forward a plan and estimate for construction of a building to house quarter-sized models of ordnance and attending pieces of equipment [now Building #21].[11]

An 1823 Plat of Washington Arsenal shows the line of the proposed Washington Canal by which L'Enfant proposed to link the Chesapeake and Ohio (C&O) Canal with the Anacostia River. From the route via Tiber creekbed in front of the capitol, James Creek Canal was to run from Virginia Avenue, along Canal Street, and empty into the Anacostia by the arsenal. Canal construction practically bankrupted the city by 1841, and James Creek was left as a stinking little rivulet.

In February 1835, President Van Buren and Secretary of War Cass visited the arsenal for a demonstration determining the effectiveness of cast iron gun carriages. This same year, Captain Bache was given funds to make wharf repairs, buy a boat and a crane, and floor the gun houses with brick. Mr St John was hired as a master workman at $2.30 per day to put in lab shops and train men to use the tools, forms, and machines making all kinds of military pyrotechnics.[12]

One of the best descriptions of the military installation at this time is in a letter dated 25 September 1835:

> The officers' quarters consist of two blocks, each containing three rooms with fireplaces, two rooms without fireplaces, and a kitchen, making in all six rooms with fireplaces, four without, and two kitchens. Captain Bache occupies one block, and Lieut Scott the other.
>
> The barracks, or quarters for the enlisted men consist of two blocks, each containing four rooms and two kitchens.

Four of those rooms are 18 x 20 feet, four 16 feet square. The kitchens are commodious. One other block containing eight rooms and four kitchens [have] rooms about 16 x 18 feet - the kitchens are the same size.

These are all the buildings designated for barracks, but there is a large room ultimately intended for a model room which is temporarily used as quarters. The barracks are disposed of between Major Mason's Company and the 29 enlisted men of the Ordnance Department, 14 of whom have families.

With respect to the officer quarters there is not the same abundance. The want of kitchens would render a portion of the rooms described unavailing - indeed, I do not perceive how...either of the blocks could be occupied by more than one officer entitled to a separate kitchen. The necessity will therefore result of providing quarters elsewhere for some of the officers.[13]

Military morale was low; 117 officers resigned their army commissions due to poor pay, lack of respect, no retirement plan, and hopeless prospects for promotion. Western posts were real hardship tours with inadequate quarters and uncertain replenishment of supplies -- which forced units to live off the land. Disease killed far more men than enemy action.

First Lieutenant John Benjamin Scott assumed command of the arsenal in January 1836 when Captain Bache died. His first problem was to retain workmen. Due to the high cost of rent and daily provisions, he received permission to increase wages from $2.30 to $2.50 per day, and to supplement the workforce with two apprentices assigned to each master workman. They were to be over 16 years of age, and be paid 75 cents a day the first year, and $1.00 a day the second.

In May, Congress approved a phenomenal $15,418 appropriation for the arsenal:

$7,500 - Buy a new site for magazine and keeper's house,
2,500 - Build a 202-foot gun shed,
1,700 - Add 40 feet to the carriage shed,
1,666 - Fill marsh on the east for gun shed,
1,242 - Build 1381 feet of stone seawall on east front,
600 - Build new casting house for cupola furnace,
200 - Install flagging for shot piles.[14]

With the building of the seawall, four more acres of land were reclaimed. Other portions of the grounds were graded and filled with earth brought over a temporary bridge from east of the creek. This

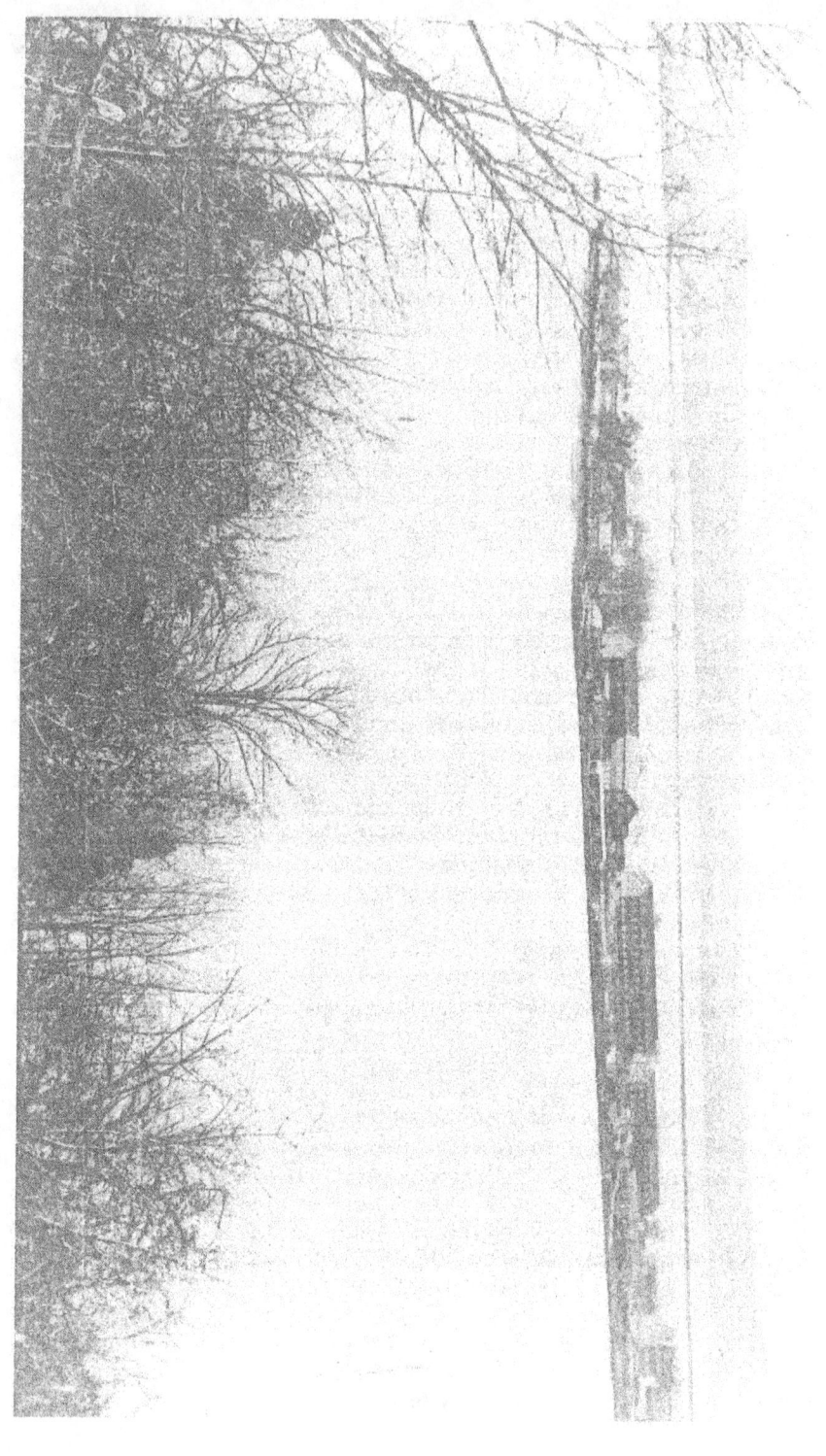

1825-1850, Peace and War

provided more useable space and symmetrical boundaries for the arsenal grounds, but the marsh east of the post was still a health hazard.

As Captain George D Ramsay took command in September 1836, distribution of ordnance materiel continued to fill such orders as that of 3 September 1836 to send the 2d Regiment of Dragoons 151,000 percussion carbines, and 1/18th of a pound ball and buckshot cartridges. The reputation of the "state of the art Washington Arsenal" is verifiable by the number of requests for copies of drawings of the engine house, carpenter shop, et cetera to be duplicated at other arsenals.

Elliot's 1837 *Guide to Washington* described the 1/4-mile-square site with one hundred workmen as having three gun sheds, a magazine, laboratories, a model office, carriage maker's shop, blacksmith shop, foundry, a 12-horsepower steam engine, screw-cutting machine, drilling machine, circular and upright saws, bellows, lathes, patented mortising machine, turning lathe and stores of 800 iron cannon, 30 brass cannon, howitzers, mortars, Revolutionary trophies, 40,000 stands of arms, 100 wooden field carriages, and cast iron fortifications.[15]

On 7 March 1837, $25,000 was allotted for certain works at the arsenal: $3,200 for construction of 1,600 feet of seawall at the north end of the post; $12,000 for fill of James Creek and repair of the wharf; and $10,000 for completion of a magazine and keeper's house on a site between the long bridge and Georgetown. By October, none of this had been done. (photo 3)

In December 1837, the arsenal commander was advised the appropriation for preventing Indian hostilities was exhausted. He was told to support the endeavor with whatever stores he had on hand. Apparently the day of free gifts of choice to agents and Indian delegations was at an end.

Colonel Bomford wrote a seven-page letter to the Honorable William Coal Johnson outlining the advisability of establishing a National Foundry on the Potomac to provide cannon in case of emergency, thus insuring a constant price and government oversight of supplies and labor. He emphasized the Potomac location could furnish cheap labor from the tidewater area; had good communication facilities; was located on a navigable river open eleven months of the year; had abundant water, and adequate dwellings.[16] Although the logic was convincing, it didn't sell.

In May 1838, a great deal of attention was given to the construction of a building to house models of seacoast artillery. There were to be models of: (1) every species of military weapon or warlike machine with their appendages, (2) complete and exact drawings so copies could be made for other arsenals, and (3) complete working patterns for all the parts involved. An appropriation set aside $6,580 for a brick building, 50 x 36 feet, two stories, a basement and a portico, "nothing extravagant or gaudy, but not to present a meager plainness." Architectural drawings were completed by 9 July 1838 with instructions to build the portico of stone, if possible, and forwarded on 29 October [present building #21].[17] Mr Miller, model master, earned $3.75 per day, and his assistant $2.50.

Captain Ramsay was transferred to Frankford Arsenal in September 1838, but he would return several more times during his career. When he graduated from the Military Academy in 1820 he chose artillery branch. In 1835 he was promoted to captain -- a grade he would remain in for the next 25 years before retiring as a Major General. Captain William H Bell replaced him in September 1838.

New orders informed the commander that the men were to work 10 hours a day, year around; that he could hire a clerk at $1.50 per day, and that Mr Buck, recently arrived as military storekeeper, was to be paid at the same rate as a captain.

An undated news account writes of this period as follows:

> In November 1840, Captain John Symington who left the arsenal seven years before...returned to command where he remained till November 1844.... This was on the eve of the Mexican War, and consequently busy times were ahead. The discarded flints from the old-style arms had accumulated in great quantities and were sold with other condemned property; but the lucifer match, introduced a few years before, was driving the flint and tinder box out of use, and there was no sale for them, the whole pile, said to weigh a few tons, being sold for a song.
>
> The percussion cap having come into use and the process of making them being slow, two of the employees, Mr George Wright and Mr StJohn, set about constructing a machine for making them. Ere much headway had been made the latter left the city and abandoned the machine. It was, however, perfected by Mr Wright and excited wonder. From strips of copper fed to it the caps were cut, shaped, charged with fulminate, varnished and dropped out ready for shipping and use. By this machine the service of the government was supplied with caps, and a quantity was sent to European nations.
>
> Captain Mordecai, after an absence of eleven years, returned to the command in October 1844, and remained ten years. In this period the Mexican War took place, and the arsenal for several years was the scene of great activity, the number of employees being augmented and new branches of industry being added, with buildings for their accommodation, and in a little time as many hundreds of persons were on the rolls as there had been dozens before. The making of ammunition was a feature, and perhaps 150 boys were

employed in preparing cartridges -- "ball and buck." The harness shop, too, became an important part of the establishment in connection with cavalry equipment, and the fitting out of light batteries.

It was told of Major Mordecai that two old men waited on him once to ask an increase of wages...and his answer was: "No, not a cent more. Others are liable to discharge whenever the work slacks. You are part of the establishment that only death can remove."[18]

A 1936 newspaper article entitled "Near Centenarian Turns Memories' Light on Post" said:

> The population of the District of Columbia in 1840...was 23,765, there being 16,843 whites, 1,712 slaves, and 4,809 free colored people...[Captain Mordecai's daughter] who is not far from the century mark, has lived to see her native city greatly increase in population and develop from one of magnificent distances to the most beautiful Capital in all the world....She says she recalls being aroused from her trundle-bed by her father in April 1841, to look from her window in the Seven Buildings at the torchlight procession that escorted the remains of President William Henry Harrison to the Capitol to lie in state until the funeral took place....
>
> In 1846 my father was ordered to command the Washington arsenal....We led a very primitive life in those days without gas, electricity, water or autos in daily use. Experiments of all kinds for the ordnance were conducted by my father, who was highly educated and a great scientist.
>
> When the first murmurs of the Mexican War began to stir the country, the shops, officers, and soldiers were full of activity. I recall the quantity of grapeshot, canisters, bullets, etc., that were manufactured -- also harness, and the most wonderful ammunition chests, with compartments not only for the missiles but for all sorts of tools to repair damage of any kind. The troops were soon called to take the field, and great was the distress among the officers and soldiers who were called to leave wives and sweethearts for the glories of the field.
>
> Four young officers were stationed under my father -- Peter Hagner, James G Benton, T T S Laidley, and Samuel Ringgold, the last named a native of the District, with a frail wife, then in a delicate condition, and a lame sister dependent upon him. But he went in charge of the battery which was afterward called for him, "Ringgold's Battery."
>
> He was mortally wounded at the Battle of Palo Alto and died in Texas in the prime of usefulness (age 46) without

seeing his infant son, who was born at the arsenal....

All sorts of things were sent to my father. A weeping willow tree from the grave of Napoleon at St Helena was brought by Commodore Porter, who represented the United States when the body was removed to Les Invalides in Paris. It was planted by the well where we got drinking water...all the willow trees on the [illegible] are descended from it.[19]

A November 1843 Ordnance Department Report described construction of a ballistic pendulum for conducting experiments to determine the proper proportion of length and weight in construction of cannon, and to find the best method of manufacturing and proving gun powder. Later the same principles were adapted for a musket pendulum.[20]

Captain Mordecai reported on 10 November 1846 that no new construction had been undertaken and only repairs and maintenance performed on the buildings. The river wall around the arsenal was filled and regraded. A new 25-horsepower steam engine replaced the old one allowing the press and trimming machine to put out 40,000 balls in ten hours. Mordecai's inventory for the year included:

      26 - 6-pounder field carriages
     200 - Wheels
     120 - Ammunition chests
      52 - 24-pounder barbette carriages
   3,100 - Rounds of ammunition for field artillery
1,500,000 - Pressed musket balls
1,000,000 - Pressed rifle balls

The arsenal was operating with 25 enlisted mechanics and laborers, 110 hired men, and 50 boys making musket and rifle cartridges.[21]

When Texas won independence from Mexico and requested to become a part of the United States of America, it provoked war with the neighbor to the south. A cavalry battle in April 1846 opened hostilities. This conflict would be the training ground for soldiers not suspecting their lessons would be put to the test a mere fifteen years later. Many future generals underwent their baptism of fire in the famous battles of the War with Mexico. Engineer Captain Robert E Lee directed batteries that bombarded Vera Cruz and other sites, and Infantry Lieutenant U S Grant fired a mountain howitzer from a church steeple at Chapultepec.

The urgent need for munitions of war placed heavy demands on Washington Arsenal. Thirty additional mechanics and laborers were hired, and 25 more boys for making small arms cartridges.[22] As a result of the War with Mexico, the emphasis was on siege and mountain artillery, heavy howitzers, and 12-pound pack howitzers.

1825-1850, Peace and War

Unfortunately, it continued to be military policy to fight the next war with the weapons and tactics of the last. Breech-loading cannon would not be adopted for many more years. Cannoneers continued to step in front of muzzle-loaders, ram down powder and shot, stand clear for the discharge, then run back to swab and load again while lead rained around them. Captain Robert P Parrott developed a rifled iron cannon which the government rejected, but an artillery instructor at Virginia Military Institute recommended its use by the Confederates in the Civil War. Captain Thomas J Rodman devised a new casting method to strengthen cannon and increase their range which Federal troops would use to their advantage.[23]

By November 1848, a site had been selected and approved for construction of the arsenal's new powder magazine and keeper's house on public grounds on the eastern side of the city known as the Hospital Reservation [later used for the mental facility now known as St Elizabeths]. The cost was to be $10,000. Building materials were drawn from the arsenal.[24]

By mid-century, Captain Mordecai's last report of the principal operations at Washington Arsenal stated extensive repairs and alterations were made to officers' quarters, but the machine shops were in bad condition. Having been built on reclaimed land, they were dangerously cracked to the point that their condition seriously interfered with the efficiency of the machinery. As others before him, he strongly recommended the acquisition of additional land to alleviate the crowded conditions within the arsenal.

Strangely, few comments are listed in arsenal records about coexistence with the penitentiary. The first reference was in July 1826 when Lieutenant W H Bell wrote to Colonel Bomford:

> Persons said to be commissioners to establish a site for a penitentiary for the District of Columbia have recently authorized certain works to be commenced at this post, and have, for this purpose, marked off 420 feet on the banks of the Potomac. I have received no official information in relation to these works, and am at a loss to know whether they are to be permitted or otherwise.
>
> I beg that the Department will be pleased to give me the earliest information to this subject; and as to the extent of ground to be turned over to these authorities; as from what I understand they intend to proceed with the works tomorrow.[25]

CHAPTER IV: *1829-1862, The Penitentiary*

In America in the 1820s, there were two types of prison systems, both based on the theory that crime was caused by idleness and laziness, and that criminals should not associate with one another thereby learning additional larcenous practices. When the District of Columbia decided a penal institution was needed to deal with and stem crime in the capital, studies were made of Auburn prison (which separated the incarcerated only at night) and the Pennsylvania system (which kept prisoners in solitary cells at all times). This was an era of prison reform supporting the theory that punishment did not reform the perpetrator whereas segregation, discipline, and hard but productive work would accomplish rehabilitation as well as offset costs of confinement.

When an Act of Congress dated 3 March 1829 (US Stat. at Large, V 4, 365) created an establishment to be known as the "penitentiary for the District of Columbia," it included the following sections which outlined the annual appointment and duties of three inspectors (under the Department of the Interior), selection of wardens, system of rules for discipline, salaries of each office, restrictions against wardens and guards, segregation of sexes and youthful offenders, powers of punishment, health care, visiting privileges, et cetera.[1]

Once Congress authorized construction of the prison, President John Adams called upon Charles Bulfinch from Boston to study the site from SW "T" Street to the arsenal and draw plans within the $140,000 appropriation. The location was considered ideal because inmates and their supplies could be transported to the prison by water instead of being conveyed through the streets of the city. The architect previously worked on the Capitol and the Massachusetts State House, as well as designing and building the Massachusetts State Prison at Charlestown in 1805. Colonel J R Raymond described Charlestown Prison as "a bastile that belonged in the middle ages, slated for demolition in 1950, seventy-five years after it had been condemned for even the most hardened criminals."[2]

Bulfinch's plan (photo 4) called for a three-story brick building 120 feet long, 50 feet wide, and 36 feet high. It contained four tiers of 40 cells (160), 3'4" wide, by 7'11" long, by 7'9" high; each opening alternately north and south to prevent contact with adjacent cellmates. No bunks were planned -- only straw upon the floor. A two-acre courtyard would contain workshops, latrines, sheds, and a gardening area.

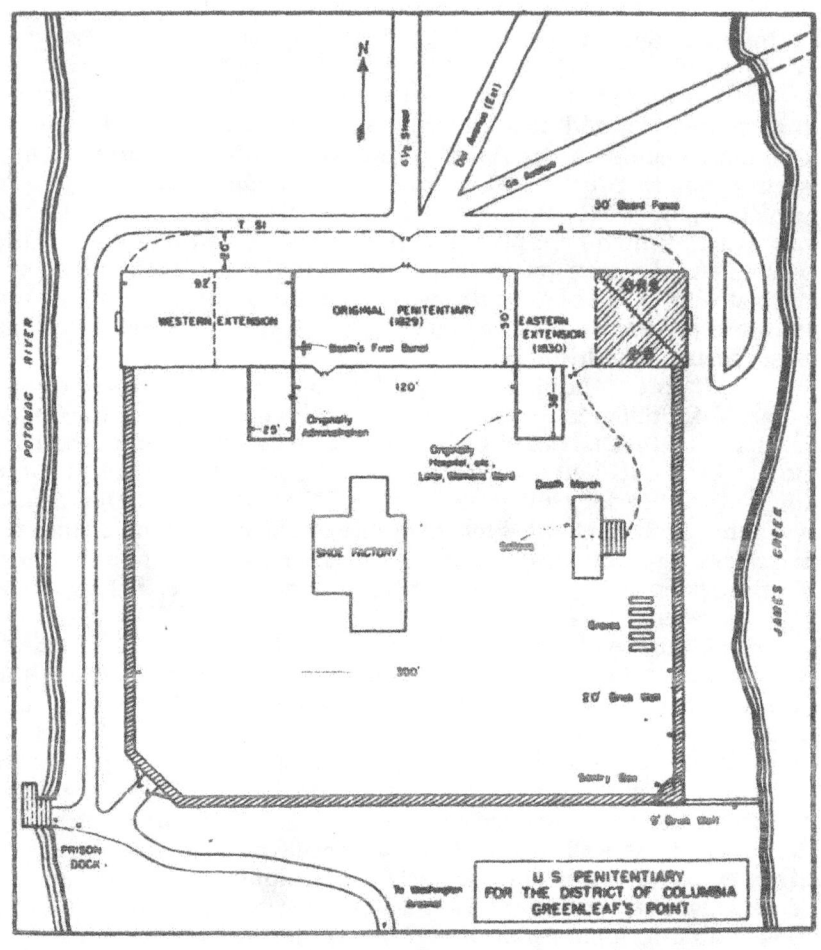

photo 4

Els 25 x 38 feet joining the main cellblock extended to the rear, or south, to accomodate administration and hospital facilities. The hospital wing later became the women's ward when extensions 92 x 50 feet were added on the east and west sides of the original cell blocks thus making the front footage over 300 feet long. Separating the prison from the city was a 30 foot board fence along T Street, and the other three sides of the institution were enclosed with a 20 foot high brick wall. The west extension was for the warden and his staff; the eastern extension accommodated the kitchen, laundry, and hospital staff. (photo 4)

On 21 August 1829, Lieutenant Symington wrote his superior:

> The inspectors of the penitentiary have requested of the Secretary of War permission to join a wall to that which incloses the arsenal grounds in order to provide a double gate way at their southwest gate.
>
> They have been informed, in answer, that it is necessary first to trace out on the ground the lines they may desire to occupy, and that you would then examine them and report thereon to this Department....
>
> I have called the attention of the inspectors to the condition of the roads between the river and the penitentiary walls, and have desired them to erect the wall according to the original understanding, designed for supporting the bank and the road, as well as to secure the wall of the penitentiary. This river wall should be at least sixty feet from and parallel to the penitentiary wall, and extend from the wharf to the north line of T Street; and be at least eight feet high above the water mark.[3]

After the prison was built, the road from 4-1/2 Street became a dead end at T Street, made a right turn to the banks of the Potomac, then ran to the south end of the prison wall where a dock had been erected for the transport of prisoners and penitentiary supplies and products. The road then angled eastward reaching the point in line with 4-1/2 Street where it turned south again to the arsenal gate.

Remnants of the penitentiary wharf can be seen in Washington Channel behind the present officers' club. (The wharf burned once due to sparks from a passing steamer, was often damaged by floods, and finally rotted away from lack of maintenance.)

The $141,000 prison was considered complete in 1829, and the first warden, Benjamin Williams, reported for duty in May 1830. Wardens were political appointees; none were trained. Warden Williams had spent the past two years awaiting completion of the governing rules, the settlement of the duties and pay of the inspectors, and visiting other prisons in New York, Boston, Philadelphia, and Charlestown.

The governing board first met in April 1829, and not having found an institution they considered to be a model to follow, the directors created a set Rules and Regulations as comprehensive as the US Constitution. This historic hand-written set of rules, bound in bound in leather and sealed in plastic is preserved in the National Archives.

The system was set in motion 9 April 1831 with the arrival of the first convict, Thomas Williams, who had been arrested for stealing a $6.00 barrel of flour and sentenced to one year. After examination by a physician, the prisoner's clothes and belongings were taken from him and he was given a striped uniform. Assigned a cell which contained a Bible, two blankets, and a coarse sheet, he was then apprised of the regulations:

> You shall be industrious and labor diligently in silence.
> You shall not attempt to escape.
> You shall not quarrel, converse, laugh, dance, whistle, sing, jump, nor look at nor speak to visitors.
> You shall not drink or use tobacco.
> You shall not write or receive letters.
> You shall respect officers and be clean in person and dress.
> You shall not destroy or impair property.[4]

Convicts received two meals a day in a dining hall where silence was strictly enforced. They were to be fed the "cheapest food that would support health and strength."[5] The cost of foodstuffs was not to exceed seven cents per day per prisoner; the total cost per inmate including bedding and clothing was to be sixteen cents per day. The annual expense of supporting the institution was $15,000.[6]

Throughout its history, the penitentiary was lighted by oil lanterns and heated by eighteen small coal burning stoves. No water was piped into the building -- a pump in the yard was the only source of supply. Prisoners worked in silence from sunlight to dusk, six days per week. Work was suspended on Sundays, but attendance at church and Sunday school was the only escape from a dank, cramped, solitary cell. There was no incentive to work except fear of punishment.

Punishment was swift and inevitable for the slightest infraction. Common regulation infractions included fighting, using vulgar language, attempting to talk to women, trying to escape, refusing to work, etc. Some of the more colorful punishments imposed included:

> -- Campbell was ironed and placed in a dungeon for fighting. He swore he would kill the guard, and was then taken from the dungeon and hung over the gallery for three hours.

-- For using insolent language and refusing to work, Williams was given twenty-two lashes on his bare back, required to work each day, and sleep in the dungeon at night.

-- Louise was maliciously malevolent, cursing, quarreling and putting pepper in Mrs Charles' tea. Considered the most depraved woman prisoner, no amount of punishment ever did her any good.[7]

By the end of 1831 the prison population was 21, including three females who were kept in a separate section and assigned work apart from the men. This was the first prison to separate young criminals and first offenders from hardened inmates, and to offer vocational training as a rehabilitative measure.

Warden Williams was accused of misappropriation of funds, incompetence, deficiency in ability and knowledge, use of prisoners to work in his home, and forged vouchers. By March, Williams had disappeared and never returned to the District. After Williams, all future wardens were required to be bonded since they handled federal funds. Acting Warden Pierce Spratt served until a new warden came.

The second warden, Isaac Clark, who served from March 1832 through May 1841, believed paddling was an appropriate form of punishment. Dr Thomas was appointed physician, and William Kirbey, Chaplain. The doctor earned $500 per year, guards $550, the Assistant Warden $750, and the Chaplain $250. The average number of new prisoners was 28 per year serving various terms of confinement.

To provide meaningful work and attempt to make the prison self-supporting, a shoe factory was established in a shop erected in the courtyard. The operation never cleared a profit. Foremen complained the prisoners were too lazy to work, wasted material trying to learn tasks they were incapable of, and were insufficient in number to accomplish a significant industrial product. Continuity was impossible due to alternating admissions and discharges.

The shoe factory ceased operation when a foreman bid on a contract to supply 15,000 pairs of shoes for the Navy. A law forbade government agencies to bid on government contracts. When the order could not be filled by the penitentiary workers, the the scandal came to light. The foreman died, and thus escaped punishment, but Warden Clark had to face a reprimand. As a point of interest, right and left shoes were not made for military personnel until so ordered by War Department GO #33 of 12 June 1851.

By 1838 the penitentiary housed 27 white prisoners and 49 colored, nine of whom were female. John B Dade arrived as Warden in May 1841, and supervised the installation until September 1845. He instituted total abstinence by all guards and workers which he found difficult to enforce. However, many convicts addicted to drink and tobacco at the time of incarceration kicked the habits with no ill effects -- not even temporary indisposition.

During Robert Coltman's tenure (September 1845 to November 1847) he reported that the prison population was 50 percent white and 50 percent black, among whom 18 percent could be considered incorrigible. Short stints as Warden were served by businessman C P Sengstack (November 1847 to April 1849) and Thomas Fitman (April 1849 to June 1850). During Stenstack's tour, Miss Dorothea Lynde Dix, of New York, donated a $100 library at her own expense.

Warden Fitman was totally against physical punishment and advocated that a positive admonition worked better than a whip. He suggested that instead of the penitentiary being restricted to District offenders, other federal offenders be sent there in order to have a sufficient number of workers to try new enterprises like a broom factory and a carpenter shop. He also recommended a task system whereby convicts would receive pay in proportion to the work they completed. This idea would not be put into practice until 1857.

Under Warden Jonas Ellis (June 1850 to June 1853), chewing tobacco was permitted, and lamps were allowed to remain on until 9:00 PM to permit inmates to read. The small library had afforded this pleasure only on Sunday afternoons, or summer evenings when the sun set very late. Warden Thos Thornley (1853 to 1856) cancelled the evening reading privilege after an escape was attempted. He also closed the blacksmith shop where the escape tools were forged. However, he added six spelling books to the library, bought with prison funds, and in 1854 he unsuccessfully tried using prison labor to turn out mechanical and agricultural implements. When he enforced the rule that inmates could not receive personal letters, a sit-down strike resulted. The prisoners refused to work and only gave in after ten days with just bread and water. Corporal punishment was reinstated.

Doctors assigned to the penitentiary all suspected that the slimy little James creek was responsible for the fevers and ailments of the inmates, but no one connected it with mosquitoes. It was assumed that the 20 foot walls should serve as protection against the swampy miasmas.

Chaplains were responsible for the welfare of the soul by providing worship services where sermons dwelt on the moral shortcomings of convicts. A Miss Martha Lincoln, of Washington, walked two miles to the prison each Sunday to bring words of encouragement to female prisoners.[8] The first female matron for six women inmates was hired in 1855. The women were assigned to do laundry and mending.

In 1858 the hospital was closed and converted into a work shop. By 1859, C P Sengstack was again appointed warden. He repeated his complaints of the noxious odors of collected sewage in James

1829-1862, The Penitentiary

Creek. He recommended the installation of iron bedsteads, and updating of lighting and heating systems. Discharged prisoners were given a new suit of clothes, not to exceed a cost of $10.00, and $2.00 in pocket money -- not even enough to get them past the first grog shop.

When Warden H J King took charge in October 1861 he found 226 prisoners, not all securely confined, and about half of the number idle. He set the convicts to work scrubbing floors and white-washing the walls. Ninety-two soldiers, sentenced by court-martial, were interned at the penitentiary between January and September 1862.

With the onset of the War of the Rebellion, the arsenal was in dire need of more space. A letter dated 18 September 1862 to the Honorable E M Stanton, Secretary of War, related that annexation of the penitentiary for additional storage space was vital.

> [There exists] the imminent risk of accident, which may destroy in a moment, the immense supplies of munitions of war collected at and daily arriving there, and on which the operation of the Armies in this vicinity are essentially dependant.
>
> Besides the want of storage room, which the use of the penitentiary would supply, its position within the arsenal grounds render it liable to such an occurrence by placing it in the power of any escaping convict to cause destruction by the simple use of a match.[9]

By order of the War Department, the building was vacated and turned over to the arsenal in September 1862.

> "The transfer to military authority was made with the greatest secrecy. Some of the prisoners were released to go to the front, and a few who had but little time to serve were pardoned. A number, however, were retained as prisoners, and one night were marched to a steamer and taken to Albany to complete their sentences. With this transfer, the history of the building as a civil prison ended.[10]

A recap will highlight the 33-year history of the penitentiary. During its period of operation, it received only 1,189 convicted prisoners, an average of 40 criminals per year, 90 percent of whom received less than two-year sentences. Of the total, 593 were white men, 506 were black men, 81 were black women or girls imprisoned for stealing or larceny, and nine were white women charged with larceny, stealing, or perjury.

Negro women outnumbered the white about four to one...Their sentences ranged from one to eight years, with the greatest number receiving sentences of two years or less. Their median age...was about 24 years....A possible reason [that Negro women outnumbered white] is that Negro women took a more active part in society than did the white women [who] led a very sheltered life and were very inactive outside the home. Another factor may have been that Negro women were not given the same respect and protection that white women were given.[11]

There were four successful escapes, three by white men convicted of murder and given life sentences. A fourth white man, William Wells, condemned to death for murder, had his sentence commuted to life imprisonment by President Fillmore, but escaped after eight years and was never recaptured. Only eight persons died in prison, and they were all white men in their twenties. Four white men convicted of rape were given ten year sentences, while six other white men received 15 years for the same offense. All of the more serious crimes receiving sentences of five years or more were committed by white men and women: murder, manslaughter, robbing of the US mail, rape, assault and battery, mutiny, arson, forgery, and counterfeiting gold coins. A farmer, Henry White, was given ten years for burning the US Treasurer's office. The only black men imprisoned for serious offenses included one for manslaughter who received eight years; one for burglary received 14 years, and a third man was given nine years for receiving stolen goods.

The penitentiary shoe shop was taken over by arsenal workers making harness, gun pouches, and other leather equipment. The prison dock was repaired and used for the shipment of supplies, movement of wounded soldiers, and docking of all manner of craft.

As the city celebrated the end of civil strife on 14 April 1865, President and Mrs Lincoln attended a performance of "Our American Cousin" at Ford's Theater. The next morning, Lieutenant Colonel Benton ordered the arsenal flag lowered to half mast in tribute to the President who had been shot in the head by a crazed actor named John Wilkes Booth.

Within twelve days, nine persons were apprehended and charged with conspiring to kill President Lincoln, Vice President Johnson, Secretary of State Seward, and Union forces General Grant. Michael O'Laughlin was arrested in Baltimore; Samuel Arnold was found clerking at the Sutler's store in Fort Monroe; and Lewis Paine was arrested at Mrs Surratt's boarding house at 604 H Street, NW, Washington, DC.

The three men were imprisoned aboard the ship *Saugus*, anchored midstream near the Navy Yard, and Mrs Surratt was placed in the Old Capitol Prison. George Atzerodt, assigned to dispose of the Vice President, was arrested in Maryland, 22 miles from Washington and held on another ship, the *Montauk* off Greenleaf's Point, as was Edward Spangler, who held Booth's horse at the theater. On 27 April, news came that Union forces had trapped Booth in a burning barn in Bowling Green, Virginia, but shot him when he refused to surrender. With him was David Herold, a mentally retarded clerk, who had met Booth outside Washington and accompanied him on his flight from justice. Herold was taken prisoner, and he and Booth's body were transported back to Washington where both prisoner and corpse were placed aboard the *Montauk*. Dr Samuel Mudd, who had set Booth's leg, broken when he leaped from Lincoln's box to the stage, was arrested and confined in Carroll Prison.

Just 26 days after the assassination, a Military Commission appointed by the Secretary of War met to consider the fate of the conspirators. The commission consisted of Major General David Hunter, President; Major General Lew Wallace (author of *Ben Hur*); Major General August Kautz; Brigadier General James Ekin and Colonel Charles Tompkins.

Building #20, presently converted to officers' quarters, was the site of the courtroom where the Lincoln conspirators were tried, and Mary Surratt was moved from Capitol Prison. The gallows for hanging the condemned assassins and their gravesites were near the present tennis courts. (photos 5 and 6)

The prosecution completed nine days of testimony on May 23rd hearing 131 witnesses. The defense rested on 10 June after examining 128 witnesses. Arguments continued until 29 June. By 5 July 1865 the sentences had been determined. Four conspirators received death sentences; three, life imprisonment; and one, a six-year prison term. George Atzerodt, a carriage painter; David Herold, a drugstore clerk; and young Lewis Paine, who had attacked Seward, and Mary Surratt were told on 6 July they had but one day to prepare to meet their Maker. The executions were carried out in the penitentiary courtyard on 7 July 1865.

Captain Watt was forced to coerce volunteer soldiers to build a scaffold, stand ready to spring the trapdoor beneath the prisoner's feet, and to dig the graves -- workers at the arsenal were too superstitious and refused to work. The carpenter shop did construct the wooden coffins. The prisoners were well aware of the sounds of preparation -- the hammering, nailing, sawing, and testing of the trap doors. Anne Surratt stayed with her mother all that long day and night, and up until a few minutes before her mother was led to the scaffold. The window in the upstairs room where the women waited inexplicably fogs up, even today.

photo 6 - Building #20 - Site of trial of Lincoln assassins. Present tennis court was where scaffold stood.

The Potomac River was filled with boats on 7 July, and dry and dusty 4-1/2 Street was crowded with the curious hoping for a glimpse of the gruesome activities. Within the prison yard were federal troops and 100 civilians with reserved tickets issued by the War Department. After climbing the steps to the gallows platform, the four prisoners were bound, hoods placed over their heads, and a noose placed around their necks. While photographer Matthew Brady recorded the event, Major General Winfield Scott Hancock, commander of the Military District of Washington, gave the order for the gibbet to be dropped. Within a half an hour, the four bodies were buried in graves beneath the gallows. Guests with tickets were served cake and lemonade. (photo 7)

O'Laughlin (accused of being assigned to kill Grant, but not proven), Arnold (who agreed to the kidnap plot, but refused to participate in murder and left Washington before the assassination), Dr Mudd (who missed hanging by one vote), and Spangler were sentenced to life in the Dry Tortugas. For O'Laughlin, it was a death sentence for he died there of Yellow Fever. The other three were later pardoned by President Jackson. To this day, Mudd descendents seek to clear the name of their ancestor.

There were many stories about the disposition of Booth's body. It was rumored he found a watery grave, or that the wrong man had been killed and identified, but the most authentic story came 46 years later. George Loring Porter, assistant surgeon at the arsenal at the time, related in the April 1911 issue of the *Columbian Magazine* that he had participated in transferring Booth's body from the ship to a grave dug in the southwest corner of a large storeroom, and the key to the room was given to Secretary of War Stanton.[12]

Stories linger of Mary Surratt's ghost pacing the floor, pleading for help. A sentry was once court-martialed for reporting he had encountered her ghost, but punishment was cancelled when his commanding officer saw the same apparition a few days later. Another warning says not to stare into the channel waters at night lest the hand of a drowned man pulls you to a watery grave.[13]

CHAPTER V: *1850-1875, Expansion*

Although the penitentiary separated the arsenal from the city, a railroad track and a half-mile of muddy road crossed a section of land between P and T Streets called the "Extension." This land bounded by the Potomac and James Creek was purchased by the Act of 2 March 1857 for the use of the arsenal. The 752,751 square feet of ground was not to cost more than ten cents per square foot; it brought the size of the military district up to 89 acres. For some years a high board fence marked the north boundary of the reservation. The increased size allowed space for a drill field, and also a 1,000 yard rifle range. The area was sparsely settled with a butcher's house on P Street and a slaughterhouse in the vicinity of Canal Street.

The main function of the arsenal was distribution, storage, and construction of gun carriages; repair of weapons; and manufacture of small arms ammunition. Stacks of cannon balls and rows of cannon lined the seawall. The ordnance stores were delivered and sent out by barge, steamers, and army wagons.

Captain Mordecai was relieved by Major W H Bell who commanded the arsenal from 1855 to 1858. Although his tenure was under peacetime operation, there were 200-300 workmen employed.

An undated news item in the Washingtoniana section of M L King Library states:

> New discoveries and inventions were made or tested here, and some which were crude were perfected. In the '40s, Colonel Colt, of revolver fame, experimented with a shell and succeeded in blowing up a small vessel moored in the Eastern branch, but he did little with the invention, the more valuable one of the revolver demanding his attention.
>
> There was also much experimenting there with explosives, the pendulum guns for that purpose having been put up near where Captain Villard's gun was mounted over sixty years ago. Some of the first tests with gun-cotton were made here, and it may be said but few explosives came into use which had not stood the tests at the arsenal.
>
> Many young officers of the past found the arsenal to be a fine place for practical work, and not a few who served as lieutenants rose to high rank afterward. Among those whose names can be recalled are Lieutenants Simonson, Childs, W E Williams, Ringgold, Brereton, Bassford, Reno, Hagner, Bradford, Babbitt and Rogers.

1850 -1875, Expansion

The work-shops contain much useful and ingenious machinery, propelled by steam...among these...the machines for planing and boring wood and iron, those for toning and mortising the spokes and hubs of wheels; Blanchard's ingenious lathe for turning irregular forms in wood such as spokes, axe handles, etc; machinery for making leaden bullets by pressing them out of a lead bar instead of casing them; and above all, the beautiful machine for making and charging percussion caps, for small arms, invented by Mr George Wright, a workman at the arsenal....

On the west side of the arsenal grounds, near the river, are two pyramidal structures which often attract the curiosity of visitors...These buildings contain an apparatus called a Ballistic Pendulum, which is used for testing the force of the gunpowder when fired in heavy ordnance, and also for trying many other interesting experiments in gunnery.

A simple explanation of the ballistic pendulum is that a weapon was placed in a sling, fired, and the effectiveness of the charge was judged by the recoil. A photo shows the pendulum houses located on the west bank, between the present officers' club and the tip of the peninsula. A target was mounted on the wharf which once stood at the southwest end of the arsenal compound. When the cannon fired, the round would pass through the target and fall harmlessly in the river beyond. In this manner, the optimum charge was determined, and the range plotted according to where the round splashed into the water.[1] (photo 8)

In June 1858, Brevet Major George D Ramsay resumed command. Although brevetted for gallantry at Monterey during the Mexican War, he did not become a regular army major until 1861. Mild mannered and unambitious, his intelligence and gumption were sometimes questioned. However, he came to be regarded as a friend of President Lincoln who often visited the arsenal to observe ordnance tests and escape advisors and job seekers.

Ramsay's first requests were for $1,000 to put the commanding officer's quarters in order, and authority to install lightning rods on post buildings. In July he requested that the road from the railroad depot to the foot of 5th Street, SW, be repaired so freight could be shipped to troops in Virginia. Even local citizens complained that 4-1/2 Street was nearly impassable since the last repairs had been made twelve years before when it was graded and graveled by the US Government. In September he stated that satisfactory tests had been made with Hale's Rocket, and suggested the arsenal be authorized to manufacture them.

An undated Washingtoniana news article entitled "Home Front, August 1861--Affairs at the Arsenal," described 800 iron cannon and 30 brass cannon in the arsenal yard. The article stated there was "much activity...the area blocked with army wagons and carts heavily loaded with arms and provisions...huge shells to be filled...huge guns ready to be mounted, while hammers clang, saws buzz...and a constant tide of muskets, rifles and bayonets roll in and out."[2]

Activity increased to the point that Ramsay requested additional help. He complained he could not act as military storekeeper in addition to other duties, and asked for two more lieutenants and two more clerks. In June he reported the arsenal could make 120,000 cartridges a day which would require 150,000 percussion caps. In November he reported the arsenal was flooded with water standing one foot deep in the machine shop, presumably from flooding of the Potomac. In addition to ordnance, the installation was also charged with making field harness for horses, and stocking and distributing saddles.[3]

By July 1862, there were 56 wagons hauling all day long. In a period of an hour and a half, 128 wagons passed through the gate. Feed bags, brushes, and currycombs were needed for care of the mules and horses. Ramsay was besieged by requests from artillery officers begging for nonexistent field telescopes. He reported that General George B McClellan often sent large orders which did not reach the arsenal until after nightfall, and then complained the post was lax in responding.

R V Bruce described an explosion when a building blew up:

> ...One afternoon...a workman used a cold chisel to cut a defective fuse out of a spherical case shot. A spark from the chisel ignited the fuse, the shell exploded. Seven or eight other shells---some in the hands of workmen--were detonated, and deadly fragments of iron flew in all directions. Surprisingly, only one man was killed outright, though three were terribly mangled. The explosion lifted the ceiling, blew out doors, buckled walls and set ammunition boxes ablaze. In the smoke-filled building were more than 36,000 artillery shells, and nearly 7,000,000 rounds of small-arms ammunition. But for the cool courage of the arsenal commandant [Lieutenant Colonel G D Ramsay], who came at once and supervised emergency measures till the fires were out, a fearful disaster might have struck Washington.[4]

Ramsay was promoted to Lieutenant Colonel in July 1861 and commanded the arsenal until September 1863 when he transferred to the office of the Chief of Ordnance. Major Benton replaced him.

During the war, women were eager for employment to support themselves and their families, even accepting hazardous positions like making cartridges at the arsenal. One of the worst catastrophes that ever occurred in the city of Washington took place on Friday, 17 June 1864. In a room where 29 girls were hand-loading cartridge cases, a spark from fireworks drying in the courtyard flew in the window and landed in an open bin of gunpowder. The fireworks had ignited from the intense heat of the sun. The resulting explosion killed 21 girls. Eight women escaped death, along with the chief clerk, Hosea B Moulton, who rescued a girl who jumped into the creek with her clothing afire. (Moulton, invalided out of the old army, would later be nicknamed "the Judge" and serve as doorkeeper at the Capitol until retirement in 1932 at age 89.)[5]

Workers saved themselves by jumping out of windows, and others were saved by the gallant efforts of storekeeper E M Stebbins, and members of F Company of the 16th Regiment under Captain Joseph B Collins, and Company D, 19th Regiment under Captain Charles H Tyler. Only six victims were identified.

An inquest held Thomas B Brown guilty of carelessness and negligence in placing highly combustible substances in a blazing sun so near a building. It also disclosed that girls wearing hoop skirts were burned the worst, the hoops allowing the flames to consume their dress faster.

A public funeral was held on 20 June. Bodies of victims were escorted to the Congressional Cemetery overlooking the Anacostia River in hearses and ambulances furnished by the Medical Department of the Army. Lincoln, himself, led the procession accompanied by Secretary of War Stanton. The War Department paid all funeral expenses and erected an impressive monument with a low relief panel depicting the explosion.

Throughout the Civil War, the arsenal at Greenleaf's Point distributed shot and shell, rifles and cannon to protect the nation's capital. The Inspector General for the District of Columbia, Colonel C P Stone, estimated the defense of Washington consisted of 300-400 men at the Marine Barracks, and 56 officers and men of ordnance at the Washington Arsenal. After the surrender of the Confederate Army at Appomattox, disbanding of the Union Army started on 1 June 1865. Within 153 days, 786,000 officers and men were mustered out of service and transformed back to peaceful citizens.[6]

The War Department cancelled all arms purchases and the rumble of army wagons was no longer heard at the arsenal. The 120 workmen turned to the business of disposing of large quantities of ordnance. Lieutenant Colonel Benton requested money to replace forty trees ruined by quartermaster wagons. He stated there were no Confederate cannon on hand, but asked for authority to sell Rebel small arms. He wanted the railroad tracks removed to do some grading, and recommended a brick walk from the outer gates to the old penitentiary area.[7]

1850 -1875, Expansion   53

The arsenal was assessed as being worth $737,881, of which $568,080 was land value, and $169,801 the value of the buildings. Peacetime requirements called for military forces to be stationed at the reservation for protection of the capital, and placed the arsenal under the jurisdiction of the War Department.[8] (photo 9)

On 18 December 1865, another explosion occurred at the arsenal in which eight men were killed--all discharged soldiers. They were sorting ammunition returned from the battlefield. Witnesses testified that ammunition containing loose friction primers exploded when a workman dropped a box.

On 7 April an unexplained fire at the arsenal damaged a large stand of arms. These later showed up at Fort Monroe, Virginia serving as a fence around the half-acre gun yard. The old-time musket barrels with bayonets attached had been sent there to be placed under the trip hammer and reworked, but with the war over they were not deemed worth the effort and expense.[9] Another explosion took place on 24 May 1866 when a 24-pound shell detonated while being unloaded. Fortunately, only two men were hurt.

A newspaper item told of changes taking place at the Washington Arsenal:

> ...The first step towards these improvements is to tear away the prison portion of the old penitentiary building, leaving those portions formerly occupied by the warden and deputy warden of the institution, which will be fitted up as officers' quarters. It is calculated that the buildings to be removed contain about three and one-half million bricks. These bricks will be cleaned and reused...
>
> The remains of the assassin Booth, which are buried just east of the new wall of that part of the building used as the warden's dwelling will be reached in the removal of the prison, but the remains of the other assassins Mrs Surratt, Payne, Herold and Atzerodt, with the Andersonville Jailer, Wirz, lie buried in the order named south of the eastern portion, and will not necessarily be disturbed...
>
> At present there is but little work going on at this post, owing to the immense amount of material remaining at the close of the war (during which the number of workmen frequently numbered as high as 1,200) and the force now is about 120, nearly half of them being laborers employed in taking to pieces the large number of gun-carriages at the post and storing them in sheds.[10]

Later, Booth's remains were reinterred in Baltimore; Mrs Surratt and Wirz were taken to Mount Olivet cemetery near Bladensburg; Herold was buried in the Congressional Cemetery; and Atzerodt found his final resting place at Glenwood. Payne was first buried at

Holmead Cemetery, but his remains were later shipped to his family in Florida.[11]

Being over age, Ramsay retired in September 1864. In June 1866, he was unexpectedly brevetted Major General and returned to command the arsenal. Never very complimentary about this officer, R V Bruce wrote that although Ramsay was relieved of command as Chief of Ordnance, Secretary Stanton "presently gave Ramsay the brevet rank of major general...and restored him to command of the Washington Arsenal until retirement in 1870." Bruce further stated that Ramsay was "straight as a rush" and "active as anybody" until he died at age 80 in 1882.[12] (photo 10)

Regarding changes in the military reservation when the the penitentiary was dismantled, Colonel Raymond wrote:

> Actually 44 feet of each end of the 92-foot extensions added to Bullfinch's original building were left standing. These were refaced with some of the reclaimed bricks, and covered with Connecticut freestone. [Architect Adolph Cluss is credited with the renovation.] Attached to the north side of each was an addition constructed of bricks salvaged from that part of the building torn down. These two "L's" [sic] were each 37 feet by 26 feet, and two stories high. The interiors were completely remodeled and modernized -- which in those days [1872] meant tin bath tubs, fireplaces, gas lights, and running water. Beautiful marble mantelpieces were imported from England and installed in each of the rooms....
>
> From the bricks obtained in the salvage operations a small guard house, presently Building 17-B [#17 in 1991], was built just east of the old prison wall between Quarters 2-B [now Building #20] and the Post Administrative Building, 3-B [now Building #21]. This guard house was one story in height, 30 feet by 25 feet, and 14 feet high.[13]

The *Outline of US Military Posts and Stations in the Year 1871* completes this description of Building #17-B:

> On the northern end is an extension 12 x 29 feet, in which are contained the cells, two in number. These cells are each 12 feet square and 10 feet high, with a passage 4 feet wide between them. They are damp within, in consequence of the floors resting immediately upon the ground. They are ventilated by skylights in the roof, but have no provision for heating. The guard-room, which occupies the entire main building, is warmed by a coal-stove, and ventilated by four windows.

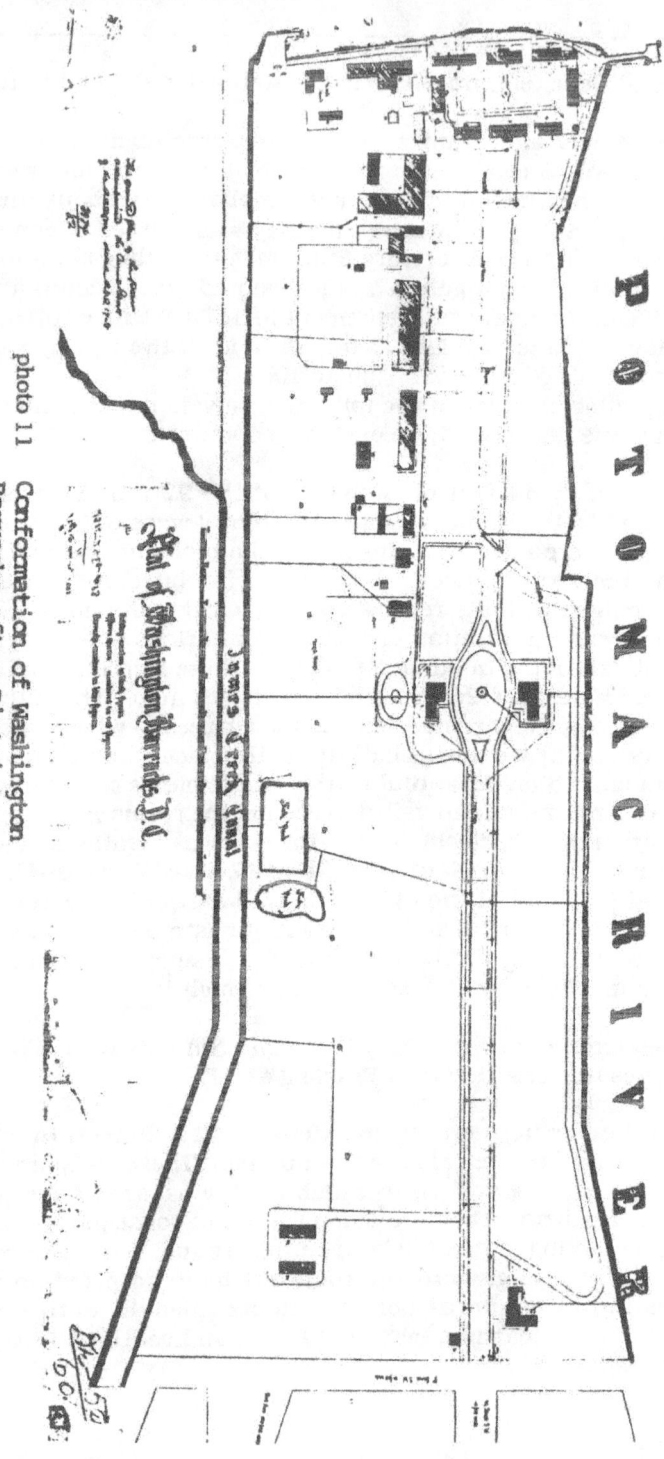

photo 11 Conformation of Washington Barracks after District Penitentiary was razed, 1867.

The building in which is the hospital is of brick, two stories in height, 76 x 25 feet. It contains 12 rooms, 6 of which are used by the hospital department, and the rest by the hospital matron and married soldiers. The hospital is heated by stoves, lighted by gas, and ventilated by windows. There are two wards with five beds each, the hospital cook and nurse occupying beds in one of the wards...There is no bath or wash room. The bath-tub is placed in a small closet, 3 x 10 feet, in the basement. The water-closet is about 40 feet west of the hospital, and is drained into the river. There is no dead-house at the post; and in case of death the body awaits in one of the hospital wards for burial.

The bakery is a small brick building, with a capacity for baking for 200 men. There is no laundry, chapel, or school-house on the post. The post library...contains about 500 volumes....

Four buildings are in use as officers' quarters. They are plain brick buildings, two stories high, 63 feet by 30, containing each eight rooms. One entire building is allowed to each officer. They are heated by stoves, lighted by gas, and ventilated by ordinary windows. Each house contains a water-closet and bath-room, and has hot and cold water throughout. The residence of the commanding officer, completed in the winter of 1873-74, is a brick building, three stories and basement in height, possessing all the modern improvements. The eastern front is plastered in imitation of Connecticut freestone.

One brick building is used as barracks. It is two stories and basement in height, 84 by 20-1/2 feet, and contains 8 rooms used as dormitories, besides a mess-room, kitchen, and bathroom in the basement....[14] (photo 11)

An undated Washingtoniana newsprint states:

The circle, on each side of which are located, on the right, the quarters of the commanding officer, and on the left, the quarters of the surgeon, marks the central point of the grounds....Now a fountain plays...in the midst of scarlet canna and colia beds. Trees, little flowering bushes, greens, and maples are planted round the grass-sodden circle, and at their base are pyramids of shining black cannon balls and several squat, smoothbore mortars painted red....The officers' mess is a one-story, slanting-roofed building full a hundred feet long and only twenty-six in width. It has more than half a dozen chimneys and the funniest little windows that were ever put into a house, having brown headings like hats too large for them to wear.

In 1870, the US Army consisted of 50,000 enlisted men on duty in various parts of the Union. It was commanded by a General, headquartered in Washington in a small red brick building on 17th Street, diagonally opposite the War Department [present Old Executive Office Building]. In addition the standing army included one lieutenant general, five major generals; 10 brigadier generals. Previously only 50 officers had been generals, and half of these had held that grade only during the war of 1812.[15]

By now the city of Washington was accessible by rail, and horse-drawn streetcars served the inner city. Luxury hotels such as the Willard and Arlington, and Ebbitt and Riggs Houses charged five dollars per day. Paved streets were beginning to make an appearance. The US Census of 1870 reported 131,700 persons in the District; by 1890, that number would double.

Colonel Franklin D Callender took command of the post when Major General Ramsay retired in June 1870. Callender is given credit for approving and overseeing the installation of the wrought iron entrance gates.

> The arsenal gates are always open from sunrise until sundown....The main supports of these gates are fashioned out of old cannon, 32- and 24-pounders, placed column-like, bolt upright, their muzzles turned up to the sky. Out from their trunnions stretch the crossbars which uphold slender iron shafts, on whose summits rear up more iron emblems of the bursting shells.
>
> On the central gate the huge letters "U.S." are woven in bronze, while on the side gates are placed crossguns and again bursting shells. The engineers' castles are soon to mount up over these artillery symbols.[16] [The central US gates have disappeared.]

Callender also oversaw the fill behind the seawall and the completion of the north wall built with bricks from the old penitentiary, each section of which is capped with a cannon ball with a flame bursting forth.[17]

By mid-1874, the arsenal commander was ordered to dispose of surplus war materiel by auction, and to give away cannon to Grand Army of the Republic Posts, to Soldiers' Monument Associations in various states, to Gettysburg Battlefield, and to townships for use in cemeteries. Although Europe used smokeless powder by 1865, the US Army was ordered to use black powder until the supply on hand was exhausted. How many gunner's lives might have been saved if the clouds of white smoke generated by black powder had not given away gun positions?

One of Callender's last orders in 1875 was to clear away the remnants of the old wharf. He was to see that the pilings were completely removed, not just sawed off, because the channel was narrow and somewhat shallow and piling stubs would endanger craft plying the river and be unsightly at low tide. Even at this time the Army Engineers had plans to dredge a channel on the west side of the arsenal using the fill to build an artificial island on a shoal in the Potomac River, thereby separating the reservation from the river, and creating a small boat channel to service the numerous commercial wharfs along Water Street. Eventually the long bridge from Virginia to the District would be replaced by a new structure anchored on the island created by the dredging.

CHAPTER VI: *1875-1900, End of an Era*

By 1875, masonry forts and smooth-bore cannon were declared "more dangerous to the defender than to the enemy." Iron-clad ships could level coastal forts. Rotting wooden gun carriages spilled their ordnance pieces to the ground, and the penny-pinching Congress refused to vote money for modernization. The Army was ill-equipped, having only modifications of old arms. It was commanded by old men, geared for administration not combat, weakened by decentralization, irrationally administered, inadequately trained, unsure of the scope of its mission, with no standardized system for recruiting and training soldiers.[1]

When Lieutenant Colonel John McNutt took command of the remnants of the arsenal in November 1875, his first mission was to arrange a military honor guard for the funeral cortege for Vice President Henry Wilson. Like his predecessor, his primary mission was to survey, sell, and get rid of old equipment such as McClellan saddles offered for $3.50 each. He was also ordered to submit estimates for repairing officers' quarters, and to compare operational costs with other arsenals and armories. The Chief of Ordnance ordered Captain Clarence E Dutton's explosives laboratory closed and all equipment shipped to the New York Arsenal.

In June 1876, McNutt was authorized to send a contingent of men to Philadelphia to attend the first International Exposition held in America. The celebration marked the 100th Anniversary of the Declaration of Independence.

Due to the impending closure of the arsenal, personnel were told to prepare to vacate and turn over to the Quartermaster Corps all facilities, plans and drawings of the grounds and buildings, with details of quarters, storehouses, carpenter shop, hospital, and married soldier houses.[2] Clearing the post of arsenal materiel continued. The boat, crane, and lathe were sent to Sandy Hook, New Jersey. The steam engine was shipped to the San Antonio Arsenal.

However, throughout 1877, Ordnance personnel were still filling requests such as: send one-hundred 3" Howitzers to Bighorn, Montana via Bismark; provide Gatling guns and ammunition for two batteries of artillery from Fort Monroe; issue the Ohio militia 1,500 rifles; and stand by to arm District militia.[3]

Lieutenant Colonel McNutt asked for a telephone to connect his office with the storehouse. The request was denied when told it would cost approximately $30 to install a wire, and $10 per year to rent a phone from the Chesapeake and Potomac Telephone Company. Telephones were not installed until after the turn of the century.

On 14 January 1878, House Resolution #2286 authorized the Secretary of War to sell the property occupied by the Washington Arsenal. This elicited hundreds of letters of protest pointing out that reacquisition of the land would be impossible and the site was essential for protection of the national capital.

A newspaper article dated 27 March 1878 stated:

> Gen. Meigs says that if the arsenal is no longer needed for the ordnance department, he recommends that it be placed in charge of the quartermaster's department, to be retained for military uses. The buildings, he says, would form a nucleus for quarters and barracks for the use of troops when passing through Washington....If sold now the buildings would go at a low valuation, and a loss to the Government....Gen. Meigs also calls attention to the fact that no great nation should be without some provision for the assembling of troops at its capital.[4]

Captain George W McKee arrived in June 1878 to take command of the post, relieving McNutt. He found the military reservation in a state of flux as Ordnance personnel were replaced by Artillery Batteries. A temporary solution was to assign half the useable facilities to the newcomers. Thus buildings such as barracks and quarters were divided between Ordnance personnel and the newly arrived B Battery of the 2d Artillery commanded by Brevet Major Joseph C Breckinridge. During this interchange of mission, some sharp conflicts occurred between post surgeon, Dr Hazen, and the ordnance and artillery commanders, but eventually even the hospital was divided. Stores were removed from the burned building which was put to use as barracks for artillerymen. Captain McKee was authorized to build a bake-house near the end of the burned building.

By June 1880, Lieutenant Colonel James M Whittemore [who would retire as a colonel in 1900] had taken command of the military reservation. He was ordered to return the land in Anacostia accommodating the arsenal powder magazine to District Commissioners to construct an asylum for the insane. Magazines were to be established on post near the stables.[5]

Five-year enlistments were recommended and adopted giving greater stability to military units, thus reducing training time. Emphasis was placed on revitalizing US military forces with new ships, forts, and guns to guard against increasing European imperialist and expansionist tendencies.[6]

In February 1881, the General of the Army directed that the garrison designation of "Artillery Troops, Washington Arsenal, District of Columbia," henceforth be known as "US Barracks, Washington, DC." For the next 20 years, Military District #5 would be the home of a five-battery artillery regiment, although the number of units would vary month to month, and year to year.

The 2d Artillery Headquarters, under the command of Colonel Romeyn B Ayers set up at the US Barracks (destined to be referred to as Washington Barracks) in April 1881 where one or more batteries had been stationed since 1877.[7] For his illustrious duty during the Civil War, Ayers, a West Pointer, received six brevets, the last being Major General in both the Regular Army and the Volunteers. He was six feet of soldierly bearing and considered a brilliant tactician. The story is told that Ayers disliked getting up early. Since reveille was supposed to be at daybreak, he issued an order that daybreak would be at six o'clock the year around.[8]

One to six batteries would constitute an artillery regiment, commanded by a major or lieutenant colonel and a staff. The number of soldiers in a battery varied from 50 to 150. Some men were reenlistees with a little training, but most troops were raw recruits with no experience nor discipline. Almost every officer was a graduate of four years training at either the Army or Navy Military Academies with technical knowledge but little leadership experience. They had learned tactics and doctrine, but implementation of theory was largely pragmatic--what worked at the moment was put to use.

Junior officers were detailed to lead a small squad of four to ten enlisted men. They learned by observing older officers and listening to experienced noncommissioned officers. First lieutenants commanded a platoon of 20 to 50 troops. Their performance and training methods were overseen by the captain battery commander.

Besides the regimental commander, the staff included an adjutant, who saw to the distribution of orders and took care of administrative duties; a quartermaster was responsible for shelter and equipment for the unit; a commissary officer saw to food and supplies needed. If available, a chaplain and surgeon would be assigned to the staff. In training environments, instructors were attached to teach specialized courses.

Garrison duty consisted of standing formations [being present at], guard duty, kitchen police, drill, weapons stripping and maintenance, marching, parade practice, calisthenics, riding, driving teams, stable duty, care of draft and saddle animals, et cetera. Daily reports indicate that units took turns going by train to Annapolis for annual firing tests and training in handling large ordnance pieces. Along James Creek there was a 1,000-yard firing range for practice and qualification with small arms (rifles and pistols).

Special duty requirements covered funerals, White House guard duty, inaugurations, ceremonies for dignitaries, and holiday performances. In contrast, daily garrison life was routine, predictable, dull, "hurry up and wait," dawn-to-dusk duty. Officers assigned to command these troops had to be firm but fair, competent, innovative, and competitive. They had to find ways to make painting cannon balls or peeling potatoes seem as soldierly as qualifying for expert marksman.

The officer roster was seldom stable for more than a year. Individuals were transferred from one battery to another to gain practical experience; they were detached to other regiments for special duty, or sent to Fort Monroe for one or two years at the Artillery School of Instruction. Other interim duties such as courts-martial, equipment inspection and surveys, and promotion boards, had to be performed without letting training suffer.

Officers on duty at Washington Barracks before the turn of the century who served with distinction include:

W E Berkheimer received the Medal of Honor for leading a charge in the Philippine Island of Luzon of 20 men against 300 entrenched Filipinos, routing them and saving the day. He enlisted as a private in Iowa in 1863 and was a USMA graduate of the class of 1870.

Captain A Capron of Battery E, 1st Artillery Regiment advanced his pieces of artillery in Cuba within 1,000 yards of the enemy to assist an infantry charge. Although the white smoke from the black powder guns gave away the artillery positions, the enemy guns were so obsolete they were entirely ineffective.

Fredrik Fuger, of German origin, enlisted as a private during the Civil War and received a battlefield promotion to 2nd lieutenant. When all officers were killed or wounded during Pickett's Charge at Gettysburg, he took command of Battery H, 4th Artillery Regiment, and with five guns disabled, he continued to fight until ordered to withdraw. He achieved the rank of major by 1899 and retired in 1900.

H L Hawthorne, a Naval Academy graduate in 1884, was awarded the Medal of Honor in October 1892 for gallant coolness and discretion in handling and serving the guns of his command in action against hostile Sioux at Wounded Knee Creek in December 1890. He was severely wounded while commanding his platoon of light artillery, but turned his Hotchkiss mountain howitzers on a group of Indians attempting to recapture the pony herd.

Officers who rose to the rank of general include Francis L Guenther, Andrew Hero, Alexander C M Pennington, Romeyn B Ayers, H G Gibson, Jacob B Rawles, Peyton C March, George D Ramsay, and Frederick S Strong. March and Strong were both four-star Generals.

The water supply for Washington Barracks came from the end of the city line on 4-1/2 Street, and ran the length of the post through an eight-inch cast iron pipe. The line served 21 of the 32 buildings. Lateral pipes had been installed, but there was no blueprint of their locations; they were discoverd only when the pipes rusted and sprung a leak. The Quartermaster did not pay for the water. In addition, a 25,000 rainwater cistern was in front of the enlisted quarters, and a well with excellent water.

In May 1885, Colonel H G Gibson, brevetted a brigadier general for action at Antietam, assumed command of the post. Projects already approved but awaiting action included a recommendation to build a new guard house, "as strong as the Capitol itself," and to use the approved appropriation of $9,777.65 to remodel an old building in the arsenal quadrangle into three sets of officer's quarters.[9]

In 1887, D R Keim's guide book stated that the US Barracks, formerly the US Arsenal, could be reached by Horse Railways passing 7th and 9th Streets en route to the terminus at 4-1/2 Street. Here could be seen

> various styles of guns and mortars....The commanding officer's quarters are in the large building on the right....The officers' quarters are in the quadrangle at the foot of the Peninsula, and for men and stables on the left....The garrison consists of Foot and Flying Batteries [horse-drawn caissons]....[10]

The Canteen Council made up of Adjutant Chase and battery commanders Turnbull, Lancaster, and Davis met on 29 October 1889 and agreed to convert the late Post Trader's store, formerly the arsenal tinshop, into a canteen. Although only 25 x 30 feet, it sat alone and extensions could be added once the dilapidated ceiling and broken floors were repaired. When partitioned and whitewashed, it could provide a library and reading room, as well as a billiard room, thus conforming to regulations to provide entertainment for enlisted men. All that was needed, as usual, was funds.

In 1890, a fire in a set of quarters prompted purchase of $540 worth of fire-fighting equipment, including buckets, hoses, and pumps. When repairs were made to 4-1/2 Street and sidewalks installed, $600 was earmarked to raise 1,400 feet of the north brick wall to a height of nine feet, requiring 150,000 bricks. The old crib work and piles of the wharf were hazards to navigation. The Light House Commission was ask to mark the area with warning buoys, but by December 1893 a repaired wharf and new boathouse were reported.[11]

The area between Washington Barracks and the White House long remained marshy and subject to flooding. Link-up of the C&O,

Tiber, and James Creek canals was not completed before other forms of commercial transportation made barging obsolete. Congress was reluctant to approve costly river and harbor bills, and ordered the Army Corps of Engineers to come up with a solution to flush the refuse away from the city. The task was assigned to Peter Conover Hains, an 1862 USMA graduate as an artilleryman. He transferred to topographical engineers, and was brevetted three times during the Civil War. He remained in the Corps of Engineers, retired as a major general in 1916, and died in 1924--the last member of his graduating class.

Major Hains oversaw a plan designed to drain and fill the low areas around the monument grounds, construct a tidal basin with gates diverting a flow from the Potomac through an artificial channel skirting the shore from Georgetown to Greenleaf's Point thereby providing a protective harbor for the commercial wharfs and docks of the city. Digging this channel created an artificial island, Potomac Park, on a shoal in the Potomac which reclaimed 739 acres.
(Photo 12)

In December 1890, a House resolution and Senate Bill 54471 proposed selling the US Barracks and using the money to enlarge Fort Myer and rename it Fort Grant. Major General J M Schofield and Secretary of War Redfield Proctor supported the proposition. They stated that no matter how much money was spent on Military District #5, it could never be a healthful spot since main city sewers emptied into it.[12] No action was taken, and James Creek continued to be the best mudhole cow-catcher in Washington, DC.

General Order 80, 1 December 1892, designated Washington Barracks as the official Saluting Station to return gun salutes of foreign vessels entering the port.[13] This custom evolved from armed warriors rendering their weapons harmless to prove their visit was peaceful. Early warship salutes would fire seven rounds, and land batteries would reply with three times that number since their supplies were greater and closer at hand. Starting in 1810, an honor salute fired the same number of rounds as there were states in the Union. Today, when gun salutes are given for American or foreign dignitaries, the number of cannon fired is in accordance with the position held by the visitor -- from 15- to 21-gun salutes.

As city transportation retired horse-drawn streetcars and installed an electrical conduit system, in 1892 the Metropolitan Railroad built a combination powerhouse and carbarn at P and 4-1/2 Streets -- directly across from the Washington Barracks entrance gate. *Capital Losses* describes the building as a conservative, utilitarian, late-Victorian design by John B Brady. On one front corner was an imposing tower, with rounded corners and patterned brick cornices resembling a church belltower. Actually the building was just a huge shed whose roof was supported by an intricate steel truss system. In 1896, a hurricane caused the tower to collapse, but did not badly damage the rest of the shed. When first built, it was used for storing and servicing streetcars; in 1934 it was turned into a paint shop; and it was finally razed in 1962 when streetcars were replaced with buses.[14]

When Colonel LaRhett L Livingston was assigned command in June 1893, a newspaper extract in the Washingtoniana section of the M L King Library in Washington, DC, gave a last glimpse of the installation:

> The first building passed is the guard house, with its vigilant sentinel pacing up and down in front. Next comes the large, solid-looking headquarters building where Colonel Livingston and Adjutant Birkham [Berkheimer] have their offices, and where the business of the post is transacted. This is truly a busy spot. A view of the clerical labor required at a post like this would surprise one not familiar with campaign and garrison duties.
>
> The busiest man, without question, in the post is Sgt Maj Frederick Semple. The sergeant is a model [noncommissioned] officer and his office is a model of method. He has charge of the correspondence, reports, returns and records of the twelve batteries that constitute the [3d Artillery] Regiment [A, C, E, K, and I batteries]....The duties are congenial to him, and he will enlist for a fourth time in a few days. He has been in service nearly fifteen years....
>
> The two next large buildings to the southward are used as barracks for the men, the small buildings standing between them being the quartermaster's and officers' carriage house and stables. The large L [sic] in the rear of the north building of this group is called a Recreation Hall, and here it is that the people living in the barracks have their amusements. Here they have their dances, parties, etc. The Women's Christian Temperance Union occupies it every Wednesday evening. The floor is well waxed and the walls are beautifully draped with old flags, guidons, and pictures which show signs of hard usage. The Maltese cross of the old Fifth Corps of the Army of the Potomac is numerously represented....There is talk of turning the lower hall of this wing into a billiard room for the use of the men.
>
> The band and part of the noncommissioned staff occupy the next building, in the rear of which is the canteen, where nearly everything a soldier needs in the way of eatables and drinkables (except wine and distilled spirits) is sold. Beer is the only intoxicating beverage allowed to be sold, and it is of the best quality made. Nearly every officer and soldier that you question on the subject will tell you that the army canteen is a good thing; that it is good for the soldier's pocket

and morals, as well as being in the interest of better discipline among the men. It is said that there is less drinking and drunkenness than under the old method. Instead of wandering around the streets, exposed to the many temptations that beset young men, the boys remain in camp and drink their beer if they feel so disposed.

Following come the offices and storehouses of the quartermaster and commissary of subsistence, the barracks, stables, sawmill, garden cottage, oil house, bake house, coal house, and workshops....In former days these old buildings were foundries, gun sheds, timber storehouses, engine sheds, driving-houses, armorer's shops, finishing shops, and a storehouse for guns, shot, shells, small arms, artillery implements, equipment for cavalry and infantry accoutrements. The buildings are painted a light-toned brown with dark trimmings, the very look of fading leaves.

The buildings forming the quadrangle in the extreme south end of the grounds on the Anacostia are occupied by officers of the post. A sun dial, time bell, and flagstaff stands in its heart. This is the oldest part of the post, and it was in this point that the old fort originally stood. The old-fashioned buildings are gathered close in a ring. Two arched gateways enter the Spanish-looking courtyard, and the southernmost quarters back right down to the water, saving for the seawall, like the houses of Venice. Then, too, every one of them is a little "picture house."

Nearly every house in the quadrangle dates back to 1829 or before, and not one has been modernized, so living there today is far from being a picnic, even if it does sound picturesque.

Truth is that the arsenal has been made over, cut and recut till its old bones ache and it can do no more, and though it can put on, and does put on, a fine-looking uniform, close inspection reveals rags and tatters beneath the coat with all of the lining gone. It has been a good soldier, and it needs a more comfortable home in its old age, and certainly some new clothes.... [No author, date, nor publication shown.]

Livingston was replaced in June 1893 by Colonel Henry W Closson, a USMA graduate of 1854. Closson had served on frontier duty, in the Florida Seminole struggles, throughout the Civil War, and attained the rank of colonel in 1888. He remained in command until May 1896 when he was temporarily replaced by Major J B Rawles until Colonel F L Guenther arrived in September. Guenther had been promoted to captain at Shiloh, major at Stone River, and permanent colonel as he assumed command of Washington Barracks; before being reassigned, he would be promoted to brigadier general. Under Guenther's tenure the post again bristled with activity with the approach of the Spanish-American War. Blue clad soldiers marched and countermarched in the cleared areas.

When the battleship Maine was blown up in Havana Harbor in February 1898 with a loss of 260 American lives, untrained troops were mustered and rushed to shoulder outdated weapons, in insufficient quantities, without ammunition to fire. The 6th and 7th Regiments of Artillery were formed at this time and batteries of these units served and trained at Washington Barracks before shipping out to Cuba or the Philippine Islands.

After the US destroyed the Spanish fleet in the Philippines ending hundreds of years of oppression, the Filipinos rallied against the occupation forces for not giving them immediate freedom. On the scene was artilleryman Peyton C March who graduated from West Point in 1888 and reported to Washington Barracks as a 2nd lieutenant. He completed the Artillery School Course at Fort Monroe in 1898 just in time to take command of the elite volunteer "Astor Battery" [privately funded by banker John Jacob Astor] en route to the Philippines.

After being brevetted several times for his service in Luzon, March spent the next 26 years with troops. He was appointed a major general in 1918, sailed to France with the American Expeditionary Force, but was called back to become Chief of Staff of the Army, charged with getting two million men overseas to win the war. He is credited with streamlining the General Staff, creating specialized branches of military service, reducing political interference in military matters, and establishing the office of Chief of Staff as the immediate advisor to the Secretary of War on all military actions.

During the Spanish-American War, a new activity was created at Washington Barracks. US Volunteer Signal Corps troops, partially organized elsewhere, came to Washington to complete unit organization, receive equipment, and move out to other locations for training. Among units accommodated at this time were the 3d, 7th, 12th, 13th, and 16th Companies of the Volunteer Signal Corps.

1875-1900, End of an Era

By the turn of the century it was obvious that Washington Barracks was too confined for field artillery training. Since the Engineer School of Application at Willets Point, New York was looking for a new home, Washington Barracks was selected as a suitable location; Artillery units made plans to depart. Artillery units that served at Washington Barracks include:

1881 - 2d Arty Regt, B Battery
1882 - 2d Arty Regt, A, B, C, D, H Batts
1883 - 2d Arty Regt, A, B, C, D, Batts
1884 - 2d Arty Regt, A, B, C, D, G, M Batts
1890 - 3d Arty Regt, A, C, E, H, K, L Battss
1891 - 3d Arty Regt, A and C Batts
1892 - 3d Arty Regt, A, C, E, M, K, L Batts
1893 - 3d Arty Regt, A, C, E, K, I Batts
1894 - 1896, 4th Arty Regt, A, G, I, M Batts
1897 - 4th Arty Regt, G and I Batts
1898 - 1st Arty Regt, E Batt
1898 - 3d Arty Regt, A, C, E, H, K Batts
1898 - 6th Arty Regt, C, D, E Batts
1898 - 5th Arty Regt, K and L Batts
1899 - 3d Arty Regt, A, C, E, H, K, L Batts
1899 - 7th Arty Regt, M and O Batts
1900 - 7th Arty Regt, M Batt[15]

At the turn of the century, the sentinel on the Potomac was assigned a new mission requiring a complete face-lift.

CHAPTER VII:
1901-1919, The Engineer School

The United States Corps of Engineers dates from the American Revolution but was officially formed in 1802 when Congress created a Corps of Engineers to establish a military academy at West Point, New York. The Corps was first charged with making coastal surveys, and planning and building fortifications. Their responsibilities gradually expanded into construction and repair of dams, roads, buildings, canals, et cetera. The Engineer Corps grew to be the largest and most diversified technical service fulfilling both military and civilian needs.

By 1900, proposals to reform the army included (1) state militias trained by regular army, (2) education of all males of military age, and (3) better branch training. Yet by the end of World War I, 48 percent of the officers had only three months more experience than the enlisted men; only one out of six had any previous military experience; and of the 200,000 officers at the time the armistice was signed, only 6,000 were Regular Army -- the rest were products of brief officer candidate schools.[1]

At the outset of World War I, the Corps of Engineers consisted of 256 officers and 2,000 enlisted men, but by 1918 it had expanded to 11,175 officers and 285,000 enlisted men.[2] Like other branches of the Army, as changes in the rules of war took place, the engineer branch saw a need for advanced training of officers, as well as for continuous training of troops who rotated in and out of the service.

US War Department General Order 117, 3 September 1901, called for the Engineer School to move from Willets Point, New York to Washington Barracks. This was followed by General Order 155, 27 November 1901, authorizing establishment at Washington Barracks of: (1) an Engineer School of Application, and (2) a War College for advanced professional study for army officers. The old arsenal buildings were too dilapidated to house the Engineer School. The cracked and decayed structures were ordered razed and new buildings erected suited to Engineer School needs, along with quarters for officer and noncommissioned officers assigned to the school. When the proposal was presented to the Secretary of War, the Honorable Elihu Root slyly endorsed the plan with the stipulation that an area be set aside for an Army War College (although the concept was still in the planning stage and not yet officially sanctioned).

The last artillery battery commander at Washington Barracks, Captain C D Parkhurst, wrote to the Adjutant General, Department of the East, Governor's Island, outlining the limitations of the reservation. He reported the old barracks could only house 300 men whereas a full battalion of engineers consisted of 418 men; 24 more rooms would be needed if the band accompanied the new school; the small drill area was unlevel and cut up with trees; and that a full battalion could not form a line in front of the barracks without extending beyond the seawall. [Hopefully the last men in line could swim.]

Parkhurst stated the old buildings were even inadequate for storage of Quartermaster and Commissary supplies, and that most of the northwest portion of the post was occupied by the General Hospital -- an entirely separate command requiring housing for its Hospital Corps of Instruction.

The Captain described the spongy, fetid ground surrounding James Creek and the sparsely settled land on the east bank which could not offer additional space unless the land were available. Because James Creek Canal was under District supervision, unknown rights would have to be investigated before the creek could be filled or bridged. He noted there was a large brick factory at Canal and P Street that barged its clay from the Anacostia River, and that the canal was bridged on M and N Streets thereby limiting its use as a waterway to gravel and sand barges. He concluded by saying cleanup and practice of modern sanitation methods could eliminate mosquito breeding, and with a bit of fill and leveling the reservation could become one of the finest posts in this part of the country.[3]

Parkhurst's unit left for Fort Myer, Virginia on the morning of 10 October 1901 and the Army Engineers moved in that afternoon.

The new post was to be constructed according to plans drawn by the architectural firm of McKim, Mead, and White. They were given instructions to completely raze the US Barracks and reconstruct the reservation in a harmonious design to accommodate a new Engineer School of Application and an Army War College. It was unusual for a civilian firm to draw up blueprints for military engineers to construct, subcontract, and supervise labor performance. It was inevitable that a few squabbles would ensue.

Despite that, reconstruction went forward swiftly and efficiently resulting in a symmetrical, park-like campus with only one flaw. Because of the immediate need for space, three old 19th century buildings in the center of the parade ground were not torn down: an old post guardhouse, a model museum, and the east wing of the old penitentiary. They effectively blocked out the "picture" of the magnificent war college on the tip of the peninsula and left only the frame. When a member of the architectural firm came to see the completed construction, the sight that met Stanford White's eyes as he entered the main gates must have been as painful as the fatal bullet fired into his chest a few years later by Harry Thaw, a jealous husband.

Under the Engineer School regime, Major W M Black was the first post commander followed by Major Edward Burr (1903-1906), Major E E Winslow (1906-1907), Lieutenant Colonel W C Langfitt (here in various capacities from 1906 to 1910), Major R R Raymond (1910-1911), Major W J Barden (1911-1913), Major W P Wooten (1914-1916), and Col M M Patrick (1916-1917). Undoubtedly, all these commanders occupied the row of handsome officers' quarters completed in 1905 along the Washington Channel seawall. Appendix B documents the occupants of these quarters.

The physical move of the Engineer School property and personnel from Willets Point took three days via the Old Dominion Steamship Line. Upon arrival at Washington Barracks, freight was unloaded by local labor but distributed for placement by arriving troops: nine sergeants, nine corporals, 71 privates, two cooks, and two musicians. Instructional material was placed in the old penitentiary building #2-B (now #20) which was to serve as classrooms. The new tenants plunged into housekeeping, teaching, and training activities. (photo 13)

Administrative duties were discharged from building #3-B (now building #21) constructed in 1838 as the Arsenal model museum to house scale drawings and one-quarter-sized models of all ordnance pieces. In 1990 when bird nests were being cleared from the eaves of the front porch, removal of a board disclosed the original name, "Model Arsenal," still very legible.[4] Building #27 (now #17) on the parade ground east of the tennis courts served as a guardhouse and later as the Engineer Photography School.

Impacting on troop discipline was a February 1902 message to Lieutenant F C Boggs, Corps of Engineers, Washington Barracks, from the clerk of the Excise Board for the District of Columbia: "within one mile of your location there are 50 barrooms (ten located on 4-1/2 Street), and two wholesale liquor dealers."[5] (The Volstead Act [Prohibition] was not enacted until late 1920.)

In July 1902, Major Black reported to Brigadier General G L Gillespie, Chief of Engineers, that the $10,000 costs for the fiscal year covered workmen, a chief clerk, a storekeeper, purchase of lumber, office furniture, and contingencies (i.e., materials, tools, ponton equipage, express, freight, telegraph and telephone, and mileage).[6]

As the Engineer School undertook its mission, the 1903 report on *Military Posts and Reservations* stated:

<u>Summary of the Post as it Exists</u>:
  Old officers' quarters for 11 married and 9 bachelor officers; noncommissioned staff quarters... one set of 4; barrack building, 1 (capacity, 186 men); band barracks (capacity, 28

men); mess halls, 2 (temporarily occupied as barracks, capacity, 93 men each); garden cottage, 1; waiting room at gate, 1; administration building, 1; Engineer School 1; post exchange 1; photographic laboratory, 1; main guardhouse 1; stable guardhouse, 1; quartermaster and subsistence storehouse and offices, 1; quartermaster stable sheds, 1; light artillery stables, 1; light battery stables, 1; temporary stables, 2; post bakery, 1; blacksmith shop, 1; carpenter shop, 1; boathouse, 1; new coal shed, 1; signal-train shed, 1; scale house, 1; battery water-closet, 1; water-closet, 1; wharf 1.[7] [All of the above was scheduled to be demolished.]

These must have been confusing times with the Engineer School set up under one commander, the Army General Hospital operating as an independent command, and an Army War College designed by civilian architects being constructed under the supervision of an Army engineer, Captain John S Sewell.

Captain Sewell had an interesting career. Graduating second in his USMA Class of 1891 he was detailed to Washington, DC to construct public buildings until 1897. As a member of the 1st US Volunteer Engineers during the Spanish-American War he rose to the rank of Lieutenant Colonel before mustering out in 1889. Returning to the rank of Captain, he again worked in Washington on such projects as the Government Printing Office, Department of Agriculture buildings, the Soldiers' Home, the Army War College and buildings of the Engineer School at Washington Barracks where he was assisted by Mr Mark Wilmarth, a civil engineer, and by Captains Markham, Benton, and others.

He resigned in January 1908 to become vice president of the Alabama Marble Company, but with the advent of World War I, he joined the AEF as a Colonel commanding a regiment of engineers. As commander of the base port at St Nazaire, France, he earned the Distinguished Service Medal. After the war, he resumed presidency of the Alabama Marble Company, and in 1933 was appointed director of exhibits for the World's Fair.

Projects already planned at Washington Barracks when the Engineer School first arrived included a November 1898 funding of $13,774 for construction of a brick quartermaster stable; $14,480 set aside in June 1900 for additions to the General Hospital; $3,172 designated on 6 June 1900 for a Hospital Steward's house; $25,186 in June 1901 for repair of the seawall and laying macadam and gravel roads; $6,000 for sidewalks; $2,725 for wharf repair and a boathouse, plus dozens of miscellaneous contracts for plumbing, heating, pilings, screens, et cetera.

In 1901, Senator James McMillan helped create the Senate Parks Commission to oversee the future development of Washington in line with L'Enfant's original plans. Charles F McKim was a member of

Washington Arsenal Model Museum, 3-B (now #21) built in 1838. Used as the Administration Building for the Engineer School, 1901-1919.

the commission. When asked to look at the Army Engineer plan for reconstruction of Washington Barracks he stated that "the heel of the stocking was where the toe should be" -- that the plan should be reversed. He proposed that the barracks, administration, and supply buildings should flank the main gate across from the Metropolitan Car Barn on 4th and P Streets, and the Army War College should be built on the tip of the peninsula.[8] On either side of a broad parade ground lined with stately trees there should be a row of six duplex quarters for noncommissioned officers on the east, and a row of fifteen officers' quarters on the west, all of dark red brick with broad piazzas overlooking the water and white columned porticos lined up like a "regiment on parade."[9] Between the quarters and the War College there should be a Commissioned Officers' Mess followed by another row of officers' quarters along the seawall toward the college for staff and faculty officers [these were never built]. At the far end of the peninsula, with a view across the Potomac, and in a direct line with the main gate, there should be located the magnificent college, with a dome and buttresses of Guastavino tile.[10]

For the north, or Engineer portion of the post, $500,000 was requested from Congress, and $400,000 more was designated for the War College and quarters. Predictably, the final costs were closer to $1,300,000. Things did not run smoothly as Military District #5 underwent reconstruction. The architects objected to the Engineer control; the Army Engineers feuded with the civilian architects over their extravagant plans far exceeding funds appropriated, and with subcontractors about quality of material and unmet deadlines.[11] Workers were hired by the government and paid by the day. All material was brought in directly and its utilization superintended by men in government employ.

By 1905 the most urgently needed buildings for the Engineer School were completed:
    2 Troop barracks at $100,000 each
    1 Band Barracks
    2 Mess Halls, $23,000 each
    2 Storehouses-Quartermaster and Engineers at $60,000 each
    2 Stables-Quartermaster and Engineers at $16,000 each
    1 Guard House $8,000
    1 Cook and Baker's School
    15 Sets of Officers' quarters for $210,000
    6 Duplex quarters for NCOs for $81,000

Still needed was a new building for the school itself, a power plant, post exchange, gym, and miscellaneous lesser facilities.

Engineer troops occupying the new barracks averaged 95 men per company. Recruited from all over the country they were taught drill regulations and guard procedures during practice marches. (photo 14)

Engineer floating pile driver. It took 8 men 6 hours to drive 1 pile.

Classroom trade school instruction included basic engineering functions such as plumbing, masonry, carpentry, and machine shop and steam plant operation. Troops scheduled for extended action in the field were taught signalling and telegraphy. Drafting, photography, and printing were a part of the curriculum, as was splicing/lashing/knot-tying, block and tackle principles, modes of moving heavy weights, and erection of derricks. For fiscal year 1911, $25,000 was expended for supplies needed for instructional use. (photos 14 and 15)

The soldiers responded to bugle calls apportioning time for activities of the day: reveille, mess call, sick call, post police, work detail, drill, retreat, roll call, and taps (or lights out). Regular calisthenics hardened muscles and built up physical stamina. The Manual of Arms was taught as well as gymnastics, wall scaling, fire drill, bayonet practice, and first aid for the injured. Noncommissioned officers and selected privates received instruction in drill regulations, Manual of Guard Duty, firing regulations, Troops in Campaign, field fortifications, military bridges, reconnaissance, and use of surveying instruments.[12] Mess Halls provided a generous, staple diet for active, hard-working men.

Newly assigned or graduated officers were also required to undergo classroom study. If the individual had already completed subjects offered, he was encouraged to study a foreign language or compose monographs. Riding was also compulsory. A story is told of a greenhorn 2d Lieutenant who put his saddle on backward and was hoorahed by onlookers. Redfaced, he yelled: "How in hell do you know which way I'm gonna go?"

A report to the Quartermaster General by Major W D Connors listed the following officers and NCOs on duty at Washington Barracks in June 1915:

Quartered on post	Quartered in the city
1 Commandant	1 Chaplain
1 Surgeon	5 Student officers
1 Quartermaster	2 Depot Engineers
19 1st Battalion officers	
2 Engineer School directors	
5 Student officers	**Total 37 officers**

Noncommissioned officers

15 Engineer Band	130 1st Battalion Engineers
17 Engineer School Detachment	12 Quartermaster Detachment
6 Cook and Baker School	5 Bakery Company
2 Hospital Corps	3 Post Detachment
	Total 189 NCOs

Masonry students of Company K, 3d Battalion at the Engineer School, Washington Barracks.

In addition, assigned to the General Staff College (an adjunct of the Army War College) were 48 white NCOs and 60 enlisted men, and 9 black NCOs and 41 enlisted men.

In 1914, when major powers of Europe declared war, President Woodrow Wilson proclaimed this nation neutral and forbade members of the Army General Staff to formulate war plans. The United states was to be a peacemaker, not an interventionist, however, the active reserve was called into service in June 1916. The Army Reorganization Act of 1916 charged unit organizations to make decisions regarding training, equipping, and supplying an expanded army recruited by draft. After numerous provocations and attacks on shipping, the US declared war on 6 April 1917.[14] Not surprisingly, this act found the United States thoroughly unprepared in all areas: industrially, economically, and militarily.

To fill the urgent need for troops, the Engineer Corps was ordered to activate a 6th Engineer Regiment at Washington Barracks. Units formed and given one to three months of training included:

56th Engineers	3d Division, 6th Engineers
71st Engineers	5th Division, 7th Engineers
73rd Engineers	220th Engineers-20th Division
464th Engineers	478th Engineers-Depot Detachment
465th Engineers	1st Engineer Training-1st Div.
466th Engineers	6th Engineer Training-3rd Div.
472th Engineers	481st Engineers
488th Engineers	489th Engineers[15]

The post became a madhouse of troops passing through to points of departure for embarkation to Europe. Portable cantonements (temporary frame barracks) were set up south of the NCO duplexes, and the parade field, and every other open area not used for drill and training, mushroomed with tents. Much of the field training had to be done at Fort Belvoir. Building #22 (which no longer exists) was hastily constructed to house the influx of officers reporting for assignment, equipment, and training. The YMCA erected a sizeable building behind the Photo Lab (#17), which they dismantled and hauled away after the war.

As the post guarded against saboteurs and spies, President Wilson was urged to curtail public appearances for fear of assassination. As it turned out, the most threatening enemy in the capital was unseen, and unexpected -- the Spanish Flu. Absenteeism soared, movies and schools closed, large gatherings were forbidden, and it was was a punishable crime to spit, sneeze, or cough in public. Over 12,000 District residents contracted the virus, resulting in 475 deaths the first month. Nationwide, over 500,000 Americans died of the Spanish or Swine Flu, including 25,000 soldiers.[16]

1901-1919, The Engineer School 83

Engineer units stationed at Washington Barracks from 1902 through 1916 include:

1902 - 3d Engineer Battalion, Major W J Borden, CO
1903 - 3d Engr Bn, Companies I, K, L, M, Major W M Black
1904-06 - 2d Engr Bn, Companies E, F, G, H, Maj E Burr
1907-08 - 2d Engr Bn, Companies E and H, LTC W C Langfitt
1909 - 2d Engr Bn, Companies A and B, LTC W C Langfitt
1910-13 - 1st Engr Bn, Companies A, B, C, D, Maj W J Borden
1914-16 - 1st Engr Bn, Companies A, B, C, D, Maj Wooten[17]

Of the Engineers serving at Washington Barracks from 1901 to 1919, the following officers rose to the rank of general: W M Black, B B Buck, Edward Burr (last surviving member of the class of 1883), W D Connor, J P Jervey, H C Jewett, J J Kingman, W C Langfitt, E M Markham, T M Robins, A E Waldron, F B Wilby, E E Winslow, and G A Youngberg.

The most noted engineer officers serving at Washington Barracks during the period 1901-1920 were Douglas MacArthur and Ulysses S Grant III. Both were here in 1907, but young Doug found the duty dull and onerous and set about finding a job more befitting his talents. As an aide to President Teddy Roosevelt, the trip from his Massachusetts Avenue Club to the White House was less onerous on Washington's unpaved streets.

President Grant's grandson enjoyed his duty as Adjutant of the 3d Engineer Battalion and rose to Major General before retiring in 1943. His marriage to the daughter of Elihu Root undoubtedly complemented his professional talents. He was selected to be a representative at the Supreme War Council in 1917-18 and at the peace conference in 1918-19. After retirement he served as Chairman of the National Capitol Parks and Plans Commission (1946-51), and of the Civil War Centennial Commission (1951-61). He died in Washington in 1968.

Serving as Engineer Commander in 1916-17, Major General Mason M Patrick's reputation was earned in service to US Army Aviation in the closing days of World War I. Appointed by General Pershing as the head of the AEF Air Service, his appointment smoothed the squabbles between Brigadier General B D Foulois and Colonel Billy Mitchell (who did not live to see fulfillment of his visionary remark that "the next war will be decided in the air").

In July 1919, Washington Barracks quartered the General Staff College, the 1st Replacement Regiment of Engineers, the Engineer Band and School, the 478th Engineers, and detachments of Ordnance, Medical, and Quartermaster corps; by October 1919, only the Engineer Reproduction Plant remained -- all other activities had been sent elsewhere after the armistice.

This picture of life within a military compound was about to fade:

> The day is punctuated by bugle calls, the band comes out and plays, groups of children disport themselves on well-kept walks, young women play tennis and older women play bridge, while everywhere men in uniform are coming and going, afoot or on horseback, the enlisted man stalking stiffly about his business, the officer snapping salutes.
>
> There is a traditional idea of an army officer as a good fighter...but in time of peace an idle sort of fellow, somewhat given to drink; and an accompanying tradition of his wife as a mere butterfly, leading a merry and irresponsible life of perpetual dancing and flirting. This was never altogether true....At present, our officer is a hard-worked man whose day is filled with duties of the most strenuous kind.... Outside of unlimited duty hours, he is obliged to take many courses of study, pass many examinations, and exert all manner of exercise. And the young officer's wife is hard put to make ends meet. Outside of his pay there is never any money. Servants are scarce, expensive and unreliable.
>
> No manner of dress is more expensive, and often when the uniform has not yet lost its first gloss, changes are ordered involving a heartbreaking outlay for a new one. To save the cost, the wife must make her own and the children's clothes -- simple ones at that, for the gorgeous plumage belongs to the male.
>
> ...offsetting miseries are the bugle calls, strains of the Star Spangled Banner, taps, quickened pulses when heads are bared as the colors pass.
>
> It is a comparatively simple life in the army. A wife once said that when she visited her family she found her friends had more money, but she didn't see they had more fun. Their chief aim was to acquire things to put around their houses, then hurry up to get more. She had gotten over caring much for things having found that one can get along so happily without them.
>
> For those whose hearts break with breaking china, and whose tempers are rasped by a scratch on cherished mahogany, the discipline of army life is indeed hard. If we have poor quarters, the next move will give us good ones. If the pay is small, we have plenty of companions in misery, and eventually there will be more rank with more pay; more obligations and responsibilities, to be sure. But we don't borrow trouble.[18]

The National Defense Act of 1920 provided for an army of 280,000 to garrison overseas posts, form small expeditionary forces, train citizen forces, and in wartime to form nine corps of regulars supplemented by reserves and national guard units. However, Congress rejected Universal Military Training and the Army was forced to rely on volunteers. Recruitment soon failed, and Congress further cut appropriations as well as the size of the standing Army.

In 1922, an article entitled "Wrecking the United States Army" reported that Congress had further cut the Army to 115,000 men and 11,000 officers, and granted only enough money to train 1,000 reservists. This action was deemed "absolute destruction" which would leave the United States in a condition of complete and costly unpreparedness -- as in all previous wars.[19]

The war to end all wars was over; no need ever to prepare for another. Let the good times roll!

CHAPTER VIII: RECONSTRUCTION: DATE AND COST OF BUILDINGS

With the exception of four or five structures, all buildings at Fort Lesley J McNair were constructed at the beginning of the 20th century. The revisal of mission from an arsenal, to an artillery garrison, to an Engineer School necessitated doing away with the old and starting anew. In the interest of expediency, it was desirable for all major structures to be built simultaneously, therefore the most important buildings were completed between 1903 and 1907. The first two years were plagued with unseasonably bad weather, slow deliveries, expensive labor, and exorbitant charges for inferior materials. This added considerably to construction costs causing many revisions of plans to keep within budget.

A report of the Chief of Engineers agreed that red brick would be an enduring and economical building material, at the same time presenting a stalwart military image. More critical was designing foundations for weighty buildings on the marshy peninsula. Since wooden pilings would rot in the shallow water level, a previously untried method of pouring concrete piles was decided upon, which has survived the test of time.[1] (photo 16)

The Engineers pitched in with zeal razing the old buildings. The west wing of the penitentiary which had served for the last 35 years as quarters for the post commander was reduced to rubble. Lost to history was a brick structure coated with mastic resembling an Italian villa with massive doors of polished oak adorned with carved lions' heads. The rooms were high-ceilinged, wainscoated, with panelled doors. A columned portico with a beautiful garden ran to the water's edge.[2] The east wing, #20, still standing, was spared to house the Engineer School until its new home was constructed. Space always being at a premium, for one reason or another the house was never razed; today it serves as five sets of officers' quarters.

This chapter will briefly outline the date of construction, cost, and usage of individual buildings. Plumbing, heating, and lighting were installed by private contractors, but construction was overseen by Army Engineers.

The 1870s "six-gun" entrance gate was moved forty feet east of 4-1/2 Street to form a central axis that would exactly frame the future War College on the tip of the peninsula. (photo 17)

Washington Barracks six-gun main gate, c 1918. Note waiting room w/prison cells

#1 through #15, Officers' Quarters

The American Colonial row of fifteen officers' quarters were completed by the end of 1905 and ready for occupancy by majors, captains, and lieutenants of the Engineer School. Since the ground was unstable, the structures were placed on concrete pilings.

Each of the two main floors have nine rooms. The cellar floor is cement; and the room partitions are expanded metal and cement. In the drawing and dining rooms there are open fireplaces, but there is also steam heat and electricity. The construction is of dark bricks, with black bricks at irregular intervals, and limestone trimmings. Servants rooms on the third floor were closed off, or used as bedrooms by large families.

The two-story rear porches were designed with open lattice work

> to afford the occupants an open air retreat in hot weather, where costumes may be negligee, without offending the sense of propriety of the neighbors....to those familiar with the heat of a Washington summer this ought to be sufficient to settle the question of arranging the houses. The second story of the porch would form an admirable open air nursery for families with small children, and if enclosed in whole or in part by wire netting...would afford a more comfortable sleeping place on hot nights than any other spot in the house.[3] (photo 18, photo 19)

The handsome front porch pillars are constructed the same as barrel staves--an art seldom used by today's carpenters--and, therefore, difficult to repair. All rear porches have since been enclosed, but previously an open or closed rear porch was important enough for a family to move. In 1925, the family of Lieutenant Colonel W S Grant moved from #12 to #14 because the porch was enclosed. *Marjory (Grant) Exton said her mother grew weary of drying out wet bedding when sudden rain squalls struck. [The * indicates correspondence or an interview with the individual named who voluntarily responded to a written inquiry for data about the period during which they lived on post.]

Quarters #1, #2 and #3 were the last to be completed inasmuch as temporary barracks were located on that site to house the Hospital Corps of Instruction. When Engineer units were sent to Cuba, the barracks were torn down and the Hospital Corps temporarily quartered in the old hospital building #54.

The center house, #8, designed for the ranking officer, has 20 rooms. It is 53 feet x 52 feet 9 inches and cost $18,000. It faced a 1916 Georgian Revival bandstand on the parade ground. The twin cannon L'Active (The Demon) and La Rusee (The Spy)[4] guarding the residence were placed there in the mid-1960s.

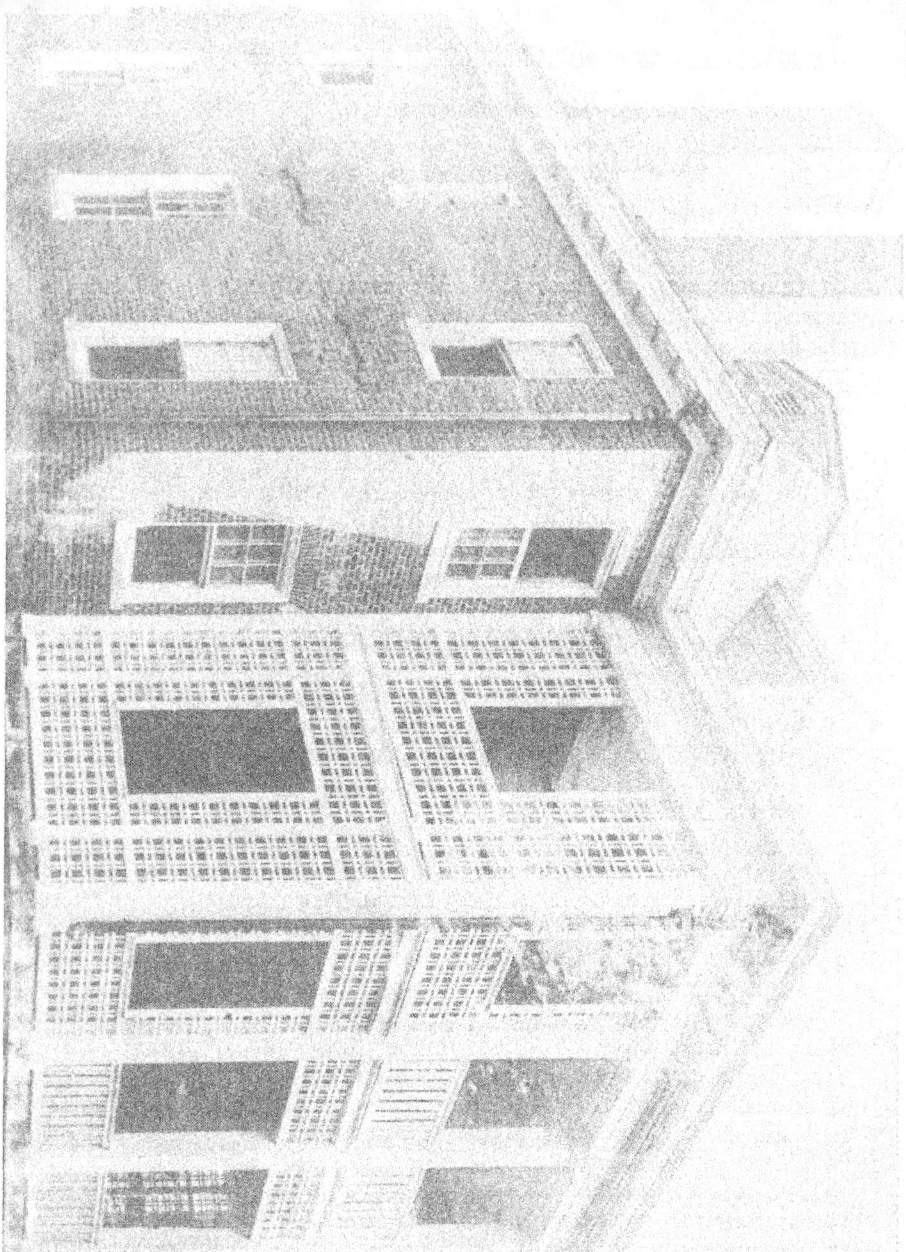

Flanking quarters #7 and #9 cost the same as #8, and each has 20 rooms, but the buildings are slightly smaller--a total of 19,497 square feet. Quarters #1 through #6 on the north, and #10 through #15 on the south have identical floor plans and cost $13,000--only $2,500 more than the estimate. They are 46 feet x 33 feet, a total of 9,017 square feet, with 17 rooms (seven bedrooms).[5]

In 1909, all quarters were issued mahogany sideboards, dining tables, and a writing desk.[6] In March 1911, a chest of drawers, bookcase, armchair, and a hall tree were added; and in March 1912, the quarters were furnished with a refrigerator, eight dining room chairs, a desk, three parlor tables, a divan, and a library chair.[7] It was determined that considerable savings could be realized by not having to pay for shipments of heavy household items.

As Engineer officers departed for Fort Belvoir and vacated the 15 sets of officers' quarters along the west seawall, they were eagerly snapped up by war college personnel. Colonel J B Gowen's daughter, *Dorothy, recalled everyone on the row in 1920.

*Marjory (Simonds) Ryan, *Marjory (Grant) Exton, and retired *Major General Sid Wooten were youngsters living on post with their parents in the 1920s. There were horse-drawn wagons to take them to school, family gardening plots located on the banks of James Creek Canal, stables of riding horses, and a bridle path around the seawall.

Today the houses are reserved for generals, admirals, or their civilian equivalents. Quarters #8 is reserved for the Vice Chief of Staff of the Army. Quarters #7 and #9 are for the commanding general of the Army Materiel Command and for the Chief of Engineers. Other residents include the commanding generals of the Office of the Surgeon General, National Guard Bureau, Military District of Washington, Inspector General, Commandant of the National War College, Commandant of the Industrial College of the Armed Forces, President of the National Defense University, members of the Joint Chiefs of Staff, and Ambassador to the National Defense University. Appendix B lists occupants from 1905 to the present.

#16 Bungalow

The date of construction of bungalow #16 is documented by a contract dated 15 June 1900 to W F Walling to construct a hospital steward's quarters with a slate roof for $3,369 plus $519 for plumbing and heating.[8] In 1939, $7,066.35 was spent adding a dining room and bath on the first floor, and a master bedroom and bath on the second floor. The kitchen was updated in 1963, and the baths in 1966. The front porch was rebuilt in 1967 replacing the round supports with square posts, eliminating the porch rail, and adding plant boxes. (photo 20)

#17 Sports Center

#17 was built in 1882, cost unknown, from bricks of the central portion of the old penitentiary. It was a one-story guardhouse on C Street and 3d Avenue which contained an office, guard room, sick room, cells, and water closet facilities in the rear.[9] The bricks were originally painted tan with brown Gothic woodwork on the porch when it was used as a photo gallery by the Engineer School. (photo 21) The building was gutted in 1938-39, leaving only the roof and exterior walls unchanged, and remodeled as quarters. It was converted into a Sports Center in 1991 when the "10th Hole" in #57 was razed to clear an entrance to Marshall Hall.

The nine-hole golf course opened in 1929 with a 1,700 yard, par 59 for 18 holes. At one time the holes were named:

1. The Straightaway.
2. Poa Annua (an unruly type of grass).
3. The Cannon.
4. Buzzard Point.
5. Channel Run (which endangered parked car windows).
6. Officers' View (which endangered cars on both sides).
7. The Slide.
8. Second Shot.
9. Right Corner Pocket.

*Retired General Phil Bolte drew a diagram of the course when the post was called Fort Humphreys from 1935 to 1939. (photo 22)

The current Guardhouse Sports Center brochure of rules and regulations describes the present course designed around an immovable historic landmark, Roosevelt Hall. The giant Parrot cannon which sits in the center of number three fairway causes more than a few tee shots to ricochet off. The cannon was named for its designer, Captain R P Parrott, graduate of the 1824 USMA class. It is made of cast iron with a jacket of wrought iron over the seat of the charge to reinforce the weapon. It is marked 1865, R P P (for Robert P Parrott), W P F (for West Point Foundry at Cold Spring, New York). From this point can be seen two 15-inch mortars at the Anacostia end of 4th Street. This sized-weapon had to be moved on a wrought iron bed with rollers, and the projectiles had to be lifted to the muzzle with a block and tackle.

Golfers are cautioned to allow helicopters to play through on number four, and the Anacostia and Potomac Rivers form water hazards along the next three fairways. Colored balls are advised when flocks of sea gull strew millions of feathers on the fairways. The golf shop has on display General Lesley J McNair's "Robert Treat Jones" #2 wood with brass inlays.

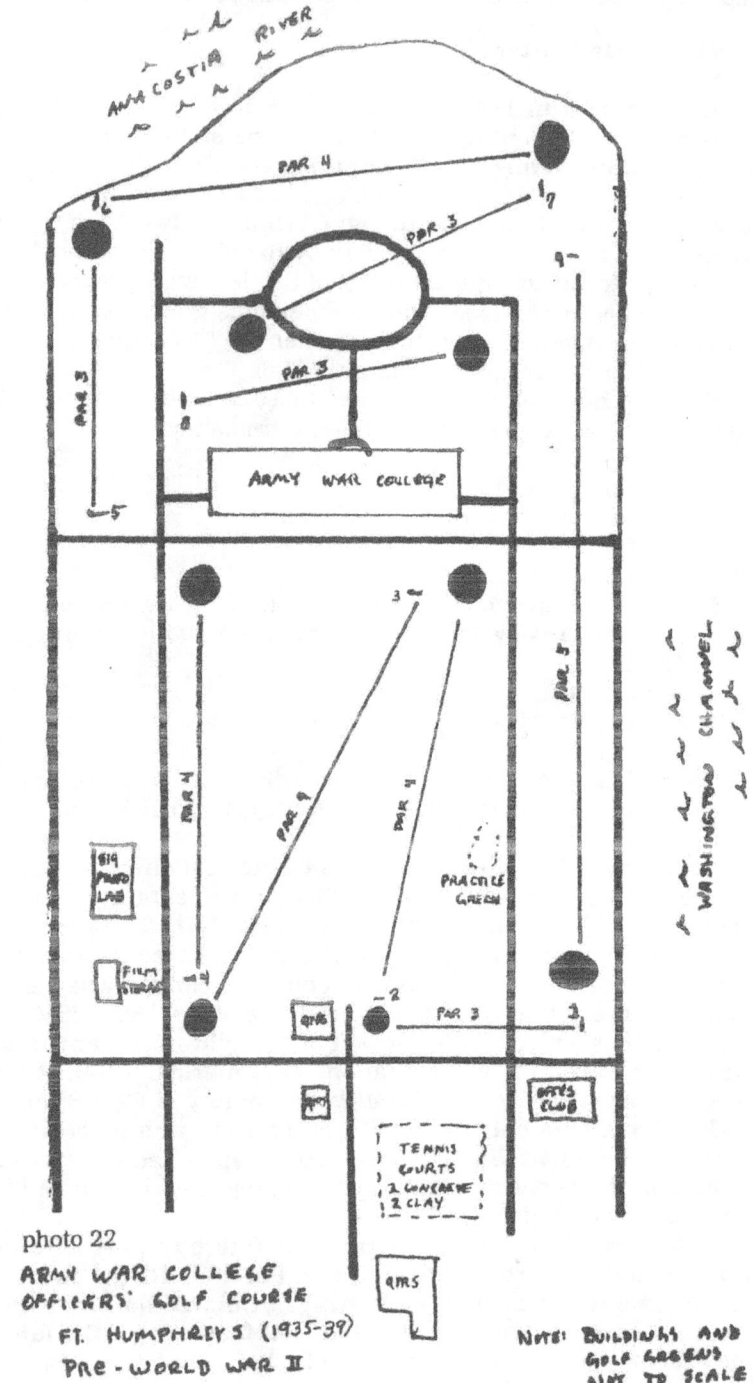

photo 22
ARMY WAR COLLEGE
OFFICERS' GOLF COURSE
FT. HUMPHREYS (1935-39)
PRE-WORLD WAR II

NOTE: BUILDINGS AND GOLF GREENS NOT TO SCALE

#18 Original Band Barracks

Building #18 (photo 23) was constructed in 1903-05 to house an average of 25 members of the Engineer Band. The building included a practice room, dining room, and kitchen. The arcaded front matched the two barracks facing the parade ground. A typical year (1909) listed band performances at the White House, summer concerts in the parks, Sunday afternoon public concerts at Washington Barracks, unveiling of monuments, reception of officers of an Argentine frigate, and the inaugural parade.[10] Band members underwent troop training and target practice. When the Engineer School left the post in June 1918, the Army School of Music was set up in barracks #52 after a $4,263 renovation.[11]

In 1919-20, $2,000 was spent to adapt #18 into ten sets of NCO quarters. The son of 1st Sergeant R P Fisher reported having lived here as a child from 1921 to 1928 at which time the building was renovated and turned into quarters for lieutenants and captains. He remembered the horse-drawn fire wagons stationed behind the present gymnasium and boats stopping at the wharf on B Street by his uncle's office (Captain John S Martin, director of the Army Band).[12] The building was last used as quarters in 1984.

#19 Bungalow

On north edge of the west seawall, bungalow #19 may be a set of quarters for a hospital matron referred to in the Surgeon General's report of 1884. [Engineer records state the house was built in 1920 for hospital staff, but the hospital moved to Georgia Avenue in 1908, and the Hospital School of Instruction moved to Fort Niagara in 1911.] No proof of the date of erection nor cost has been found, but the house appears to predate #16 on its left, since a bathroom was awkwardly added (indoor plumbing was introduced on post in 1886), and the outside entry on the upper floor appears to have been made to give access to eight small sleeping rooms.

The first oral report of an occupant of #19 was from *Colonel A P Nathan's wife who lived there in in 1956-57. They had been told that house was once General Patton's "office." The house was painted battleship grey and the sun porch had been added. Mrs Nathan welcomed repainting the house red, as were the nineteenth century buildings in the middle of the parade ground.

The National Archives has an 1887 drawing and floor plan for a two-story, frame, gingerbreaded hospital stewards' quarters with a bay window which appears in a 1903 (photo 20) showing quarters #16, however the view south of #16 is blocked by the Dispensary, so it cannot be determined if #19 was in existence at that time.[13] The gingerbread house would have had to be razed when storehouses #46 and #42 were built in 1912.

#20 (old #2-B), Lincoln Conspirators Trial Building.

At C Street and 3d Avenue, building #20 sits in the middle of the parade ground. It was built in 1831 as female quarters and laundry rooms of the penitentiary. When the central portion of the prison was razed in 1867-68, architect Adolph Cluss was commissioned to design officer's quarters from the two ends of the building. The inner side was refaced and a basement added.[14] The west wall is Renaissance revival style; a roof parapet has been removed. The north wing was redone in 1874-75.[15] (photo 24)

Building #20 was the site of the Lincoln conspirators imprisonment and trial held in the northeast corner room, top floor (which eventually became the kitchen of one of five apartments). On 7 July 1865 Mrs Surratt, David Herold, Lewis Paine, and George Atzerodt were hanged and buried beneath a scaffold temporarily erected where the tennis courts are now.

Many are the ghost stories told of Mrs Surratt's footprints melting the snow between the prison and the gallows, of a window mysteriously steaming up in the room where Mary and her daughter Anne kept vigil all night before the hanging; of lights, noises, and footsteps on the stairs, and window shutters flying open in the rooms overlooking the gallows.

The Jim Droskins lived in apartment #20-5 from 1977 to 1980 and told of trying the get their son to sleep when the boy looked over his father's shoulder and abruptly stopped crying. Jim had felt a hand on his shoulder, but there was no one in the room. They often felt a presence in the house.

Peggy Cook wakened to find all the lights on at 4:00 AM, got up and turned them off, and before she could return to bed they were all on again. Another time she found the Venetian blind pulled up cockeyed with the cord hooked over the bedpost.[16]

Building #20 housed the Engineer School from 1901 to 1914 accommodating a lecture room, drafting room, electricity lab, and library.[17] Rooms in the north wings were used for offices. In 1914 when the school failed to move into newly constructed #32, it moved into rooms in #48 until transferred to Virginia after World War I. Money was made available to adapt #20 into a BOQ, but part of the engineer library was still in this building as late as 1923.[18] No date was found for the conversion of #20 into five sets of officers' quarters, but the first occupants recorded were in 1935.

Major J E Raymond lived in #20 from 1937 to 1944. He described the basement when he first saw it as follows:

> The basement of the house in which I was to live was a musty, decayed wood, rotten floored place. The window casings were rotted. The wooden floor had been laid directly on the ground and was completely deteriorated; old whitewash plaster was hanging in chunks from a moldy ceiling; the old cupboard was chewed up with rat holes; a tin sink was rusty and an old cooking stove was a pile of red rust. It had been the old kitchen of that once quite palatial set of quarters, but the building had been used as the academic building of the Engineer School. WPA [Works Progress Administration] money and labor were plentiful at that time, and General DeWitt had the entire basement repaired so that when I moved in I had adequate hobby and storage space. Within the next few years a large amount of money was spent in sanding floors, putting in hardwood, a new roof and the ornamental woodwork around the top of the building just below the roof.[19]

The building had a complete facelift in 1940 making five apartments available where only three formerly existed. An open fireplace was built in each of the four corner rooms, and later the entire building was heated by a steam plant installed in the reconstructed basement.[20] Weatherproofing and screens were added in 1962. Apartment #20-5 had a fire in October 1967 and remained vacant for nearly two years before repairs were completed.

Building #20 was described as being red in 1971, but returned to original tan brick with brown trim in 1976. The fire escape was replaced in 1989. The structure was reroofed with copper, copper drainpipes were added, and two underground fuel tanks were replaced in 1992.

#21 Model Arsenal

Classical Revival style building #21 was constructed in 1838 for $6,850, at 3d Avenue and C Street, as a model house for the Arsenal. Architectural drawings and correspondence authorized construction stating: "...nothing extravagant or gaudy, but not to present a meager plainness...and build the portico of stone if possible."[21] Drawings of all pieces of ordnance and 1/4 sized models were displayed here and used for reference by other arsenals. In 1865, #21 was converted into a writing office, and when the Arsenal closed in 1881, it was made into quarters for artillery officers whose troops trained at Washington Barracks until 1901. (see photos 9 and 14)

When the Engineer School arrived from Fort Totten in 1901, the building was used for administration offices until 1918, despite a May 1910 engineer evaluation that it was too old to repair and was inadequate and unsafe.[22] It has served as quarters from that time on. The brick walls originally were unpainted with grey wood trim. The building is now divided into two apartments: one with three-bedrooms, and another apartment with four bedrooms. A photo of the interior shows the first floor living room as it was decorated when Major J B Ord (later Major General) lived here in 1935-37. (photo 25)

Major General Poore's daughter married Captain Charles L Bolte who brought his family to live in #21-1 from 1937-40. At age 92, *Mrs Bolte remembers that in the large living room divided by two huge pillars there were eight tall windows. It took 20 yards of fabric to curtain each window, an expense they could ill afford. In desperation she bought woven peanut sacking whose selvage edges needed no hemming and the cost was only three cents a yard. Her curtain problems were solved, but not the furnishings. Her husband declared that for the first time, he understood what "an occasional chair" meant.

#22 Officer Apartments

Number 22 was a three-story brick building constructed in 1919 as a Signal Corps Photo Lab. A sum of $70,000 had been earmarked to build a bachelor officers' quarters (BOQ) south of C Street, facing both 4th and 5th Avenues to accommodate 14 officers in two-bedroom, sitting room units; then, in times of necessity, the units could house 28 officers. Construction started 1905, but just as the foundations were finished, the seawall on James Creek caved in and all work stopped.

Nothing further was done until 1919 when plans went forward to use this area to house a Signal Corps Photographic Laboratory. (For a short period in 1919-20, the building was used for transient quarters.) When the Signal Corps activity moved to New York, the building was converted in 1947 into quarters for 20 families, and was later made into 12 apartments for officers. This was always considered a temporary building, but because it was used to processing highly inflammable film, it was made of reinforced concrete and looked permanent. Still it was a eyesore and really didn't belong to the grand scheme envisioned by the architects. However, it was not demolished until 1985.

#23-A and -B through #28-A and -B, NCO Quarters

To replace prior NCO quarters (photo 26) inherited by the Engineer School when they moved to Washington Barracks in 1901, six duplex quarters #23 - #28 were constructed on the east side of the parade ground in 1905-06 on the banks of James Creek at a cost of $13,500 each. Rear sun porches were added later. At times when the post was crowded, these houses were assigned to officers' families. Ghosts occupy some of these quarters also. Sergeant Major W Knauss told of locking up quarters #26 one night, and the next morning finding the front door open and a heavy chair moved across the living room. Another time their washing machine turned clear around on its own.[23] (photo 27)

#29 US Post Office

The Post Office was built on the site of a 1904 reception area/waiting room with two prison cells. Constructed in 1939 with WPA labor it cost $17,002.

#30 Guard Post

The guard shed across from the post office dates from 1951.

#31 Ordnance Building

On the northeast corner of A Street and 4th Avenue stands guardhouse #31. Conflicting opinions exist about the date of construction of this one-story and basement brick building with a gabled roof. Although the AGO approved $4,368 in April 1882 to build a guardhouse "as durable as the capitol itself," no structure is shown in this area on the 1893 map. A contract was let to Hobbs and Parkingson in June 1900 to build a guardhouse to be completed by November not exceeding $8,000. Another document further confirms that a guardhouse for 20 prisoners, 47 feet x 48 feet with 1,958 square feet of floor space was completed at a cost of $7,700.[24] The basement had three rooms and a hall; the first floor had five rooms.[25] In June 1910, a contract was entered into with Hourson and Skinner to extend the guardhouse by 30 October for $4,952.[26]

The building was proposed to serve as a Finance Center in 1954, and to accommodate a mail unit in 1967. It presently houses the 67th Ordnance Detachment which serves as a bomb disposal unit for the national capital. The unit moved from Indiantown Gap to Fort McNair in March 1955 and was housed in the basement of the West Mess Hall #52 for a while. The building has its own ghost--a parachute wind dummy. The dummy moved around at will for several years, sometimes getting into locked rooms or standing guard in an unusual place. Finally the detachment sergeant grew tired of its antics and hung it securely upon a nail where it has been content to remain.

The 8'2" World War II aerial bombs displayed on the porch were once on the pedestals in front of Roosevelt Hall. The modern fin-driven bombs are a Mark 82, 500# low-drag, and a Mark 83, 1,000# laser guided unit.

#32 MDW Headquarters

Building #32 abutting the north wall on the site of an old 1883 picket guardhouse was completed in 1914 to house the Engineer School. Erection had been delayed because the McKim, Mead, and White plan called for the school to be built on the east side of the reservation along James Creek, but the land was too spongy to support the structure. The total cost for this building, and the Central Heating plant and Carpenter Shop #34 was $88,900.

The Engineer School never occupied #32--the building was usurped for Administration, the Post Exchange (PX), and Telephone Exchange. In November 1955, the PX moved to the old stable area adjacent to the Commissary and Post Headquarters took over the building.[27]

Since 1966, Headquarters, Military District of Washington (MDW) has been quartered here. (Chapter XI describes the responsibilities of MDW.) In 1989, the basement windows were bricked in and the air wells filled. Bullet-proof glass was installed in windows facing 4th Street.

#34 Central Heating Plant

The present building was completed in 1914 in conjunction with building #32.[28] In 1920, $16,000 was spent on an addition to the north end of this building to install two 150 horsepower Erie tubular boilers with a Dorrance rocking grate manufactured by the D A Farrel Company of Philadelphia. Underground steam lines cost an additional $8,500.

In November 1923 the boiler was replaced by two "B&W" boilers from surplus. In April 1934, a Flynn and Emrick automatic coal stoker was added for $8,490. In December 1939, a $60,085 contract was given to C T King to replace the boilers and smokestack. The chimney has been struck twice by lightning without serious damage, and was caulked and inspected in 1987.

#35-A, Commissary and #35-B, Movie Theater

In August 1919, an expenditure of $150,000 was authorized to make alterations, repairs, and additions to several Washington

Barracks buildings to house Selective Service Draft Records.[29] With the advent of World War I, the Army increased from 263,000 to over 2,500,000 men through draft registrations in all 48 states. These records were boxed and forwarded to Washington, DC to file for future reference. A memo asked the War Department for instructions for disposition of 90,000 wooden shipping crates cluttering the post. File cabinets to hold the records were requisitioned from every post in the eastern half of the United States. To serve as a storage site, $44,000 was used to frame in, floor, and ceil the corral area between the Quartermaster and Engineer stables in the northeast corner of the post (the forerunner of the present Commissary #35).[30]

The north stable was first shown on a 1901 map and referred to as the "old quartermaster stable relocated to this site" at a cost $13,774 to provide 35,748 cubic feet of storage and forage room to care for 74 horses. It was renovated again in November 1941 to serve as a quartermaster clothing and general supply storeroom. A second floor was replaced, a hand-operated elevator was reinstalled, guard grates placed on the windows, and the wiring and fixtures replaced for a cost of $16,600. The work was accomplished by WPA labor. At the same time the south stable was converted into a movie theater.

The building was converted into a commissary in 1963, and underwent a complete renovation in 1968-69 which cost $224,325; new equipment cost an additional $72,990.[31] The commissary was gutted and redone again in 1988-89.

#36 Carpenter and Paint Shop

Between the storehouses and the Central Heating Plant, building #36 was erected in February 1940 for a paint shop with an attic for storage of carpenter materials. It cost $24,184.

#37 Transportation Motor Pool

A fuel pumping station was constructed in 1930 in the northeast corner of the post. It was superceded by the new service station adjacent to the theater.

#39 Built as a Commissary Storehouse

Building #39 (54 feet x 251 feet with two stories and a basement) which cost $60,000 was completed in 1905 for use as a Commissary storehouse. It was steam heated and lighted by gas (electricity was introduced in 1907).[32] The main entrance has been altered and some arched windows bricked in.

In 1920, $13,067 was spent on alterations for storage of the Selective Service System (SSS) records of the Adjutant General's

Office (AGO), and additional plumbing was installed. Eventually, these records would fill seven buildings.

From June 1963 to 1992 the PX occupied the main portion of #39. The Post Credit Union moved from the old tempo buildings on 2nd Street into the north end of the building in 1973. There is a bowling alley in the basement which was mentioned as early as 1923. The exterior was restored in 1980, and windows replaced in 1985.

#40 Facilities Engineer Shops

The one-story warehouse #40 was completed in November 1910 for additional ponton storage. A contract was let to Hoge and Luebkert in June 1910 for $7,884.[33] The building was converted for AGO use in 1919-20 at a cost of $5,252 by framing in the open bays, adding doors, windows, toilets and heat.[48] When the old records were disposed of, a segregated noncommissioned officers' club was located here in the 1950s. Sheds attached to the rear of these buildings are due to be removed leaving the scenic area along the seawall for recreational use.

#41 Community Facilities Building

Building #41 facing north on A Street is a cluster of buildings added at various times for specific uses. The Post Engineer office states that foundations may date to 1880, however the only structures in this area shown on a 1887 map were two ammunition magazines. The portion attributed to be the original blacksmith and carpenter shop (corner of 4th Avenue and A Street, appear to be "footed" on one of the magazines.

An 1871 reference says that a small brick building was constructed on the south end of the post capable of baking bread for 200 men, and a reference in 1902 states that existing bakery buildings were moved to the northeast corner of the fort.[34] The Engineer Annual Report of 1905 says that a one-story bakery, 51 feet 8 inches x 31 feet 10 inches, was completed in October for a cost of $3,600 to provide for a Cook and Baker School.[35] An April 1909 document stated the post was crowded since being placed on a war footing and additional space was needed to house bakery cooks forced to sleep in the guardhouse and band barracks, as well in bakery itself.[36]

An addition to the Cook and Baker's school was completed in August 1913 at a cost of $8,551. This was a two-story brick building 37 feet 2 inches x 32 feet 2.5 inches with wings 51 feet 7 inches x 22 feet 2 inches. The first floor contained an entrance hall, a lecture room, a dining room and a kitchen. The second floor had a dormitory 28 x 30 feet with a capacity of 20 men. The school operated for at least 30 years with 25 to 30 students in training.[37]

Residents of the 1930s recall buying fresh baked bread for two cents a loaf.

In December 1929, a Completion Report costing $6,493.23 states #26-A, labeled Post Bakery (now #41), had the northwest room, first floor, converted into a meat room, a dairy room, and a vegetable room which indicates the commissary was located there. These rooms were insulated with two layers of 2" corkboard, and meat racks, shelves, and cooling coils were installed. The wood flooring and all plaster were removed as was a brick wall between north and south rooms west of east hallway on the first floor. Steel I-beams supported in the center by a column were installed to accommodate electric wiring. A new cold storage room costing $3,750 was installed in the commissary (#41) in April 1941.

A Completion Report dated 23 March 1939 outlined the enlargement of the Post Commissary and Bakery for a total cost of $59,246:

> ...[to] extend the east wall of the east wing and the west wall of the west wing; removing the west wall of the east wing and the east wall of the west wing; joining the east and west walls, as extended, by a wall along the south elevation; covering the space which formerly existed between the east and west wings, also the extension of the east wing with a tin roof; re-locating the compressor for the refrigerating room; connecting first floor of Bldg 26-A with the first floor of Bldg 27-A by means of a passageway, consisting of brick walls and slate roof; covering the extension of the west wing with a slate roof; moving all bakery equipment into the south room of the west wing; providing a room at the southwest corner of the west wing for wagon and truck scale; changing doorway of bakery proof room from north to south side of proof room; removing steam radiators from remodeled portion, and replacing with 10 unit steam heaters.
>
> Further modifications: addition of a toilet and shower bath for use of the bakers. Floor level of original east wing was not changed....A double doorway was cut at south end of the east east wing, as extended, to afford direct access to bakery storeroom. Covering space between Bldgs 26-A and 27-A, on north side of passageway joining the buildings, with a tin roof. Constructing a brick wall from the southwest corner of Bldg 27-A to the east wall of Bldg 26-A, on the south side of passageway; placing a doorway in the wall as constructed, on the south face, and covering the storage space thus created with a tin roof. Constructing a concrete floor in the room above.

#42 Engineer Administration Offices

Along the northeast seawall there are three storehouses built for the Engineer School. Building #42 was completed in April 1912, with two floors 33 feet 8 inches x 159 feet 8 inches for storing 16 ponton wagons. The cost was estimated to be $15,000.[38] The cast iron bollards at the base of the building served to minimize damage when these were open doorways. In 1920 the open bays were framed in with doors and windows to convert them for use as AGO storage. Toilets and heat were added, and the renovations cost $7,925. The roof was replaced in 1983.

#43 Gas Station

The Gas Station (#43) was built in June 1941 costing $11,148.39. It contained 648 square feet and had an office, toilet, storage room, grease pit, and a 5,000 gallon storage tank. In the 1960s, the station provided lube jobs, tire sales, oil changes, and minor repairs. The east end of the building served as a Class VI (beverage) store. In 1991-92, the storage tanks were replaced, the area repaved, and a mini-market added.

#44 Meter Building

The small brick building #44 in the extreme northwest corner of the post contains the Washington Gas and Light Company meters. A 1928 map shows a double set of NCO quarters in this spot.

Just outside the north wall at this point, at the foot of P Street, stands a statue of a man with flowing robes with his arms outstretched. This is the Titanic Memorial which used to stand on Rock Creek Parkway overlooking the Potomac until it was moved in 1966 to make way for the Kennedy Center. The inscription on the statue reads: "To the brave men who perished in the wreck of the Titanic, April 15, 1912. They gave their lives that women and children might be saved. Erected by the women of America."[39]

#45 NCO Club and Craft Shop

The east mess hall #45 costing $23,000 was completed in March 1905 to serve barracks #47 and band building #18.[40] Half of this building has been converted into a Craft Shop, and the other half serves as an open club--The Fort McNair Inn. The Inn contains a Honduran mahogany bar which "could tell a tale or two." Installed in Hall's Tavern on 7th Street about 1860, it served libations until prohibition when Hall's turned into a restaurant. A half-section of the bar ended up in Christian Heinrich's brewery, and when that closed in 1956, the NCO Club bought the lovely relic. (photo 28)

The NCO Club Bar Could Tell A Tale Or Two

From the earliest days, "the bar" has had a colorful existence.

Reputedly fashioned of mahogany which traveled from the jungles of Honduras by clipper ship to Baltimore, Md., by an old world artisan from Germany, the bar was transported to Washington's southwest area and installed in Hall's Tavern on 7th Street during the 1860's.

Hall's was a colorful place during the gaslight era, with its long bar, gold-plated cash register, family room and private dining rooms off the upstairs iron-railed balcony. Old pictures of the tavern bring to mind the French Quarter of New Orleans.

Many of the great and near-great of Washington's past as well as men of the Washington Arsenal bent elbows over the bar at Hall's.

During the era of prohibition Hall's became a restaurant and the bar moved again, this time only to the garden where it remained until some time between 1945 and 1949 when a half section of it was sold to Christian Heirich of brewery fame.

According to Earl Gilbert, sales manager at Heirich's, the bar was a prized conversation piece in the brewery garden.

When the brewery closed in 1956, Mr. Heirich sold the bar to the NCO Club here for a nominal sum and this weathered relic of Washingtoniana traveled to its present location where new friends stripped it of the weight of many coats of paint and varnish to restore it to the present beauty of its natural wood.

Mrs. Julie Hall, owner of Hall's Restaurant, commenting on the beauty of the NCO Club bar, regrets that it was necessary to sell this twin half of the bar. The other half is still in use at Hall's.

She nostalgically tells of the many personages famous in Washington's history "who have draped their elbows over the bar," including General Grant, Mary Pickford, men of the press and theater such as Ernie Pyle, Daryl Zanuck and Cecil B. DeMille, to name a few.

At Hall's, the name "F. X. Ganter, Baltimore, Md.," appears on a pair of swinging doors of the same era as the bar.

Some research led to the discovery that two individuals by the name of Ganter live in Baltimore; one, a newcomer to the area, had heard of a cabinetmaker by that name, but was not related to him.

A reply to a letter to Carl Ganter and Associates, Architects, indicates that an uncle, A. Carl Ganter, designed the bar at the woodworking plant established by his grandfather, Francis X. Ganter, a cabinetmaker who was born in Baden-Baden, in the Black Forest of Germany.

Mr. Ganter wrote: "If the wood is mission finish and looks like oak, it is chestnut. If the wood is close red grain, it is mahogany. These bars haven't been made for over 60 years."

In 1920 the toilet facilities were upgraded at a cost of $1,450, and at one time the plumbing shop was located in the basement of this building.

#46 DCS for Operations, Plans, and Security

This building was completed in April 1912 (at the same time as #42) to serve as a ponton storage shed for the Engineer School. The original cost was estimated to be $15,000,[41] and renovation for AGO storage in 1920 cost $6,600.

#47 East Barracks and West Barracks #52

Buildings #47 and #52 facing the parade ground on B Street were built as barracks for enlisted personnel. A concrete marker near the roof beam is dated 1903, but they were not ready for occupancy until 1905. Note the concrete lintel on the roof above the main entrances which once held large crenelated Engineer Castles--the branch insignia.

Barracks #47 is the home of A Company, 3d Infantry Regiment, the Commander and Chief's "Old Guard." It is made up of six officers and 175 men who, with the rest of the 3d Infantry stationed at nearby Fort Myer, perform ceremonial duty in the nation's capital. The west area of the first floor was remodeled in 1950 to serve as a chapel, and a complete face-lift was given this building in 1979.

Barracks #47 and #52 were erected with a planned cost of $115,000 each. First lighted by gas, electricity was added in 1907. Heat came from steam boilers located in the basement of the mess halls in the rear of the buildings. Planned for four companies of 100 men each (or a wartime strength of 164), besides dormitory areas there were rooms for one to three NCOs, with water closets, urinals, and lavatories on the same floors as the squad rooms. Company officers were on the second floor with bathrooms in the basement. The loggias, or porches enclosed by brick arcades, were large enough to hold inspection of a full company in inclement weather.

#48 Built as an Engineer Depot and Storehouse

Building #48 on 3d Avenue was completed in 1905 at a cost of $60,000 as offices and storage areas for the Engineers. Major Burr reported in 1906 that the building had engineer tools, ponton bridge equipment, survey and astronomy instruments.[42] The basement was designed as one large room 50 feet x 245 feet; the first floor contained a room 50 feet x 20 feet and another 50 feet x 225 feet; the second floor had two rooms: one 50 feet x 135 feet and another 50 feet x 110 feet. It was heated by steam and lighted by gas until 1909.[43]

In 1919, the Engineer Map Reproduction Plant moved into #48. This activity was formed by consolidating the Central Map Reproduction Plant, the Central Photographic Laboratory, and the Engineer School Press. During and after the war, maps, posters, circulars and other printed matter needed by the Army were produced here. A 1928 map shows this activity still occupying the area.

From 1912, a small arms range with 1,173 square feet and four targets with a range of 75 feet was located in the basement of #48. Sheets of lead prevented stray rounds from penetrating the first floor. The range was dismantled in the mid-1980s.

The the frame addition on the west wall now serving as offices of the Inspector General (IG) dates back to July 1941 when a 48 x 119 foot storehouse was added at a cost of $12,968. The small, old brick structure attached on the west side was a transformer house.[63] A new roof and fire escape were added to #48 in 1963; the building was "modernized" in 1974, and the exterior restored in 1979.

Guarding this building are two 9-pounder trunnion type naval carronades--a short cannon of large caliber designed to smash in the target. They are so named because they were first made at the Carron Foundry in Scotland; they were first used during the Revolutionary War.[44]

The buttressed, flank facades between the storehouses and barracks buildings facing the parade ground were constructed in 1905 to shield interior courtyards containing mess halls and areas for maintenance of equipment and accoutrements.

#49 Gymnasium

On the southeast corner of B Street, building #49 was completed by the firm W H McCray in October 1908 for $36,703 (plus cost of pilings) to be used as a post exchange and gymnasium.[45] In October 1910 a door and steps were added on the west end.[46] When building #32 was erected in 1914 the PX moved there, and #49 became the gym. During World War II, temporarily assigned troops were billeted in the large unpartitioned rooms.

#50 West Mess Hall

The west mess hall #50, designed to feed two companies, remains in daily use serving members of the Old Guard, students of the Inter-American Defense College, and other uniformed members of the post. The 89 feet x 104 feet one-story brick building completed in 1905 for $23,000 contained ten rooms. The basement held the steam heat equipment for both the dining hall and the west barracks #52 facing the parade ground.[47] Toilet facilities were upgraded in 1920 at a cost of $1,450.

#52 West Barracks (see also #47)

Built at the same time as the east barracks, construction was halted on #52 in 1905 as can be seen by the last row of bricks in the west walls (photo 29); they remain staggered to accept the planned completion--forestalled because the existing hospital #54 would have to have been torn down. The Army General Hospital was an independent command in 1903, and its services were essential to the post. When the hospital was moved to Georgia Avenue, NW in 1908, the vacated rooms were needed to house Company D of the Engineer Command. The old facility always seemed too important to discard and thus it remains today.

In 1921, the Army Music School transferred from Governor's Island and occupied #52. Until the start of World War II, the school trained classes of up to 100 who went to various army bands upon graduation. Warrant Officer J Stannard was the first leader of the Army Music School from September 1922 to June 1935.[48]

*Sylvia Ruth (Hoffman) King recalls that her father, Elzie S Hoffman (1871-1946) often played for social functions at Washington Barracks in the 1920s. He was not only an accomplished concert director and conductor, but also a noted and proficient band leader, jazz artist, and vocalist.

In 1962, building #52 was modified to house the IADC (Inter-American Defense College) operating under the auspices of the Organization of American States. The curriculum is devoted to studies of political, social, economic, and military factors that contribute to inter-American defense. New steps were installed at the entrance in 1968. The cannon mounted at the front entrance are Revolutionary War pieces made in France, and are named La Mignarde, (the gentle one) and La Vedette (the guard, sentinel).[49]

#54 Built as Army General Hospital

The first hospital on this installation was located in the Arsenal compound. It was a two-story brick building, 76 feet x 25 feet, with 12 rooms. A second hospital was described in an Inventory of Buildings at Washington Barracks in March 1882 when Colonel R B Ayers reported to the Quartermaster General: "The post has a new frame, regulation hospital, with authorized departures, 36 feet 4 inches x 84 feet, with two wings 45 feet 8 inches x 25 feet 4 inches. It has been built since the last report."[50] (photo 30) A subsequent letter to the Adjutant General dated May 1882 requested additional funds "to complete the new hospital at this Post, and to make certain additions not contemplated in plans of Cir No 10, AGO 1877." Besides minor alterations, the plan proposed construction of a store room and a "dead room" (morgue) which would cost $12,000 if built of brick, or $10,000 if made of wood.

1880 Frame Hospital, replaced in 1894 by building #54.

Rather than put $10-12,000 into a 13-year-old hospital needing additions it evidently was preferable to build a new and more substantial structure costing only $6,000 more. In 1893-94 a contract was let to W W Winfree to build a third hospital whose final cost was $18,875.[51] In 1896, Contractor J S Reynolds was paid $1,157 for finishing three rooms in this new hospital; and, in 1898, contractor W E Spier was paid $6,450 for adding two pavilion wings. (photo 31)

During the Spanish-American War, the Post Hospital was designated as one of three Army General Hospitals, and expanded with framed and waxed-floored tents for army cots. (photo 32) The tent extension gave enough space to handle 753 cases, not all of whom were due to war wounds or fever. The Surgeon General's Report of 1895-96, stated Washington Barracks personnel had an excessive number of venereal cases, and twice as much alcoholism as was ordinarily found at military posts due to the wickedness of Washington City.

The Surgeon General's Report of 1897-98 stated that in conjunction with the establishment of an Army Medical School by AGO General Order #51, 24 June 1893, a Hospital Corps of Instruction would be trained at Washington Barracks to complete and record physical examination of recruits, make out enlistment papers, and complete sanitary inspections. It further stated that a third ward for twelve beds was provided in the hospital at Washington Barracks by completing the third floor under the mansard roof.

In June 1900, Scott and Loveless were given a contract for $14,480 to enlarge the hospital by September. When they failed to meet the deadline, the contract was voided and work was completed by Army Engineers.[52] A report in 1901 said that the hospital at Washington Barracks had been enlarged and now had a capacity of 50 beds and was an entirely separate command.

There may once have been an unique fence at the hospital according to a letter dated March 1902 by Major W M Black which stated he had no definite information about the date of erection of a fence made from old muskets and bayonets.[53] A confirming article in the 10 November 1904 Washington Post stated:

> The river runs close alongside here, in the rear of the arsenal hospitals. Willow trees and maples droop over the sea wall and at one point there rises up from the stone a long fence made of bayonets used in the Mexican and Civil War.[54]

The bronze plaque in front of #54 refers to Army Major Walter Reed who found the cause and cure of Yellow Fever. He was commissioned as an assistant surgeon in 1874 and reported to Washington Barracks as Regimental Surgeon with the 2d Artillery in 1882. He must have noted the mosquitoes infesting James Creek, and the nauseating odors emitted by a soap factory at the foot of 1st Street Southwest, which operated until 1889 converting every variety of animal offal to fat or bone meal. The factory attracted swarms of troublesome blowflies who also spread disease.[55] After serving in Cuba where he did research on the mosquito spread fever, he returned to Washington Barracks. Major Reed had an attack of appendicitis and requested Major W C Borden, his friend and fellow surgeon, to operate. He died of peritonitis November 23, 1902. (photo 33)

Major W C Borden commanded the hospital from June 1898 to September 1908. He realized the post was too small for an Engineer School, a War College, and an Army General Hospital to care for patients as well as train medical personnel. He presented a plan which was approved, "Borden's Dream," to erect a new general hospital in the northwest portion of the city. The hospital moved in 1908 and was named in honor of Walter Reed.

The rooms of the old hospital, #54, were used as barracks for Company D of Engineer School from 1908 to 1919. The building subsequently served many purposes until 1962 when the rooms were converted into quarters for bachelor students of the IADC.

#55 Swimming Pool

The first swimming pool on post was located on the site of Eisenhower Hall (#59). Built in June 1940, the 100' x 30' pool was constructed with WPA labor and cost $15,616. The present pool which cost $75,000 was started in November 1958 by Paddock Engineering and opened 1 May 1959.[56]

#56 Dental Clinic

In 1899 a contract for $1,823 was awarded to Meads and Reynolds to build a morgue, part of which is #56, now used as a Dental Clinic.[57] At some time it was enlarged and had new windows installed. The older portion appears to be that nearest the seawall. This building was known to have been used as recruiting office and photo room in 1911.[58]

#57 Film Storage, later, the Golf Club "10th Hole"

Building #57 located on the southeast corner of C Street and 5th Avenue was demolished in 1991 to give an unobstructed entry to Marshall Hall. It was originally built in 1918-19 by Weller Construction at a cost of $25,761 to store highly inflammable nitrate training films produced by the War College Division of the General Staff.[59] The building was doubled in size in 1942 to store ammunition. After

the war it was used for various purposes: a storage area for liquor, landscaping material, and golf course needs. From 1964 to 1991, the newer portion became the "10th Hole"--the golf shop and canteen.

#58 Dispensary

In 1911 the west wing of the hospital was converted into a Dispensary and has served since as a Clinic. In April 1941, $9,638.55 was spent remodeling the building, putting on a new roof, inclosing two stairways, placing linoleum on the floors, replacing the metal ceiling, and painting inside and out. The porches were still on the north end of the building.[60]

In 1976, Bonnie Slocum, secretary to the MDW Staff Medical Advisor, noticed a slim man in dark clothes standing at the top of the stairs watching her as she arrived for work. She asked the Sergeant Major who he was, and after a thorough search he found no one in the building. Sometimes the dark man knocks on the door of the examining room, and has opened a drawer as if to reach for a test tube or doctor's implement.[61] The present resident doctor, C Lateri, has experienced this phenomena during her tenure. Since Walter Reed died in this hospital in 1902, his ghost may still pay calls.

#59 Industrial College of the Armed Forces, Eisenhower Hall

The history of this building is described in Chapter XI.

#60 Officers' Mess

The officers' mess, #60, situated at the southern end of the row of quarters, is American Colonial. It is 54 feet x 108 feet, with two-stories, a basement, and an attic. A 1905 report quoted the cost of this building as $45,000, although the original estimate was $27,000 for a building to contain 20 rooms.[62] The main entrance faces south flanked by two bronze cannon which bear US markings: one is stamped Boston, the other says Ames Company Foundry, Chicobee, Massachusetts.

On the east side of the main floor is the dining area with built in china cupboards containing beautiful plates, steins, a soup tureen and a platter--replicas of the china Queen Elizabeth gave to the United States when she visited in 1976. It was made by Mottahedeh in Portugal, and is marked "Vista Alegre, 1776-1976."

McNair Room No. 160, Officers' mess, c. 1910. Called the Reading Room

The McNair Room (photo 34) on the west was originally a reading room, and the Gold Room across the hall was the billiards room. The second floor is a ballroom with crystal chandeliers and specially milled overmantles on the fireplaces.

A complete renovation took place in early 1967 when the "Scenic America" wallpaper was added in the entry hall. First printed in 1834 by Deltil, 1,690 wood blocks were required to print this magnificent multicolored scene which has 223 colors. The right wall, east of the entry contains a small section of New York Bay and the left is a scene of Boston Harbor. The walls west of the entry show the famous natural bridge of Virginia and a view of Niagara Falls. The opposite wall showns a military review at the United States Military Academy at West Point.

The furnishings in the main hall are reproductions of the American Federal Period from the famed Colonial Williamsburg antique collection. The folding card tables are Duncan Phyfe styles circa 1815; the two tall back chairs are "Martha Washingtons;" a small sofa is a duplication of a 1810 Salem piece in the Coke-Garrett House in Williamsburg; the small desk is a copy of an 1812 cabinet made by John Needle of Baltimore; the console table is a reproduction of an 1810 Massachusetts original, and the miscellaneous end tables were originally termed sewing tables.

In 1987, the Tavern was redone as the Copper Top Lounge, and in 1992 new carpets were installed in the main floor, and the walls repapered and woodwork painted.

The McNair room contains an oil portrait of General Lesley J McNair painted by Sergeant W W Cummings and unveiled on 14 November 1942. (photo 35) McNair was a Lieutenant General at that time, but when he was promoted posthumously, the portrait was touched up to turn the epaulet button into the fourth star--"a gratuitous gesture that doubtless prompted a wry smile in some corner of Valhalla."[63] The general's framed medals are displayed in this room including the Distinguished Service Medal presented by Marshal Henri Petain, himself, to the youngest general in the AEF.

Near the Club parking lot is a 14" mortar with its muzzle sunk into the ground which once stood near the old Arsenal Headquarters. It would be a son-of-a-gun to move.

#61, Built as the Army War College, (Roosevelt Hall), now National War College

See Chapter IX.

#62, Marshall Hall

See Chapter XIII.

Other Post Features

The first flagpole was within the central building of the Arsenal compound at the tip of the peninsula. The second flagpole was erected in an ellipse in the main road just south of the Penitentiary and north of the Arsenal area. The present flagpole at 3d Avenue and B Street is an unique structure; its 55-foot base built in 1914 is reinforced concrete. The total height is 90 feet. It was struck by lightning in 1937 without serious harm.[85]

Two modern field artillery pieces on caissons, and cannon and mortars around the flagpole have plaques explaining their origin. Starting from right to left:

1. A French 6-pounder bronze cannon made by Berenger at Douay named "Kimi." The date of casting is unknown, but an inscription reads "Berenger Donicourt Fecit Duaci 24 Decembre."
2. A Spanish bronze cast in the early 1500s, used in Louisiana during the Spanish occupation. Named the "San Mateo," one of four cannon called the Four Evangelists, it is believed to have been cast in Morocco as it has a design of trees.
3. A Spanish bronze mortar, made in Seville in 1780, used in the Spanish American War in Cuba in 1898.
4. A .75mm salute cannon.
5. A US Civil War 10" mortar made in 1863 at Fort Pitt.
6. A bronze British Howitzer made by A Schalch at Woolwich Arsenal in England in 1744. It has the imprint of a direct hit which would have killed the entire gun crew.
7. A Spanish Bronze cannon made in Seville in 1789, a trophy of the Mexican War in 1846.
8. A Bronze British cannon dated 1797 which was captured at the Battle of Niagara, 25 Jul 1814 by the 21st Infantry.[64]

The ceremonial firing of the reveille and retreat cannon, and the raising and lowering of the of the flag takes place daily in this location. Whether in uniform or civilian attire, everyone on post must stop, face the flag or the music, and salute or remain respectfully motionless until the ceremony is over. *Professor Denver Fugate recalls a squirrel who appeared regularly at retreat and stood at attention throughout the ceremony.

During Arsenal days there was a small wharf where James Creek entered the Anacostia River. The Arsenal also tried to keep in repair a 45 x 125 foot wharf at the western tip of the peninsula which was often set afire by steamboats loading and unloading and was eventually ordered completely dismantled and old pilings removed. During the operation of the Penitentiary, a wharf for their use was located at the west end of C Street. At low tide, large, cut stones can be seen just below the surface of the channel on which gulls often perch making them appear to be "water-walkers."

Reconstruction: Date and Cost of Buildings

In June 1902, $2,725 was allotted to build a new wharf at the foot of B Street. By August, the new Quartermaster wharf and boathouse were completed at a cost of $2,058.[65] A 1951 map showed a wharf still at this location, but it had disappeared by 1960.

Seawalls shoring up the reservation were always being worked on, but the main effort came at the turn of the century. The dredging of Potomac Flats and deepening of the channel started in the 1890s under the direction of Army Engineer Peter C Hains. This effort coincided with the construction of new seawalls for Washington Barracks. As the old arsenal buildings were razed, the debris was used to fill behind a new seawall. An allotment in 1901 of $50,650, and a March 1902 grant of $107,600 was set aside to construct a seawall on the south and west boundaries of the reservation.[66] In the 1907 Report of the Chief Engineers, $7,500 more was allotted for rebuilding the seawall between the Arsenal and N Street.

As for the east side of the reservation, the Surgeon General's Report of 1886 reported "the mile-long sewer called James Creek flooded daily due to tidal action and flushing waste from the city." Colonel Hains submitted a report that a retaining wall of 3,600 feet would cost $55,000, but could not be undertaken since District Commissioners controlled the old proposed canal site. It would be another thirty years before that problem would be solved. A 1931 photo shows a brick wall along the east side of the reservation, and a 1934 aerial photo shows the canal filled, a marina replacing the wharf.[67] A Completion Report dated December 1935 states that an interception storm water drain to the Anacostia costing $11,615.35 was installed after James Creek was filled.

By 1928, there were only a few horses and mules on post but according to *Mrs C L Bolte, through the 1920s, commissary orders could be placed by telephone in the morning, and be delivered by a horse drawn wagon in the afternoon. The parking lot between the guardhouse and the post office was a post greenhouse from 1928 to 1960.

From 1907 at least until 1930 a chapel stood about where the swimming pool parking lot is now located. It was a frame structure with wooden floors costing $551.50 with a capacity of 125. It contained 1,594 square feet, had electricity and was heated by hot air. It had one room 63 feet x 22 feet, and a wing 9 feet x 8-1/2 feet.[68] From 1950, church services have been held in the west end of barracks #47.

The Potomac Construction Company was given a $14,829.67 contract in November 1925 to install 57 street lamps on the post. In 1939, 22 more street lights were added at a cost of $4,918.43. This installation was updated in March 1941 by Plymouth Electric Company who installed a new electric distributing and lighting system running duct lines and manholes from the switching station to the Signal Corps Lab and Officers' Mess. They remodeled all of the transformer vaults in building #22, the barracks, the mess and the AWC. The total cost was $43,982.29. The washroom by building #32 was converted into a switching station.

The handsome buildings of the military installation and elegant quarters for officers and noncommissioned officers upgraded the quality of life, and Washington Barracks became a coveted duty assignment.

Hoisting the 20-ton lintel above the entrance to the Army War College, 7 March 1906

CHAPTER IX:
1904-1941, The Army War College

At the turn of the century, the United States was fortunate to have a sagacious and energetic Secretary of War, the Honorable Elihu Root, who devoted much thought to reorganization of the military services; the need was blatantly obvious.

Following the Civil War, military units were small in size and dealt primarily with Indian conflicts. Although there was a Commanding General of the Army, his voice was far from the widely dispersed troops, and his wishes were often overridden by those of the Secretary of War or the Chiefs of individual Bureaus (Adjutant General, Inspector General, Quartermaster General, Paymaster General, Chiefs of Ordnance, Engineers, Artillery, etc.), all of whom thought they were a universe unto themselves.

The miserable conduct of the Spanish-American War highlighted the shortcomings of the joint forces. Poorly led troops were sent to Cuba wearing wool uniforms, on civilian ships unsuitable for military transport, using outdated black powder guns and cannon, and poorly provisioned. The situation begged for resolution. The Army needed a complete reorganization with provisions for a staff with overall responsibility for the conduct of war, formulation of plans, anticipation of contingencies, supervision of the branches of military service, and development and distribution of tools of war. These principles could be taught to selected professional officers in a postgraduate school capping the military educational system.

Secretary of War Root appointed the Ludlow Board to outline a course of study for such a school which resulted in War Department General Order #155. It directed the establishment of a system of professional education for military officers to include an Army War College to be supervised by a War College Board. The Board consisted of the Chief of Engineers, Superintendent of the United States Military Academy, Chief of Coast Artillery, Commanding General of the General Service and Staff College at Fort Leavenworth, and five members at large.

When the 1903 General Staff Act passed, the Army War College was formed as an adjunct to the War Department General Staff, with Brigadier General Tasker Bliss as its first President. The General Staff Corps was to be a supervising, coordinating, investigating, advising, and planning organization responsible for mobilization planning, contingency planning, intelligence, joint operations, and combat developments.[1] [This work will not dwell in detail on the operational evolution of the Army War College which is finitely covered in two excellent references: G S Pappas, *Prudens Futuri. The US Army War College 1901-67*, and H P Ball, *A History of the US Army War College*.]

In 1902, General Order 68 granted $400,000 for erection of a physical facility to house the War College. Construction commenced in 1903 in conjunction with the reconstruction of the rest of the post for an Engineer School, and General Order 76 in 1904 granted another $300,000. The site selected placed the War College on the southern tip of the military reservation, in line with a central axis formed by moving the entrance gates forty feet east of 4-1/2 Street. At the flagpole, the street would divide to pass along either side of a broad expanse of a parade ground, thus framing the three-story and basement neoclassical college fronted by a broad terrace. The McKim, Mead, and White plan called for a "cohesive" style using tile and concrete mortar introduced by the 19th century Spanish father/son firm of Guastavino. No structural steel or concrete was used in the octagonal dome which supports a 3,000 pound chandelier. Held by four pillars, the capstone is 80 feet above the floor of the rotunda.[2]

The building is made of granite, limestone, and beige-toned brick. It is 308 feet long and 104 feet wide. A flight of steps leads to the main entrance flanked by Ionic columns and enclosed in an arch 32 feet wide and 128 feet high giving light to the rotunda. The eagle above the front entrance sits atop a twenty-ton lintel; carved eagles just below the slate roof also guard the east and west wings. (photo 36)

When bird droppings began defacing the building, librarian J T Russell read that owls would scare away the birds. He bought a stuffed owl from a taxidermist, installed it on an upper ledge, then charged his staff to make regular reports on the amount of droppings. The owl may have scared away the pigeons, but it turned out that owls attract crows. No longer relying on old wives' tales, the upper edges of the building were strung with an electric wire to discourage roosting birds.[3]

The vaulted rotunda is 100 feet square and 128 feet high, opening on the right and left to two vaulted wings 110 feet long and 116 feet high lighted at the ends by arched windows. Corridors flanking these rooms gave access to two tiers of offices. On the south, opening off from the rotunda is a semi-circular lecture hall. The rotunda, map rooms and corridors were finished in brick and terra cotta with vaults of Guastavino tiling, and floors of brick and terrazzo.[4]

An article in the *Cincinnati Inquirer* entitled "Uncle Sam's Temple of Mars" described the recently finished interior:

The War College building is one of the most beautiful specimens of architecture in the country. On the main floor is a large rotunda where a bust of Napoleon occupies a conspicuous place. The groined arches of the ceiling cannot be excelled. On the left is a great long chart room lined on all sides with steel fireproof chart cases....On the other side of the great rotunda...is the library, stored with books of military lore.

The lecture hall is unsurpassed for beauty, arrangement and ventilation. Large American flags are entwined about the walls....The tiers upon which the seats are arranged are of cement. In the basement is a large vault, where all the more valuable and secret plans and maps are kept...[and] an elaborate photographic room.

Whenever the President, the Secretary of War, and Army officers desire to formulate some military plan, they meet...around a great oak table [which is still in the Commandant's office]. Many days and nights President Roosevelt visited the building going over details for the cruise of the Battleship Fleet.[5]

The Commandant's office contains a handsome mahogany desk which once belonged to General Philip Sheridan. The desk's right hand pedestal has a built-in liquor cabinet. The office also has an original Gilbert Stuart portrait of Thomas Jefferson. [The first copy hangs in Boden College in Maine.]

In 1910 the War Department library was transferred to the college adding more than 59,000 military references to the 32,000 volumes on hand. Colonel C W Thomas, librarian in 1936, describes the origin and its contents.

> The War College Library was started in 1794...the present library having been consolidated in 1910 from the war office, war intelligence, and War College libraries. It is known that no funds have ever been available for buying rare books, and it is supposed they may have been willed to the library by Army people... [The Library] has been rescued from three fires, some of the books showing signs of scorching.
>
> More than 12 books bearing sixteenth century dates are in the library, and one incunabula printed in 1494, two years after the discovery of America. The volume is in Latin, "Epitome of Military Instruction," by Vegetius. The first regulations used by the newborn American Army during the Revolution are there, written by a German, Baron von Steuben, whose statue stands today in Jackson Square.[6]

President Teddy Roosevelt at the laying of the cornerstone of the Army War College, 1903

The library was extensively remodeled in 1920, and will celebrate its 200th anniversary in the newly constructed Marshall Hall. It is credited as being "the largest and most complete military collection in the world."[7]

Of the architects who designed the AWC, McKim was a member of the McMillan Commission overseeing parks and plans for the capital city, and his associate, Stanford White, was called the Captain of the Ship of Fine Art. White had transformed New York City brownstones into handsome private residences as well as built himself a penthouse above Madison Square Gardens atop which he placed the shockingly nude statue of Diana saying "there are no moral values in architecture."[8] Since the total amount of funds granted were not enough to meet their elaborate plans, much ornamental interior finish had to be omitted.

Captain John Sewell oversaw the construction of the college as well as the other 57 buildings comprising the Engineer School. Trying valiantly to keep within the budget, he carefully checked the work of independent contractors. In one instance he wrote to the Chief of Engineers explaining that although a certain firm submitted the lowest bid, he knew the bidder was a notorious drunk, not to be trusted to pay his bills nor perform acceptable work. He cited a case where the contractor's wife and son pleaded to be advised before final payment was made, for his wife's inheritance financed materials used and she wanted her money back. Sewell agreed that final payment would not be made until the man obtained a signed release from his wife. When the contractor came to Captain Sewell with the signed document he was promptly paid. The wife and son returned in great distress. The man had forged her signature, gone off on a spree, and spent every cent.[9]

The cornerstone for the Army War College was laid on 21 February 1903. The order of troops conducting the ceremony consisted of the 1st Engineer Battalion, the Engineer Band, the 3d Engineer Battalion, the 2d Provisional Battalion and Signal Corps Detachment, Company G of the 8th Infantry Regiment, the 44th Company of the Coast Artillery, and an Ordnance Detachment.[10] (photo 37)

President Roosevelt came by carriage down Pennsylvania Avenue escorted by cavalry troops at the trot, then turned south on 4-1/2 Street. Two NCOs were detailed to ride at the head of his carriage horses to control them during the firing of salutes. As the President entered the post, the Presidential flag was raised on the flagpole, and gun salutes began. The Grand Masonic Lodge of the Potomac was present to offer George Washington's trowel to cement the cornerstone in place. In an elaborate ceremony the cast bronze box was cemented in. It contained blueprints and a history of the building, coins, newspapers, 1902 *Army Register*, copies of speeches delivered, and the ceremony programme.[11] Secretary Root declared the institution was founded, not to promote war, but to preserve peace by intelligent and adequate preparation to repel aggression.

When work resumed, the statue of Frederick the Great was put in place to watch over construction of the college. Through the American Ambassador, Emperor Wilhelm II of Germany offered the school a bronze reproduction of the Uphues sculpture of his illustrious ancestor. Since it was customary to add statuary to lend elegance to public buildings, the architects provided for that eventuality. The front plaza was designed to accommodate equestrian statues on either side of the front door, and allow spaces for six others, all of whom would have to be donated since no funds had been so designated. A study group suggested the terrace statuary should include Caesar, Hannibal, Alexander, Frederick, Suvaroff, and Wellington, and so the Emperor's gift was gratefully accepted. Congress approved the expenditure of $8,000 to prepare the pedestal, raise the statue, erect stands, prepare invitations, and hire chairs and carriages for distinguished guests attending the dedication in November 1904 presided over by President Roosevelt. *The Evening Star* reported that

> ...the American wife of Baron Von Sternberg released the bunting..."discovered to a waiting throng the grim features of one of Europe's greatest war lords"...as twenty trumpets sounded. [Present also] was a body of troops which represented every branch of the military service....The list of American officers present included: Maj Gen G W Goethals, Brig Gen F D Grant, Maj Edward Burr, and Capt J J Pershing.... Speeches were made by President Roosevelt and Lt Gen Adna R Chaffee, and Charlemagne Tower, American Ambassador to Germany.[12]

Since no other gifts were offered, Freddy, as he was affectionately known, stood alone. Some factions felt the esplanade should feature American heroes such as Lee, Grant, Sherman, Jackson, et cetera. This reopened the Civil War and no choice proved acceptable to all. Just two months after the dedication, an unidentified person hung a bag filled with explosives over Freddy's outstretched arm. A colored workman named George C Ellis noticed the fleeing man, grabbed the satchel from the statue and threw it to the ground where it exploded, knocking him to the ground and injuring his eardrums. For his bravery, he received a letter of thanks from Secretary of War Taft, and an inscribed gold watch from the Kaiser. Mr Ellis served on at Washington Barracks until 1930 when his retirement was reported in *The Washington Star*.[13]

Freddy watched fourteen classes graduate before bowing to anti-German sentiments forcing the statue be removed in April 1918 and stored out of sight. On 29 November 1927 the Secretary of War ordered the statue to be replaced inasmuch as America again had diplomatic relations with Germany. Eisenhower passed the statue day-in and day-out when he was a student without being disturbed, and Lieutenant General L J McNair never felt Freddy exerted a seditious effect on students, but threats were again made in 1940. However, the statue remained in place, unscathed, until after World War II when Building #61 was announced as the new home of a multiservice National War College. The pedestals on the esplanade would better exemplify the joint aspect of the student body if they displayed symbols of the all of the armed forces. So, Freddy was again stored away in the summer of 1946. In 1954 the statue was requested by the Army War College which had reopened at Carlisle Barracks, Pennsylvania. It was installed near the Guardhouse Museum built by Hessian prisoners of war captured at the Battle of Trenton.[14]

The trophies now displayed on the pedestals in front of Roosevelt Hall represent the combined military forces. Propellers represent the air arm. The sea forces are honored by World War II cast-iron anchors weighing 1,800 pounds each. Ground forces are symbolized by the bronze cannon: one marked "Le Passe Partout" (the key that opens all doors) with dolphin handles which was cast in 1693 in Zurich, Switzerland; the matching cannon cast by Schalch in Holland in 1739 is an English trophy taken at the Storming of Stoney Point in 1779.[15]

The college was initially engaged in forming and training a General Staff. In November 1904, the first Army War College class of nine members was assembled under the first commandant, Major General S B M Young. Majors W A Mann, C G Morton, D D Gaillard, and Captains J K Thompson, R E L Michie, J J "Black Jack" Pershing, L C Scherer, R H Van Deman, and J C Gilmore met in an old brownstone house at 22 Jackson Place, NW. This private home leased by the government was erected in 1830 for President Polk's Secretary of War, William Marcy. The home had been leased for President Theodore Roosevelt to live in while the White House was being remodeled in 1902.

The criteria for selection to attend AWC included graduation from the College at Fort Leavenworth, Kansas; graduation from the Coast Artillery School Advanced Course at Fort Monroe, Virginia; or by special selection, combat performance, or written examination. No diplomas were given, but an entry noting attendance was made by the officer's name in the Army Register -- an important steppingstone to higher command.

Included in this first class was Major G W Goethals whose name would become well-known in conjunction with the construction of the Panama Canal. Pershing only attended for two months and was then assigned as an observer in the Russo-Japanese War. He stopped en route to wed the daughter of Senator Francis E Warren.

1904-1941, The Army War College   139

The Army War College moved four miles from Jackson Place into Roosevelt Hall (building #61) at Washington Barracks, on 20-21 June 1907. Patterned after the German War Academy, but modified to American needs, the curricula consisted of war studies, map exercises, lectures on military history, battlefield studies, monographs, and horseback rides over nearby Civil War battlefields. During the 1910 76-mile staff ride of six faculty members and 40 students to a Camp of Instruction at Gettysburg, it took nine wagons and teams to haul their gear, and a stable of 70 able horses.[16] The first historical battlefield trip by vehicle was in 1921 in a fleet of Cadillac touring cars carrying extra gasoline since service stations were scarce.

There were no quarters on post for either the General Staff or War College personnel. Both faculty and students rode to work on streetcars which had a terminal at 4-1/2 and P Streets, SW. Lieutenant Colonel W W Wotherspoon, was the first war college president to have an official automobile, a Stanley Steamer.

There was some justifiable criticism about spending $700,000 of public funds on such an elegant building for instruction of only a handful of students. However, activities at the military reservation in southwest Washington DC were of little importance in a city with such high profile stories about Solons and the fashionable set. Students were pleased to be expected to present calling cards at the White House and stand in line to attend the New Year's Day reception.

By 1906, the General Staff underwritten by Secretary Root had demonstrated its practical value in directing the reoccupation of Cuba. From the broad brush mandate given for creating a general staff evolved designations of staff responsibilities (still applicable today at all levels of command):

(1) Recruitment, career development, promotions and awards are responsibilities of **P**ersonnel.

(2) Collection, assessment, and distribution of information are the missions of **I**ntelligence.

(3) General and specialized instruction of every military man must be planned and accomplished by **T**raining and Operations.

(4) **S**upply covers logistical support and distribution.

Thus evolved the acronym for staff positions, **PITS**: Units commanded by a general officer use G-1, G-2, G-3, G-4; subordinate units use S-1, etc. After World War II when the United States left an army of occupation in Europe and Asia, specialized training was needed for military units overseeing the reconstruction of devastated countries until reestablishment of a national governing body. A new staff responsibility was added for Civil Affairs and Military Government (G-5/S-5). When it became apparent that Joint (Army, Navy, Marines, Air Force, Coast Guard) planning was needed, "J" staff positions were instituted.

In 1907, the AWC library moved 1,326 books, 7,658 maps, 178 chairs, 96 bookcases, 23 desks, 27 tables, and one globe to its new home.[17] Later, the War Department library merged with that of the Army War College which added 90,000 items.[18]

With the loosening of Congressional purse strings at the turn of the century, rewards of military life improved with more meaningful duty, new facilities throughout the United States, better living conditions, overseas duty, new ships, guns, and tools of war.[19] Teddy Roosevelt ordered promotions to be based on efficiency ratings, which not only moved a professional career forward faster and more fairly, but also eliminated patronage and politicking.

By 1909, America grew tired of governing new territories, pacifying populations, and intervening in affairs abroad. The lure of expansionism faded. Acquisition of added responsibilities lessened concentration on self-defense.[20]

War Department General Order 118, dated 15 June 1909, authorized the President of the AWC to organize school detachments from noncommissioned officers and enlisted men from the Engineer School, the Army Medical School, and Cook and Baker's School. "The institutional administrative staff expanded (like a good Washington bureaucracy) to include 19 officers, 74 clerks, messengers, laborers, firemen, watchmen, stenographers, draftsmen and charwomen."[21] Enlisted men thus drafted for office duty were placed on a Detached Enlisted Men's List (DEML). Pushing a pen was far preferable to pushing a broom.

During this period the AWC student body expanded to include Navy, Marine Corps, and National Guard officers. Diplomas were issued. Noted civilians, experts in their fields, were invited to lecture, as were combat veterans of the Caribbean and Mexican forays. A motto was adopted, *Prudens Futuri* (Provident for the future), and an official coat of arms was designed with an eagle denoting national character, three stars for the combat arms services, and a torch of enlightenment grasped by a mailed fist.[22] The faculty members were classified as administrators and discussion leaders.

In 1915, *The Baltimore Sun* reported that students were making plans for war with Germany. President Wilson ordered Secretary of War Breckinridge to investigate and send every officer so involved out of Washington. When informed that the purpose of the Army War College was to prepare for national defense, the President said to go ahead, but please disguise the fact.[23]

By World War I, 13 classes had graduated. From July to September 1917, the War College lost one-third of their staff to the war: "Fifty-seven percent of the army graduates went on to flag rank before death or retirement. One-third of the army's general officers on Armistice Day 1918 had graduated from the War College, as had more than 45 percent of the division and larger unit commanders, and 20 percent of major unit chiefs of staff."[24]

The National Defense Act of 1916 separated the College from the General Staff, but it was not until after the war that the actual changes took place. By 25 May 1917, the need for officers overseas caused an early graduation of the current AWC class, and future classes were indefinitely suspended. Graduates had studied terrain analysis in staff rides, troop movements by historical examples, written estimates of the situation, conducted maneuvers and planned war games, but the officer corps was not ready for an expansion from 133,000 officers and men to four million by November 1918. Half that number never received training and were inadequately equipped, however they were shipped to Europe at the rate of 10,000 men per day. (photo 38)

*Brigadier General R C Richardson III furnished the following information about his uncle's participation in the establishment of the military intelligence service. Lieutenant E E Farman left a written reminiscence of his experience in being ordered from Mexican Border duty to Washington, DC in April 1917. He reported to General J E Kuhn in a small room in the northeast corner of the Army War College and met Major (later Major General) R H Van Deman and Captain (later Colonel) A B Coxe. Along with a clerk, they were to establish the Military Intelligence Division (MID).[25]

They were shown stacks of boxes containing reports from military attaches and foreign agents and told to make some sense out of them. It soon became apparent that valuable intelligence was ignored and grew stale within a short time. Also it was obvious that attaches needed funds to operate and acquire enemy secrets. Since disbursement of public funds required signed receipts, secret funds would have to be approved. Lieutenant Farman was flabbergasted when he was given control of $1 million dollars and told to set up a system for its use.

Van Deman, Coxe, and Farman saw the need for more attaches, and recommended commissioning civilians such as Mr Henry Stimpson (later Secretary of State). In addition, interpreters were needed both at home and overseas. Many qualified people wrote offering to serve in these positions; more were recruited from universities. Captain Mason was assigned to sort, translate, and distribute military intelligence to the General Staff for action. A 27-year-old State Department code expert, Mr H O Yardley, was called in to recruit and train cipher experts, and to rewrite the *US Military Code Book* which had been stolen in Mexico in 1916. In war, it was said, that "one brilliant cryptographer was worth four divisions."[26] This section alone rapidly grew to 200 men and women. By November 1918, MID had ten generals and 272 other officers. The activity had outgrown the AWC facilities and moved to 1330 F Street, NW. Farman had left the section to go overseas and retired as a colonel. Yardley was demobilized as a major and given the Distinguished Military Service Medal.[27]

At the close of the war, the State Department had money to keep the service alive, but the funds could not be expended in Washington, DC. Therefore, MID packed up and moved to a brownstone in New York City.

The Army War College would assimilate lessons learned in France and enter a new phase of existence after the Armistice. Classes resumed in September 1919 under the old name of the General Staff College. MG J W McAndrew was Commandant, and the first faculty occupant of Quarters #8 after the departure of the Engineer School.

The following generals were commandants of the AWC:

BG T H BLISS	1903 - 1905
BG T W BARRY	1906 - 1907
BG W W WOTHERSPOON	1907 - 1912
BG W CROZIER	1912 - 1913
BG H LIGGETT	1913 - 1914
BG M M MACOMB	1914 - 1916
BG J E KUHN	1916 - 1917
MG J W McANDREW	1919 - 1921
BG E I BROWN	1921 - 1921
BG E F McGLACHLIN JR	1921 - 1923
MG H E ELY	1923 - 1927
MG W D CONNOR	1927 - 1932
MG G S SIMONDS	1932 - 1935
MG M CRAIG	1935 - 1935
BG W S GRANT	1935 - 1937
MG J L DeWITT	1937 - 1939
BG P B PEYTON	1939 - 1940

As a result of the reorganization of the Army at the close of the first World War, the Signal Corps transferred all aerial and ground photography to the Air Corps, but were responsible for historical files of "still" and "motion" pictures, and production of training films. (photo 39) Construction of a photo laboratory, building #22, started at AWC in 1919 on the site selected in 1905 for Bachelor Officers Quarters (BOQ) where work had been discontinued when the James Creek canal seawall caved in. Much had been done since then to stabilize the ground in that area. The new photo lab was completed in early 1920 and the motion picture activities formerly located at 6th and F Streets, NW, Washington, were moved to the new building.

In 1925, still picture activity was moved to #22, thus bringing all of the Signal Corps photographic facilities in Washington under the same roof. Here enlisted men were taught photography for the next ten years, and old training films were edited and updated. With the advent of talking pictures, the activity moved to New York City.[28]

In October 1919, Snead and Company were given a contract for $41,000 to rebuild the interior of the Army War College Library and extend the bookshelves to the fifth tier.[29] A photograph shows the post gym temporarily filled with books during this renovation.

The AWC class of 1920 included 33 students who had served as generals during the war, but had to revert to their permanent rank (usually two to three grades lower). The 75-member class was directed to place greater emphasis on "command" as Congress enacted the National Defense Act of 1920 which created new branches of service: Chemical Warfare Service, Finance Department, and an Air Service.

In August 1921, General Pershing directed the title of the installation, General Staff College, revert to the Army War College to reflect the emphasis on the command, and end confusion about the location which was no longer recognized as Washington Barracks.[34] This year's class had 84 Army officers including one from the Air Service, and two Navy and two Marine officers. Brigadier General E F McGlachlin had succeeded McAndrew as Commandant and revamped the curricula to instruct along the lines of the PITS staff responsibilities. He believed the art of command could be taught, but that a good commander had to possess character, good judgment, and common sense. With the advent of aerial bombardment, AWC planners and students grappled with defense against this threat. Although grades were not given, not every student attending received a diploma. When the 1922 class of 98 students only graduated 74, a more careful selection of students was demanded.

The 1923 class consisted of 65 Army students, 50 of whom had attended the Command and General Staff School at Fort Leavenworth. There were five National Guard and four Reserve officers as well as six Department of State and six Department of Commerce students. In teaching the art of command, guest lecturers formed the basis for seminar groups. Hypothetical problems had no school solutions; no tests were given, nor were research papers graded nor required.

Of graduates during this period, three became associated with misfortunes during WWII. Thomas C Hart commanded the Asiatic Fleet, and Walter C Short the Hawaiian Department on 7 December 1941. Lloyd R Fredendall was at Kasserine Pass in 1943.[29]

At the graduation of the 1925 Class of AWC, an honorary diploma was given to Black Jack Pershing who had dropped out of the first class. A portrait of the General done by Dana Pond was presented to the school by the American Red Cross. The Carnegie Institute gave a larger-than-life-sized bust of Elihu Root which stood in the rotunda until it was sent to the reopened AWC at Carlisle Barracks.

*Marjory (Grant) Exton and her brothers Walter and Francis lived in #12 (1923-27), but moved to #14 because the sleeping porch was enclosed. *Francis C Grant wrote:

> I remember a Captain Cleland who was General Ely's aide; Sonny Miller, the son of the Commissary Sergeant; and another long, lanky sergeant's son who gave us our first glimpse of dirty pictures.
>
> Mrs Kitts, who ran the Officers' Club, lived in the house where Mary Surratt was imprisoned. I once wrote a very bad story, "The Ghost of Mary Surratt." I saw her ghost one night when I was hurrying home at the sound of tattoo. I had not known about her being hung.
>
> During soccer season, there were semi-pro games on the parade ground on Sundays. Big crowds came to see them. The Army Music School and Army Band were on post. There was a colored detachment who worked as "dog-robbers" [aides who took home table scraps].
>
> The old canal bounded the post behind the NCO quarters. It was being filled in as a dump. There was a chain link fence between the post and the dump. Black kids would come and hurl insults at us, and we would throw lumps of coal at them. Our enemies then collected the briquettes to carry home. Although we traded taunts back and forth, it was understood that we were supplying them with coal.

Brother *Walter F Grant recalled:

> Henry Gibbons; Guy and Pete Glassford and their two sisters; the Sweeney son who became a Lieutenant General in the Air Force, and his sister who became a WAC officer; the Simonds girls; Jimmy Humphrey; Madge Ely and her brother; a Kilbourne boy and girl; and the Rehkopf family.
>
> On Sunday, Father Hubert, a Franciscan, who came to say mass, often had dinner with us. He built the first vacuum tube radio set we ever had -- at dad's expense, of course.
>
> Jack Turner was in charge of the gym. He organized a basketball team for we boys called the Washington Barracks Wild Cats. Somehow he got us uniforms.

In 1941 a $14,383 contract was let to N W Martin Brothers to install a slate roof on the AWC building. In October, $4,067 was used to install fluorescent lights in the message center under the auditorium where the teletype, coding and decoding facilities were. In March 1942, the rest of the college received fluorescent lighting.

CHAPTER X:
1925 -1950, Out of One War, Into Another

During the next few years, there were no major changes at the post. Money was scarce; only enough was parceled out for maintenance and repair of buildings and grounds. Forces of nature took their inevitable toll as paint blistered and peeled, wood rot set in, and neglect allowed deterioration.

At the Army War College, the 1927 class participated in a joint exercise with the US Fleet, and in 1928 a new course called Historical Studies was introduced. Major General W D Connor replaced Ely as Commandant in 1928. His objectives of instruction stated that students were to be versed in political, economic, and social matters which influence the conduct of war, and in strategy, tactics, and logistics of large operations in past wars.

He conceived the idea of bronze plaques designed by the Federal Commission of Fine Arts bearing names of graduates of each year's class. To underwrite costs of plaques for the past classes, previous graduates were asked to contribute. The first ones were installed on the walls of the main hallway in 1929. After that, each class provided its own plaque. In August 1965, the 1905-1940 plaques were finally sent to the AWC relocated at Carlisle Barracks. The monument company who made the first set of plaques has continued to be the source of supply, and has a master file of every class of graduates through 1991.

In looking for ways to economize due to decreasing funds, General Connor wrote to the Adjutant General on 15 October 1929 saying that the launch *Enterprise*, maintained at the AWC by funds allotted to the Quartermaster, was almost always idle. It only acted as a substitute for the supply ship *General Rucker*. If discontinued, it would effect a savings of $3,600 in salaries for the crew, and $500 for repairs.[1] This gesture was no doubt accepted, however, children of officers on post remember the boats as the *Big Rucker* and the *Little Rucker*, often available for birthday parties. The wharf had recently been repaired with "28 [new] dolphin piles and new decking for a total of $4,400." The work was done by a company of Engineers detailed from Camp Humphreys.[2]

Just seven months after Herbert Hoover became president, the New York Stock Market collapsed on 29 October 1929. Hard times hit with a thundering crash that enveloped the nation. Eight percent of federal workers were laid off, while others accepted involuntary furloughs without pay. Salaries declined 23 percent by 1933 while unemployment soared to a record high of 25 percent. Thousands of "hunger marchers" besieged Washington demanding food and jobs. The so-called Bonus Army camped along Pennsylvania Avenue demanding early payment of a promised cash bonus. The Army was ordered to evict the demonstrators who were driven to Anacostia Flats by mounted cavalry, armored tanks, and soldiers with fixed bayonets led by General Douglas MacArthur, resplendent in full uniform.[3]

Although the austere times called for reduction in military spending, and Congress called for cutting back programs in line with dollars available, the only concession General Connor offered was to cut the size of the AWC classes. Since 23 students failed to complete the 1929 course, Connor stated that only a limited number of officers were capable of higher command.

Then the 32nd President, Franklin D Roosevelt, was sworn in bringing his promise of a New Deal and swearing "This great nation will endure as it has endured; will revive and will prosper...The only thing we have to fear is fear itself."[4]

Major General George S Simonds, a former assistant commandant and a veteran of the budget battles took command of the school in 1932. Over-strength in the Army was a favorite target of economizers, but a bill to reduce the officer corps 17 percent failed to pass. Roosevelt then proposed to furlough 3,000-4,000 officers on half pay, but backed off when it was pointed out the remaining officers could not even provide caretaker duties. During the cutback debates, the Army went for three months without receiving a pay check. Local bankers underwrote bare-bones expenses of regular military depositors on the basis that an officer's word was his bond, and they had never lost a penny on a military client. Grocers extended credit, and utility companies waited for payment. During this period, teenager *Jane (Honeycutt) West lived on post with her parents from 1931 to 1935. When asked if she remembered the "great depression" she recalled that it had not affected post residents at all, but she did remember her father's pay had been cut, and when times improved Congress forgot to raise it again.

A New Deal program was conceived called the Civilian Conservation Corps (CCC). Three thousand Army officers were assigned to oversee 275,000 unemployed men in work camps set up to undertake government sponsored projects throughout the United States. The workers were housed in rough barracks, furnished sturdy, practical clothing, and fed simple but hardy fare keeping them out of bread lines and preserving the dignity of the unemployed. Supervisory military personnel learned how to lead men by cooperation instead of coercion. However, the price paid by the Army was reduction of Reserve officers, cancellation of ROTC camps, and a cutback of half of the officers attending schools. The Army War College attendance was not affected inasmuch as those officers were too senior to administer the construction camps. General MacArthur fought hard to preserve the budget. After one bout in the White House where he almost became insubordinate, he threw up on the steps when leaving.⁵

General Simonds is credited with adding Air Corps and Navy faculty members to the War Plans Division, and conducting the first command post exercise at Fort Monmouth, New Jersey.

Staff and faculty member Lieutenant Colonel Simon Bolivar Buckner, Jr would become a general only to be killed on Okinawa in 1945. Son of a Confederate general, he graduated from West Point in 1908 and returned there in 1933 as Commandant. He served on the Mexican border, and twice in the Philippines. He was executive officer of the Army War College from 1929 to 1931 and lived in quarters #1. Son *William, only six years old when they departed, remembered the post well enough to draw a diagram and mark the spot where their house stood. His sister, *Mrs Ed (Buckner) Brubaker verified the location of the quarters.

*Dorothy (Anderson) Goodpaster, the daughter of an AWC instructor, lived in #12 for three years from 1930 to 1933. At that time there was one general and two colonels living on the row, and the rest were all majors, and had been since the end of World War I. The teenagers were bussed to Western High School, but most of their social life was right on post.

Lieutenant Colonel Francis W Honeycutt, an instructor who lived with his family in #14 from 1931 to 1935, would die in an air accident in 1938 after being promoted to Brigadier General.

*Alice (Gibson) Tucker lived with her parents in #2 from 1932 to 1936 and recalled going to Panama with Frances Simonds in 1933 where Frances met her future husband, Lieutenant N A Costello. Alice recalled taking the 7th Street streetcar to town and back, bowling, parties at the "O Club," and the overnight steamer between Washington and Norfolk which berthed at a dock just above the post. Other friends were Rosetta Kromer, the Grunerts, and Ella (Cooper) Thomas who introduced Alice to her husband, B S Tucker, in Honolulu.

*Marjory (Simonds) Ryan's memories of the different periods they lived on the post is phenomenal. That anyone would be able to recall almost all of her childhood neighbors is a tribute to selective memory. Marge furnished many family names, married names, and addresses of former occupants of quarters.

Major General Malin Craig was commandant of AWC for a short period in 1935 until he replaced Douglas MacArthur as Chief of Staff. He reintroduced historical rides through nearby Civil War battlefields via bus. In the AWC classes of this period:

> ...[were] a number of officers who in later years would hold positions of prominence. During WWII, Jacob L Devers and

Omar Bradley commanded army groups. Courtney Hodges would command First Army. After the war, Bradley would serve as Army Chief of Staff... Jonathan M Wainwright had the unhappy task of surrendering American troops in the Philippines in 1942; Lewis B Hershey would direct the selective service system through three wars; and in the Pacific, William F Halsey would become an Admiral of the Pacific Fleet, and George C Kenney would lead the Fifth Air Force.[6]

By 1935, Congress became alarmed at the number of officers leaving the Army. Many had remained in the same reduced rank for 17 years (Eisenhower, for one). To provide hope for professional officers, Congress authorized automatic promotion to first lieutenant after three years of service, and to captain after ten. Since there was practically no active Army, the school systems were the only alternative to experience.

Just as the name "Army War College" was beginning to replace the old name of Washington Barracks, General Order No 1, 14 February 1935 ordered the name of the post to be changed to "Fort Humphreys, District of Columbia." When the Engineer School moved to Virginia in 1919, the Belvoir area was temporarily named Camp A A Humphreys in honor of Major General A A Humphreys, a Gettysburg veteran and once Chief of Engineers. Pressure was brought to bear to rename the area in accordance with old land grants stemming from the royal patent covering the Belvoir tract. When Camp Humphreys was renamed Fort Belvoir, the AGO decided to bestow the Humphreys name on the college reservation. After five years of confusion, General Order #5 gave the Army War College back its name on 1 September 1939; however, this name was to last only nine years.

Few changes would take place in the AWC program before America began to mobilize in 1940. When Brigadier General W S Grant took command (1935 to 1937), a preliminary Command Course was introduced at the beginning of the academic year, and the school was ordered to conduct combat developments studies of infantry divisions and echelons above.

Retired *Lieutenant General Kenneth Cooper recalled his childhood when his father was an AWC faculty member from 1935 to 1936 and they lived in #11. At that time the buglers (really trumpeters) blew the calls live and unmagnified except for the megaphone near the flagpole.

*Henry S Aurand, Jr recalled when his father, a Major (retired Lieutenant General) lived in #4 from 1933 to 1937 as an instructor at the AWC as well as the Post Ordnance officer. His quarters (#4) were in a direct line with the maximum muzzle blast of the saluting gun. To reduce the shattering sound, Major Aurand had the gun replaced with one of smaller caliber. When that did not help, he had the charge reduced until there was no report at all -- the gun just went "poof." The commandant ordered things returned to the original state.

When Major D W Eisenhower was a student at the AWC, on Saturdays he would bring son John to visit the Aurands. While the boys played with a model railroad in the basement, the fathers held heated discussions in the living room above. Later the sons were 1944 classmates at West Point, along with Phil Grant and Kenny Cooper.

Henry Jr also remembers the elms that made cathedrals of the streets, even beautifying 4th and 7th Streets in what then was not a very fine neighborhood. Although he resigned from the Army Corps of Engineers in 1954 as major, he remained in engineering.

The area between the post and Independence Avenue and South Capitol Street was the beneficiary of one of the first urban renewal efforts -- also a job-creating New Deal project. Congress authorized the Alley Dwelling Authority (ADA) in 1934 to demolish slums and replace them with public housing. Starting in 1951, this was the forerunner of the Redevelopment Land Agency which initiated the restoration of southwest Washington, DC.

The post further benefitted from the New Deal program through the Works Projects Administration (WPA) -- another government effort to put the jobless to work. Quarters #20 was completely renovated in 1937-38. The dirt floor in the cellar was replaced with concrete, paint was removed down to the original walnut base, and the floors sanded. In 1939, the cracked "Connecticut freestone" surface on the front of the building was removed and replaced with new plaster and repainted.

Major General J L DeWitt, a Princeton graduate, was commandant from 1937 to 1939. As he assumed command, the War Department directed the Army War College to conduct studies of cavalry divisions, corps, and field armies, and reinstituted the Mobilization Course. As war in Europe became a threat, Congress authorized a 20 percent increase in the Navy, and a Regular Army strength of 14,000 officers and 165,000 enlisted men.

*Mrs C L Bolte and her sons Philip and David recounted stories of post life when they moved into #21-1 in 1937. The boys often tangled with the MPs who patrolled on bicycles. The kids could outride them and often got away with pranks their father had to answer for such as painting zebra stripes on the mules, rolling the stacked cannon balls out onto the parade ground, playing on the golf course, and riding bikes on the narrow seawall. Once when delivering newspapers, the post commander was heard to tell his wife to bring in their dog lest the Bolte boys bite him. The Boltes would again live on post in #4 from 1948 to 1952 before the general retired as Vice Chief of Staff of the Army in 1955.

The wharf had deteriorated since its last repair in 1928. General DeWitt wrote the Quartermaster General on 26 Aug 1937 that it would take $7,500 of material, providing labor could be supplied by the Engineers as it was last time. He pointed out that since proposed plans to improve Washington Channel called for a permanent structure to replace the present wharf it would be more practical to build it now.[8]

*Betsy (Barnett) Forsythe lived with her parents in #1 from 1937 to 1940. She would return to live in #4 from 1970 to 1972 when General Forsythe served as head of the Volunteer Army.

Retired *Colonel J B Bonham's father attended the AWC in 1935, and after a tour at Fort Meade (where his wife shortened the long curtains which fit quarters at West Point in 1918) was assigned as intelligence instructor at AWC from 1935 to 1939. They first lived in an apartment in #21, then moved to the second floor of #20. In the spring of 1937, the Bonhams moved to #6. As one might guess, long curtains were needed for this house.

Of JB's friends during those years he recalled Thurman, Jim, and Anne Malony (who married Bill Neely); and Bill Weissinger's Christmas party. His father had bought him an old Ford. One warm summer evening, Ham Bonham, Nardy Rehkopf, and Bob McClure (who had a driver's license) drove out to Hains Point where the car quit. By the time they'd pushed the car home they no longer considered a car a luxury.

In 1939, Brigadier General P B Peyton replaced DeWitt as Commandant of AWC, and also as the occupant of Quarters #8. Peyton was a Virginia Military Institute graduate and also the distinguished graduate of his Leavenworth class. He was directed by Chief of Staff George Marshall to have the staff of AWC draft plans for a Hemispheric Defense Force, and to revise *Field Service Regulations* and manuals for command post and major field exercises.

As US involvement in the European conflict became inevitable, courses of instruction at the AWC were suspended on 11 June 1940. Without a school commandant, the senior officer of the post complement became acting commandant. Lieutenant Colonel E A Williams was the first officer so designated, followed by Lieutenant Colonel P J Lloyd, Colonel T F Bresnahan, Colonel G I Smith, and Colonel W N Todd, Jr. Thus the college remained officially active on a stand-by status.

> Of the last five classes before WWII were many officers who distinguished themselves as combat commanders of divisions and corps, and as staff officers at all levels....Mark W Clark commanded Fifth Army and Fifteenth Army Group in Italy. Walter B Smith was Eisenhower's Chief of Staff, and Hoyt S Vandenberg lead Ninth Air Force in Europe....After the war Smith became Ambassador to the Soviet Union. During the

Korean War, J Lawton Collins was Chief of Staff and Charles L Bolte Vice Chief of Staff of the Army. Vandenberg was Chief of Staff of the Air Force, and Clifton B Cates was Commandant of the Marine Corps.

In the Far East, Walton H Walker, Matthew B Ridgway, and Maxwell D Taylor commanded Eighth Army in Korea. George E Stratemeyer commanded Far East Air Forces. Ridgway served also as Commander of the Far East Command, followed by Clark. William K Harrison, Jr was chief of the truce team that finally brought about an armistice in the Korean War. After the Korean War Ridgway was Chief of Staff of the Army, as were Taylor and Lyman L Lemnitzer who subsequently became Chairman of the Joint Chiefs of Staff and NATO's Supreme Allied Commander, Europe, a position held also by Ridgway and Alfred M Gruenther. [Later] Collins was Special US Representative to the Republic of Vietnam in 1955-56, and Samuel T Williams was Chief of the Military Advisory Group. Taylor was Chairman of the Joint Chiefs of Staff, and Ambassador to the Republic of Vietnam in 1965.[9]

During the summer of 1940, the college building housed a small group of officers preparing a survey of British-owned sites that could be leased for US bases in exchange for 50 destroyers. At the north end of the post, the Adjutant General offices were still in place, and the AGO conducted a series of schools from September 1940 until July 1941 at which time the operation was moved to Fort Washington, MD.

Since World War I, draft records had been stored at the post, so it was natural for the Selective Service System (SSS) to set up offices at AWC in June 1940. Needing more space, they moved after a few months. The stored records were the subject of the following newspaper article:

> With the latest draft tabulation now being catalogued, the War Department had before Congress a proposal to dispose of 21,000,000 file folders of men who were not inducted during the first World War....the folders occupy 112,000 square feet of floor space in seven buildings at the Army War College....Depending on the recommendations of Congress, the records will be destroyed, sold or transferred to a non-Government agency or institution without expense. It would cost $3.5 million to microfilm the records.[10]

Space was already at a premium, but the situation would become worse with the creation of a new organization on 26 July 1940 called General Headquarters (GHQ). Studies following World War I assumed that in the event of another war, a General Headquarters, such as that of the American Expeditionary Forces of 1917-18, would be needed. The Chief of Staff of the Army would command the field force and general headquarters when mobilization began, but the President would choose the overall commander. The creation of a GHQ would decentralize training supervision. Brigadier General Lesley J McNair was named to head the group that would concentrate on training. The nine Regular Army Divisions and 18 National Guard Divisions were already in training camps throughout the 48 states, and the SSS was augmenting the ranks with newly inducted men.[11]

General McNair arrived at the Army War College on 7 August 1941 with his aide-de-camp, Major T E Lewis. Major J E Raymond was assigned to McNair's staff. Two days later, Raymond accompanied the general and his aide on an air trip across the country to observe field maneuvers in progress under commanders of the four geographical armies.[12]

For several months, the GHQ staff consisted of 11 officers with a few clerks. Raymond describes these opening days:

> ...the atmosphere [of McNair's headquarters] was most informal. A brief pencilled note from Gen McNair would start inspection parties to all parts of the country, and their reports, in many cases, were delivered informally to their "Chief," who like as not, would be sitting on their desk top. He set the pace for the staff in minimum paperwork and maximum performance. He was indefatigable, and an endless source of amazement to all members of his staff for his keen analysis of any problem, and his unlimited capacity for work. In such a simple matter as going up a flight of stairs, he never ascended one step at a time if he could make it three at a clip -- his normal method of going from floor to floor in the War College building. [McNair was 58 at this time.] He was first at work in the morning, and last to leave at night, and with him went a briefcase of papers to be "looked over." Actually, they were "worked over" on his battered typewriter. The beautiful training directive which had been prepared by one of his staff, checked and double checked as a result of "staffing," and ready for his signature, was next seen the following morning when the officer received an "As sent by L J McNair." [The paper] still said the same thing, and had the same end result, but it used half the words. The expression "in the vicinity of" had become "near," and it meant the same thing. As General Marshall stated publicly, General McNair was "the brains of the army."[13]

On 25 March 1941, GHQ was empowered to supervise and coordinate plans of the four Defense Commands under Generals H L

Drum, J L DeWitt, W Krueger, and Ben Lear. The staff had to be expanded to undertake these responsibilities. In the event of an invasion, each Defense Command could become a theater of operation. By July, GHQ authority was extended to include planning and command of military operations in the Zone of the Interior, including the newly leased bases obtained from England.[14]

A red/white/and blue shoulder patch was created for GHQ designed by the Heraldic Division of the Quartermaster General's office. The patch was properly authorized and created, but it was sewed on uniforms upside down: red, white, and blue. Since blue is the "honor color," it should have been on top. "Fretful wives and post tailors did a land-office business of ripping off the patches and sewing them back as blue/white/and red."[15]

To gain extra space for the growing GHQ, the Engineer Map Reproduction Plant was moved from building #48 to MacArthur Boulevard in Washington, DC, along with the extensive map library formerly housed in the east wing of the Army War College. In the handsome rotunda of the college building, trophies and art work were put away, and a two-story wooden structure for office spaces was built in the central portion between the four great columns supporting the dome.[16]

GHQ vanished as suddenly as it had been established when War Department Circular 59, 9 March 1941, renamed the activity Headquarters, Army Ground Forces (AGF). *Nancy (Stilwell) Easterbrook, whose sister married J Lawton Collins, wrote to verify that her father, Lieutenant General J W (Vinegar Joe) Stilwell commanded the AGF in 1945 and lived in #8. He was followed by General Jake Devers. General McNair and his staff took their place in his command. Even the blue/white/red shoulder patch was transferred to Army Ground Forces.

*Jane (Christiansen) Walker's father was General McNair's Chief of Staff of AGF, and lived in #1 from 1941 to 1945. Jane was married in the post chapel in May 1944. Her mother was chosen to notify Mrs McNair of the general's death at St Lo, France, and a few weeks later had to tell her of her only son being killed in action in Guam.

Retired *Colonel Robert M Ward and his sister *Peggy (Ward) Ballard recall visiting their parents in #6 during 1943-44 when their father was G-3 of AGF with offices in a temporary building on the parade ground. Their mother was with the Office of Strategic Services (OSS) and served as a Grey Lady (volunteer nurse's aide).

*Major General Alexander R (Bud) Bolling, Jr's father was the G-1 on General McNair's AGF staff and lived in #3. Major General Mark Clark was the Chief of Staff until he left to lead the Africa campaign. All officers serving together at this time were War College graduates and knew one another well since the Depression Army was very small. Therefore, their children became life-long friends, dating, and sometimes marrying each other.

General Bolling's daughter Kathryn was christened in #6 by the Chief of Chaplains, Major General L D Miller. The family remembered to remove the antique Chinese Buddha from the living room mantle where the ceremony was to take place. Bolling recounted how efficiently General McNair's small staff worked activating a division of troops per day, supervising training, moving troops all around the country, and coordinating the entire "get-ready" effort -- with about one-tenth of the manpower seemingly needed today.

The Bolling name was given to the air base across the Anacostia from Fort McNair. Colonel Raynal Cawthorne Bolling, a distant cousin, was a pioneer of aviation in the US armed forces. Sent to France in WWI to organize a structure for cooperating with allied air arms, he was ambushed and shot, but his efforts had been so successful that the Air Base was named for him.

Retired *Colonel H W Lange still had an October 1945 Organization Chart of Headquarters, AGF, then commanded by General Jake Devers, listing the officers on post at that time. Lange had lived in a temporary building on the parade ground.

A noted resident of the post from 1938 to 1941 was Major J Lawton Collins (later to become Chief of Staff of the Army) who lived with his family in #3. His son *Jerry and daughter *Nancy (Collins) Rubino recall being bussed to NW schools, and trying to roll the flagstaff cannonballs onto the parade ground without being apprehended by the Military Police. Collins received the nickname of "Lightnin' Joe" in the South Pacific as a member of the 25th Tropic Lightning Division, whose swift thrusts through the jungle once literally caught a Japanese officer with his pants down.

Due to unusual circumstances, the J Lawton Collins family returned and lived in Quarters #8 for nine years -- from 1947 to 1956. For the first two years he was Deputy Chief of Staff of the Army; followed by four years as Chief of Staff [who normally is assigned Quarters #1 at Fort Myer, but Collins was succeeding General Omar Bradley who had been appointed as the first Chairman of the Joint Chiefs of Staff. Bradley did not want to move, so Collins remained at Fort McNair]. Collins remained in quarters during his next three-year assignment as US Representative to the NATO Stranding Group, and 6-1/2 months as President Eisenhower's Special Ambassador on mission to Vietnam. Both Collins' daughters married while their parents were at Fort McNair, and held their wedding receptions at the Officers' Club.

Sunday, 7 December 1941, is a day every American clearly remembers where they were and what they were doing. In Washington, DC, the Redskins were playing the Philadelphia Eagles in Griffith Stadium. Excitement was so high over the home team victory that no one noticed loud speakers paging government officials. The crowd learned of the Japanese bombing of Hawaii from newspaper

1925 -1950, Out of One War, Into Another

headlines as they left the stadium. War with Japan was declared the following day.[17]

Fighting a two-continent war placed unbelievable strains on United States citizens. As America "blacked out" against aerial attack, tightened belts due to rationing, called all able-bodied men to form a 7,000,000 man fighting force, and recruited women to fill the labor shortage, Americans instantly became versatile and fluid -- willing to do anything or go anywhere. Not only did they give of their time, working several jobs; their money, buying war bonds; they also were willing to give their lives. Never in our history had such patriotism and united effort been exhibited by so many individuals.

Washington during wartime was an exiting place for newly arriving federal workers and the myriad of soldiers passing through. The United Service Organization (USO) coordinated accommodations and social activities for the transients. Meals, beds, dances, movies, tours, tickets, were arranged, as well as places where servicemen could relax, listen to music, and write letters. Cocktails cost thirty cents, and the Shoreham Hotel offered dinner and a show for $2.50 per person. Glen Echo and Marshall Hall amusement parks were popular, but movies probably drew the greatest number of pleasure seekers.[18]

The rapidly expanding activities of AGF headquarters urgently needed additional office space. Besides adapting the rotunda and old map wing of the college, five temporary buildings had been hastily erected -- four on the parade ground, and a large one between the War College building and a small marina.

October 1942 brought the worst flood ever experienced in Washington, DC. The river rose to 12 feet above normal inundating the northwest section of the reservation. Basements flooded causing damage to electrical transformers and equipment. The wharf and boathouse by Quarters #1 had to be tied to trees to prevent them from floating away. The wharf was up six feet at one time, completely detached from its pilings.

The AGF had a strength of 780,000 officers and men when General McNair took command. By July 1943, it had reached a peak strength of 2.2 million. In addition to his headquarters at the Army War College, General McNair oversaw a variety of schools, boards, replacement training centers, and special commands whose activities pertained to the combat arms. He spent much of his time traveling and observing progress. In 1943 while visiting US troops in North Africa he was severely wounded by an enemy shell fragment. On 25 July 1944, as the General stood near St Lo, Normandy, observing Eighth Air Force bombers soften the French coast prior to the landing of VII Corps, a string of bombs fell short killing over six hundred Americans, one of whom was Lesley McNair, the first Lieutenant General to die in combat. Just twelve days later, their only

son, Colonel Douglas McNair, Chief of Staff of the 7th Infantry Division, was killed on Guam by a Japanese bullet.

On 13 January 1948, the name of the post was changed to Fort Lesley J McNair with appropriate ceremonies attended by his widow, Clare (Huster) McNair, and General J Lawton Collins, Chief of Staff of the Army. (photo 40)

> While icy winds whipped in off the Channel, the widow of the general who was killed in the front lines in Normandy in 1944 heard the official orders read and stood at attention while troops passed in review over the frozen parade ground.
>
> Also in the reviewing stand were...Vice Admiral Harry W Hill, commandant of the National War College, and Brigadier General Edward B McKinley,, commandant of the Industrial College of the Armed Forces...and Brigadier General Hobart R Gay, commanding the Military District of Washington.
>
> General McNair, once stationed at the post which now bears his name was largely responsible for the speed and thoroughness with which the early expansion of the Army's Ground Forces was accomplished. [19]

It is fitting that the post containing three of the highest schools for military instructions be named for General McNair who was called "The Educator of the Army."[20] Sir Winston Churchill gave credit to the US military school system for producing so many outstanding leaders in World War II. In an address on 19 April 1946, he said:

> ...the rate at which the small American Army of only a few hundred thousand men, not long before the war, created the mighty force of millions of soldiers is a wonder of history....Professional attainment, based upon prolonged study and collective study at colleges, rank by rank, age by age -- those are the title needs of the commanders of future armies and the secret of future victories.[21]

Following World War II, the atmosphere on post changed little. The 15 sets of colonial quarters, originally built for Engineer school majors, captains and lieutenants were now entirely occupied by generals, admirals, or ambassadors. The Chief of Staff of the Army reserved seven sets for general officers assigned to his staff, and the War College staff and faculties claimed an equal number. The remaining set was reserved for the Post Commander. There were insufficient quarters for officers holding key positions who by virtue of their duties should live on post.

Colonel Raymond wrote in 1950:

> A Post Theater was made from the original Engineer stable, and a commissary was devised by adapting the Quartermaster stable and the roofed over area between it and the stable now converted to a theater. Post Headquarters, after removal from the Band Barracks was set up in the original Quartermaster warehouse, and a clothing sales store occupied the rest of the warehouse space. A Recreation Center for the enlisted men was placed in the north end of the original Engineer warehouse, formerly used by the Map Reproduction Service, and now housing troops of the 3d Infantry Regiment.
>
> A chapel was constructed in the barracks in space which had previously been made over for use as a practice auditorium for the Army Band when it had been stationed at the post. The only building ever erected for worship was a temporary one of WWI, then chapel services had been conducted in the gymnasium, T-5, the theater, and now the barracks.[22]

CHAPTER XI: *New Missions*

The criterion for a military officer to advance remained "seniority" until World War II. *Fortune* magazine denounced the career system: "By and large, one reaches the top in the Army by avoiding syphilis and reckless taxi drivers, also by refraining from murder, rape, and peculation."[1] "A three-star general credited his rise to designing a garbage-can rack, recruiting a post orchestra, writing an Engineer Corps song, mapping the post, and building a polo field."[2] Such jibes are leg-slappers, but at most contain only a grain of truth.

Following World War II, many young men riding the crest of patriotism felt a deep sense of pride for having served their country. However, as much as they may have wanted to make the military a career, severe cutbacks in defense manpower made retention almost an impossibility. Reserve officers lucky enough to be selected for a one-year "competitive tour" worked like demons to outdo their peers, but due to limited vacancies in the Regular Army, from a group of 25, only three or four officers could be accepted -- heartbreaking for contestants with equal capabilities.

In 1962, a centralized Officer Personnel Directorate was created with 15 career branches to develop a 30-year career pattern with school, command, and staff assignments. After World War II, about half of the Army officers and one-fourth of the Air Force officers had college degrees. To ensure future leadership, career management was needed to groom carefully selected commanders, stabilize tours, and enhance professionalism. One criterion for selection for higher schooling was to have commanded a unit; however, there were many more qualified officers than there were commands.

Officer's promotions depend on good or poor assignments, an individual's personal effort to be considered "well-rounded" by touching all bases ["getting one's ticket punched"], officer efficiency ratings (OERs), and often -- just being in the right place at the right time. Rating forms are constantly redesigned to establish a fair scale that nullifies personality conflicts or defies eccentric raters. A blank descriptive block on a rating can elicit such remarks as:

Unfit for anything.
Able to express a sentence in two paragraphs.
Needs watching since he borders on the brilliant.
An independent thinker with a mediocre mind.
Recently married and devotes more time to that than the job.

More fit to carry the hod than the epaulette.
Outstanding leader except for inability to get along with subordinates.[3]

With V-E Day and V-J Day ending the continental conflicts, the Army Ground Forces moved from the AWC to the Pentagon in 1945. Even before hostilities ceased, the disorganization and chaos that would take place in defeated nations was recognized. Commerce would be paralyzed, industry and agriculture suspended, schools closed, utilities decimated, and food and medicine scarce -- public order would have to be restored rapidly. The AGF recommended a School of Military Government be established. To train a military group to cope with such a situation, emphasis was placed on language ability as well as knowledge of the history, politics, and economics of the specific country.

Provost Marshal Major General Allen Gullion set the operation in motion at the University of Virginia where the first class opened in May 1942. Both military and civilian applicants from every part of the country were selected to attend. This expertise would eventually be centered in a new staff responsibility (J-5 and G-5) called Civil Affairs and Military Government. In the interim, civilian specialists were commissioned to fill such positions.[4]

Recent wars highlighted shortcomings in joint service efforts. Too often the right hand didn't know what the left was doing. The Army (with its Air Corps), and the Navy (with Marine Corps and carrier-based planes) had worked together as a team in such places as Normandy, Leyte, and Okinawa; while the outcome was successful, there had been difficulty in coordinating and planning with fierce rivalry for the lion's share of command, responsibility, and credit.

To integrate the roles and functions of various armed services, the Joint Chiefs of Staff ordered an Army-Navy Staff College to be established where State Department and Foreign Service personnel would be included. [The Air Force did not become a separate department until passage of the National Security Act of 1947.] General J L DeWitt was to be the Commandant. Classes were to consist of 30-40 students, and instruction was to cover logistics, joint command, and unified use of military forces. One-third of the six-month course was to be conducted at the old AWC building. [This concept of joint service instruction was later taught at the Armed Forces Staff College (AFSC) located in Norfolk, Virginia.]

A group appointed to study future educational needs for military and diplomatic personnel headed by Lieutenant General L T Gerow recommended a multiservice university composed of five different schools: a National War College, an Industrial College, a State Department College, an Administration College, and an Intelligence College. Regretably, the latter three recommended colleges never materialized.

Since this plan eliminated the need for an Army War College, this left the handsome building on Greenleafs Point available for use by the National War College (NWC) which was established July 1946. The school was charged with development of carefully selected officers and civilian personnel to be trained for future leadership in the field of national security policy and military strategy. The NWC inherited the valuable AWC library containing 300,000 volumes and 50,000 documents, and assumed responsibility for all AWC custodial, administrative, and property records.

Despite establishment of joint schools as the apex of the educational ladder, the Army, Navy, and Air Force clamored to retain their own senior service colleges. Ever competitive, and wanting assurance they were touching all bases, a 1948 Board headed by Lieutenant General Manton Eddy assured graduates that equal consideration for high level command and staff positions would be given graduates of the service colleges. The Army War College was reopened at Carlisle Barracks, Pennsylvania; the Air Force College at Maxwell Air Force Base, Alabama, and the Navy War College at Newport, Rhode Island.

NATIONAL WAR COLLEGE

This high level school was to:

> prepare selected ground, air, and naval officers for the exercise of command and the performance of joint staff duties in the highest echelons of the armed forces; and to promote the development of understanding between high echelons of the armed forces and those of other agencies of government which are an essential part of a national war effort.[5]

Also, students were to study the military force necessary to implement national policy in peace and war, the strategy and integration of military policy and foreign policy, the impact of science and technology upon the armed forces, and war planning and the employment of Joint Forces.

The temporary construction in the rotunda in the former AWC was dismantled as over $140,000 was spent to alter the east map room into 14 offices on the first floor, and an auditorium and projection room on the second floor, all equipped with air conditioning.

The 1947-48 class had 100 students: 30 each from the Army, Navy, and Air Force, and 10 from the Department of State. The method of instruction included lectures, committee discussions, and seminar groups. The selection criterion was not to accept borderline students, so no grades were given -- merely pass or fail. Field trips were planned, but the first two classes were confined to visits to US installations. The range was expanded in 1950 with trips to the

Pacific, Caribbean, and European areas, and with trips to Northern Europe, the Mediterranean, and the Far East in 1952. The first class visit to the USSR was in 1960.

In 1959, $70,000 was set aside to construct a reading room over Auditorium B. The housing question for staff and faculty was again raised but not acted upon.

As the size of the classes increased to 120-130, a two-week Defense Strategy Seminar was established to update members of the Reserve and National Guard forces. In 1961, an arrangement was worked out with George Washington University to grant master's degrees in International Affairs by giving credits for the subjects covered at the National War College, and outside study in specified courses to complete degree requirements. This placed an increased load on students, but enabled them to achieve dual goals in 11 months.

By 1965, classes had increased to 140 students. The War College building was bursting its seams and seriously outdated. A whole year was spent in renovating 93,000 square feet of the interior of Roosevelt Hall installing new heating equipment, plumbing, lighting, and air-conditioning. The area under the front terrace was enlarged by 10,000 square feet to accommodate a printing plant and a visual aids facility.

The computer age was impacting upon business and industry, and schools saw the enormous advantage offered by permanently stored and instantly retrievable historical data. In addition, the medium offered analysis of current data and future predictions. Not only would computers create a whole new recreational fad (game arcades), but serious gaming and planning could also utilize the capabilities. The first time-shared computer was installed at NWC in 1966. Students were introduced to the computer as a research tool and a thesis aid, but it would be another 15 years before students learned to type well enough to take full advantage of the new science.

In 1970 both auditoriums were named and dedicated honoring Air Force General "Hap" Arnold and Army General "Ike" Eisenhower. At the same time, a seminar room was refitted and named for Navy Admiral H W Hill.

The following year, the library started compiling a research collection of National Security Affairs. The nucleus consisted of the papers of General Lyman Lemnitzer and General Maxwell Taylor, plus dozens of lesser luminaries. These collections would serve as valuable research aids for students, faculty, and historians. The east basement wing was redesigned to install vending machines and laundry facilities for sports attire for student baseball, basketball, tennis, and golf teams.

The NWC building was reroofed and the dome recoppered prior to its dedication as a National Historic Landmark on 24 June 1974.

For the next year and a half the building underwent extensive renovation to the Guastavino cohesive tile and mortar dome and vault areas.[6]

In 1974 the class had 35 students from civilian agencies, seven former prisoners of war, and five military and civilian women. Their average age was 41, and the average length of service was 18 years. Further statistics as of that date indicated that of 4,000 graduates, 43 percent had attained general or flag rank; 25 percent of State and Foreign Service personnel had attained the rank of ambassador; and 60 military graduates had attained four-star rank.[7] The cost of the course was roughly $20,000 per student.

In 1976, the National War College fell under an umbrella designated as the National Defense University which included the Industrial College of the Armed Forces at Fort McNair, and the Armed Forces Staff College at Norfolk, Virginia.[8]

National War College Commandants include:

1947-49	Vice Admiral Harry W Hill, USN
1950-52	Lieutenant General Harold R Bull, USA
1953-55	Lieutenant General Howard A Craig, USAF
1956-58	Vice Admiral E Tyler Wooldridge, USN
1959-61	Lieutenant General Thomas L Harrold, USA
1962-64	Lieutenant General Francis H Griswold, USAF
1965-67	Vice Admiral Fitzhugh Lee, USN
1968	Lieutenant General Andrew J Goodpaster, USA
1969-70	Lieutenant General John E Kelly, USA
1971-73	Lieutenant General John B McPherson, USAF
1974-75	Vice Admiral Marmaduke G Bayne, USN
1976	Major General James S Murphy, USAF
1977-78	Major General Harrison Lobdell, Jr, USAF
1979-80	Rear Admiral John C Barrow, USN
1981-83	Major General Lee E Surut, USA
1984-86	Major General Perry M Smith, USAF
1987-89	Rear Admiral John F Addams, USN
1990-92	Major General Gerald P Stadler, USA

ARMY INDUSTRIAL COLLEGE (AIC), RENAMED THE INDUSTRIAL COLLEGE OF THE ARMED FORCES (ICAF)

Recognizing the need to train officers in procurement of war supplies in the event of mobilization, the Army first sent eight officers to Harvard Graduate School of Business Administration. On 25 February 1924, General Order 7 established an Army Industrial College in the old Munitions Building to train Army officers to supervise procurement of military supplies in time of war, and to insure adequate mobilization materiel and to learn the art of management.

To meet the need for emergency office space during the "Great War," temporary, frame, barracks-type buildings covered the mall along the south side of Constitution Avenue between 17th and 21st Streets. The Munitions Building was one of these. Franklin D Roosevelt was Secretary of the Navy in 1917, and he urged President Wilson to place the temporary buildings on the ellipse in front of the White House, thus assuring they would be demolished shortly after the war. Wilson refused saying he couldn't put up with the noise of construction and fight the Kaiser at the same time.

By the time Roosevelt became President, the structures were still standing, and with the coming of World War II, they were still needed. They remained in use for 53 years, finally being demolished in 1970. Only then did the mall present an uninterrupted vista from the Capitol to the Lincoln Memorial.

At the onset of World War II when more temporary wartime buildings were needed, they were designed with built-in obsolescence, the idea being to make them so flimsy they would fall down of their own weight in ten years. Tempos A, B, and C built on 2nd Street, SW (east of Fort McNair's brick wall) withstood their shoddy construction for 45 years and were only razed in 1987 to allow construction of the National Defense University Administration Operations Center in 1991.[9]

Starting in 1924 with only nine students, by 1935, the AIC had seven instructors, and had graduated an average of 55 students per year. The three outstanding graduates would attend either the Army or Navy War Colleges.

The last AIC class was in 1941 where 75 students were graduated in three months. The school was ordered closed on 15 December and its library was transferred to the Commanding General, Services and Supply and combined with the Law Library in the Pentagon in 1942. The Army Industrial College was reopened by Circular #337, 18 December 1943, with classes to be held in the newly opened Pentagon.

After the war, the AIC moved to a temporary building overlooking the marina at the Army War College. The resident course was lengthened to ten months, the name changed to the Industrial College of the Armed Forces (ICAF), and its program expanded along the joint service concept. Its mission was redefined:

> To train officers of the armed forces for duties involving procurement planning, procurement, mobilization of the national economy and economic warfare; evaluate the economic war potential of foreign nations; conduct studies and research in above fields; and foster close relationship between the armed forces and civilian engineering, scientific, educational, and industrial groups in the study of the social, political, and economic impact of war.[10]

World War II experience at revving up production and distribution from a standstill to high gear emphasized the importance of skilled military and civilian professionals in the economic and procurement areas of war. No matter how large or well-trained the armed forces might be, they couldn't move an inch without logistical support. The importance of this matter caused the size of those classes to almost double those of the NWC. Co-location at one installation allowed students of both schools to attend one another's lectures, and be aware of the importance of mobilization of the industrial area at the same time strategic and tactical plans were formulated.

In 1948, a two-week National Security Seminar was instituted to alert Reserves as well as civilians of the complexities of gearing up from a complete standstill to provide military supplies in the event of war. Whereas our national proclivity had always been to enter war totally unprepared, this approach would anticipate future needs by combining input from both the military and industry.

By 1955, a correspondence course and extension courses had been set up for Reserves, National Guard, and students wanting the knowledge, but not fortunate enough to make the selection for on-campus study. These additional functions further strained the old, inadequate building. After years of requests for money to build a new facility, Congress finally approved $4.1 million on 28 August 1958, and the low bid went to G A Hyman Construction Company who started work on 12 December. The building was fireproof construction with 775 tons of structural steel, and 1.2 million bricks specially baked in wood burning kilns which causes them to give off varying colored highlights at different times of the day. The interior walls were masonry with vinyl covering to permit cleaning. The lighting was recessed fluorescent. A cafeteria and kitchen on the first floor provided messing facilities for approximately 400 people. A 71,000-volume library was planned as well as a classified library of 1700 volumes. The school would accommodate 240 students.[11] (photo 41)

Ceremonies for the 1960 graduating class were held in the new building. The dedication of the completed structure was in September with President Eisenhower as the guest of honor at the building named for him. The old temporary building was destined to be razed and a parking lot constructed on the site, but on 30 August 1960, the empty building burned to the ground. The fire was linked to a blowtorch.[12]

The enlarged facility admitted 160 students, an increase from an average of 130 students per year. The position of Commandant was upgraded to a three-star slot (Lieutenant General) on a par with that of the NWC. In addition, this was the first year a Master's Degree in Business Administration was offered in conjunction with George Washington University.

In 1962, the Department of the Army allotted one supergrade space (GS-16) for a senior educational advisor for the staff who was given the title of Ambassador to the school. The following men have served in that capacity:

1961-62	W L Beaulac	1971-77	W Leonhart
1962-64	W G Brown	1977-79	J B Kubisch
1964-65	S D Berger	1979-81	M Stearns
1965-66	J M Cabot	1981-86	L B Laingen
1966-69	E A Lightner Jr	1986-98	R H Miller
1969-71	J W Jones	1989-92	W E Stadtler

A two week National Security Seminar group toured the country during the summer months to present an information program in principal cities to Reserve, National Guard, and civilians. It gave 14 presentations in as many states.

By 1965, it was realized that automatic data processing equipment was needed to upgrade capabilities of the large enrollment of resident, correspondence, and extension course students. Also computers would expand research, study programs, and gaming projects. Three years later, a Simulation and Computer Directorate was established.

By 1968, the school was publishing a journal, *Perspectives in Defense Management*, with a circulation of 35,000. Funds were obtained to improve classrooms with updated presentation equipment, new carpets, drapes, and furniture. New artwork for the walls was obtained from military services.

The incoming class of 1970 was the youngest and the best prepared ever, with 50 percent already having master's degrees. Graduates could apply for a newly established Research Fellow Program. If selected, a researcher could remain on campus for a specified period at full pay and allowances with no other duty than to complete an approved project.

Space again became a problem, and agitation started to build for an additional structure. The 50th Anniversary class of 1974 had an enrollment of 190 which included 12 returned Prisoners of War -- eight Air Force, and four Navy -- and over 10,000 students enrolled in correspondence courses.

ICAF was designated as part of the National Defense University in 1976.[13] Officers serving as Directors or Commandants of AIC and ICAF are as follows:

1924-27	Colonel Harley B Ferguson, USA
1928-29	Colonel William P Wooten, USA
1930	Colonel Irving J Carr, USA
1931-34	Lieutenant Colonel William A McCain, USA
1935-38	Colonel Harry B Jordan, USA
1939	Lieutenant Colonel Francis H Miles Jr, USA

1940	Lieutenant Colonel John E Lewis, USA
1941	Colonel Frank Whitehead, USMC
1946	Brigadier General Donald Armstrong, USA
1947	Brigadier General Edward B McKinley, USA
1948-52	Major General Arthur W Vanaman, USAF
1953-55	Rear Admiral Wesley McL Hague, USN
1956-57	Major General Robert P Hollis, USA
1958-61	Lieutenant General George W Mundy, USAF
1962-63	Vice Admiral Rufus E Rose, USN
1964-67	Lieutenant General August Schomburg, USA
1968	Lieutenant General Leighton I Davis, USAF
1969-70	Lieutenant General John S Hardy, USAF
1971-73	Vice Admiral J V Smith, USN
1974-75	Lieutenant General Walter J Woolwine, USA
1975	Major General Edward A McGough III, USAF
1976-78	Major General T Antonelli, USA
1979	Major General J E McInerney, USA
1980	Major General John E Ralph, USAF
1981	Major General James E Dalton, USAF
1982-83	Rear Admiral Ronald E Narmi, USN
1984-85	Major General C D Dean, USMC
1986-89	Major General A G Wheeler, USA
1990-91	Major General D M Goodrich, USAF

Goddard identifies ordnance pieces at Eisenhower Hall: a 10-inch Fort Pitt mortar at the southwest corner; guarding the front entrance are two French cannon cast by Berenger in 1756 named "La Biche," (the doe) and "La Licorne" (the unicorn); and on the northwest corner of the building is a French cannon made in Strasbourg about 1736 named "Le Partisant" (the guerrilla).

INTER-AMERICAN DEFENSE COLLEGE (IADC)

Of several sites offered, the Organization of the American States (OAS) selected Fort McNair for establishment of an Inter-American Defense College -- an advanced studies institute for senior officers of 19 member nations of the Inter-American Defense Board. Each member nation sends up to three students of the rank of colonel or equivalent, whose backgrounds qualify them to participate in the solution of hemispheric defense problems. The maximum student load was expected to be around 60, and the length of the course was to be 22 weeks. The first staff in October of 1962 was headed by Major General Thomas F Van Natta, US Army, Director; and Army, Navy, and Air Force leaders representing Argentina, Columbia, Brazil, Uruguay, and the US. This college is not connected with the other two senior service schools at Fort McNair (NWC and ICAF).

To make room for the new institution, barracks #52 and the east wing of the old General Hospital, #54, were vacated for use as classrooms and student's quarters. The 1903 mess hall #50 was converted into an open mess for IADC use. Occupancy of #54 took place in September 1962 when furniture was moved into the 31-man bachelor officers' quarters in the old hospital building. Students assigned duty in the US upon completion of the course prefer to establish homes for their families in the Washington area.

The academic building, #52, contains an auditorium with a seating capacity of 100, administrative offices, and classrooms. The auditorium has the latest electronic simultaneous translating equipment to permit students to hear guest lecturers in their own language.[14]

A formal inaugural ceremony was held on 9 October 1962 to welcome the first group of students. The Honorable Dean Rusk, Secretary of State, officially presented the buildings and furnishings of IADC on behalf of the United States Government.[15] Guarding the front entrance to building #52 are two French bronze cannon cast around 1756 named "La Mignarde," (the gentle one) and "La Vedette," (the sentinel).

By 1991, 1,540 students had graduated from IADC representing Argentina, Bolivia, Brazil, Chili, Columbia, Dominican Republic, Ecuador, El Salvadore, Guatemala, Haiti, Honduras, Mexico, Nicaragua, Panama, Paraguay, Peru, Uruguay, and Venezuela.

THE OLD GUARD

Units of the 3d US Infantry Regiment are quartered in barrack #47. This military organization traces its origin to the First Sub-Legion of a body of militia raised in 1784 and has been designated as the 3d Infantry since 1815. In the Mexican War of 1847, the 3d Infantry participated in the battles of Palo Alto, Monterrey, and the fall of Mexico City. During the unit's triumphant entry into the city, General Winfield Scott turned to his staff and said: "Gentlemen, take off your hats to the Old Guard of the Army" -- thus, the origin of their name.

During the Civil War, the 3d Infantry was credited with saving the rear guard of Union troops at the Battle of Bull Run. Units of the 3d saw action in Cuba and the Philippines at the turn of the century, and fought Pancho Villa in 1916. Since 1947, the unit has been assigned to guard the Nation's capital and perform ceremonial duties.[16]

The Old Guard has three distinct missions: to provide a force to: (1) conduct infantry missions as specified in existing war plans; (2) provide forces for the defense and support of executive mansions, key facilities, and key officials in times of natural emergency or civil disturbances, and (3) represent the Department of Defense and the US Army at official ceremonies and funerals. Among their tasks are forming the Army's honor guard to greet and bid farewell to official visitors to Washington, participating in military funerals at Arlington National Cemetery, and keeping a constant vigil at the Tomb of the Unknown Soldier.

In 1957, there was a proposal for motor vehicles to replace the traditional horse-drawn caisson used in military funerals for more than 92 years. The plan was to memorialize the caissons and equipment by transferring them to the US Military Academy Museum at West Point, New York. Because of the public hue and cry, Secretary of the Army Wilber M Brucker reversed the Army's economy-minded decision to discontinue the use of the horse-drawn caissons, the 16 matched grey horses, and the riderless black horse which carries the officer's boots reversed.[17]

In 1960, the first performance of the "Prelude to Taps" pageant was performed by the Old Guard and the Army Band. This was a dazzling demonstration of Army skills and drills, with a Fife and Drum Corps in Continental Army uniforms, the story of the American flag, and a presentation of a "Day in the Life of a Revolutionary War Soldier" presented to 10,000 guests the first year.

The company quartered at Fort McNair drills and rehearses on the parade ground. *Jane Merryman recalled Vice President George Bush jogging the two mile post perimeter, accompanied, of course, by secret service personnel. As the joggers rounded a corner, barring their path was a rehearsing honor guard with their bayonetted rifles pointing directly at the runners. Neither group had been alerted as to what the other was doing.

It is somewhat disconcerting to come upon a battered and patched casket sitting catty-wampus on sawhorses behind the barracks. It is used by the Old Guard to practice funeral rites.

MILITARY DISTRICT OF WASHINGTON (MDW)

The US Military District of Washington traces its origin to 1921 with the creation of what was then called the District of Washington. The Commanding General of the 16th Infantry Brigade headquartered at Fort Hunt was responsible for conducting military ceremonies and administering discipline to the military personnel in the District of Columbia. When the Brigade moved to Fort Meade, Maryland, in 1939, its duties were transferred to a newly established Washington Provisional Brigade under control of the War Department. On 5 May 1942, the Provisional Brigade was restructured and named the Military District of Washington. At that time the headquarters were in the Potomac Park Apartment Building at 21st and C Streets NW. In October the unit moved to the old Munitions Build-

New Missions

ing on the mall, and later into the newly completed Pentagon in February 1943.

After the war, the headquarters moved to temporary building 7 at Gravelly Point, Virginia, in July 1949, and to Fort McNair tempo building B in June 1957.[18] The unit had formerly been known as the 7001st Enlisted Detachment made up of personnel who perform duty with the various activities of District. The command was consolidated inside the fort in 1966.[19]

The shoulder patch representing MDW reflects its history and mission. A blue oval bordered in scarlet surrounds a white Washington Monument upon a green mound. Halfway up the monument, is a scarlet, double-handled broadsword with a gold hilt and pommel. The Monument represents the domain of MDW, and the broadsword symbolizes protection of the national capital. The wartime tactical force of MDW was made up of all branches of the military forces. The blue in the patch represents the Infantry and Navy; the scarlet/gold the Marine Corps, the scarlet the Field Artillery and Engineers, yellow the Cavalry, and the green the Military Police.[20]

In 1971, MDW was reorganized giving the Commanding General responsibilities previously held by the commanders of Fort Myer, Fort McNair, and Cameron Station. The first MDW general to live on post was MG J B Adamson who lived in #3. That house continued to be reserved for that position until 1983, but since that time the quarters assigned may depend on which set is available.

In 1973, the MDW assumed responsibility for supporting the Army Staff in the areas of personnel security, military personnel, civilian personnel, and equal employment opportunity. Over the years, the command has gained, lost, and retained various installations and support responsibilities.

When the Secretary of the Army decided to move the Engineer School from Fort Belvoir, to Fort Leonard Wood, Missouri, MDW assumed operational control of Fort Belvoir on 1 June 1988. The congressional Base Realignment and Closure Commission's recommendation to close Cameron Station, Virginia, and relocate those activities to Fort Belvoir by September 1995, became binding in May 1989.

The Commanding General of MDW is in charge of all US Army troop units in the geographical area not expressly part of another organization. He is responsible for organizing, training, and equipping units and individuals to perform their missions and to assure combat readiness. A primary mission is to prepare and maintain plans for the rescue, evacuation, and security of the occupants of the Executive Mansion, protect the seat of government and Department of Defense agencies, and assist civil authorities in restoration and maintenance of law and order in the event of civil disturbance.

In addition to responsibility for participation in ceremonies, MDW furnishes aviation and ground transportation for the White House, provides bus transportation service for Department of Defense within the area, and provides many thousands of active and retired military personnel and their families with post exchanges, commissaries, libraries, hobby shops, clubs, and other activities.

With the end of the Cold War and the dissolution of the USSR, Base Realignments and Closures (BRAC) was formed to streamline the armed forces. "Project Vanguard" in 1990 proposed for MDW to assume management of five additional Army installations by October 1993: Forts Meade, Holabird, and Ritchie in Maryland, and Fort A P Hill and Vint Hill Farms Station in Virginia.[21]

Past commanders of the District of Columbia and MDW:

COMMANDERS OF THE DISTRICT OF COLUMBIA

COL	H Burbeck	1810 -
BG	H H Bandheits	Aug 1921 - Sep 1922
MG	H A Smith	Oct 1922 - Apr 1923
BG	L S Upton	Nov 1923 - Mar 1927

COMMANDERS OF THE 16TH BRIGADE

MG	M T Donaldson	May 1927 - Dec 1927
BG	H G Williams	Dec 1927 - Aug 1930
BG	E T Collins	Nov 1930 - Feb 1932
BG	P I Mills	Apr 1932 - Mar 1936

COMMANDERS OF WASHINGTON PROVISIONAL BRIGADE

BG	C D Roberts	Apr 1936 - Jun 1937
BG	D T Merrill	Jul 1937 - Nov 1938
BG	M Murray	Dec 1938 - Jun 1940
BG	J I Devers	Jul 1940 - Oct 1940
BG	J M Greely	Oct 1940 - Apr 1941
BG	A L Cox	Jul 1941 - May 1942

COMMANDERS OF THE MILITARY DISTRICT OF WASHINGTON

MG	J T Lewis	May 1942 - Sep 1944
MG	C P Thompson	Sep 1944 - Jul 1945
BG	R N Young	Jul 1945 - Jun 1946
BG	C B Firenbaugh	Jun 1946 - Jul 1947
MG	H R Gay	Jul 1947 - Aug 1949
COL	J Cole	Aug 1949 - Feb 1950
MG	T H Harris	Mar 1950 - May 1952
MG	E K Wright	Jun 1952 - Apr 1954
MG	J A Stakes Jr	Apr 1954 - Feb 1956
MG	J D Van Houten	Feb 1956 - Aug 1959

MG	C K Gailey	Feb 1956 - Aug 1959
MG	P Gavan	Jun 1961 - Jul 1963
MG	P C Wehle	Aug 1963 - Sep 1965
MG	C J Herrick	Oct 1965 - May 1967
MG	C S O'Malley Jr	Jun 1967 - Nov 1969
MG	R M Glezer	Oct 1969 - Apr 1972
MG	J B Adamson	May 1972 - Oct 1973
MG	F E Davison	Nov 1973 - Dec 1974
MG	R J Fairfield Jr	Jan 1975 - Jul 1975
MG	R G Yerks	Aug 1975 - Jul 1977
MG	K E Dohleman	Aug 1977 - Jun 1979
MG	R E Arter	Jun 1979 - Aug 1981
MG	J R Curry	Aug 1981 - Oct 1983
MG	J L Ballantyne	Oct 1983 - Jan 1986
MG	D C Hilbert	Jun 1986 - Jun 1990
MG	W F Streeter	Jul 1990 -

CHAPTER XII: *Life on Post, 1950 -1975*

Following the allied victory in World War II, the United States emerged as a world superpower. The wartime alliance with the Soviet Union quickly collapsed, and communism was viewed as the new threat to world peace. International tensions, the Iron Curtain, and Cold War politics dominated the news. The already bulging federal bureaucracy continued to grow instead of reverting to prewar levels. Thousands of veterans relocated in the capital area attracted by the promise of jobs and low-cost housing. Suburbs erupted whose malls drew shoppers from the city leaving the downtown area to become empty and shabby.

The area outside Fort McNair's gates was a neighborhood of poor, working-class blacks and whites living in dilapidated housing. From Independence Avenue to the waterfronts, the southwest sector of the city consisted of docks and warehouses, a fish market, run-down buildings and wholesale grocery businesses interspersed throughout the ugly neighborhood.

In 1949, Congress passed a national housing act giving power to the Redevelopment Land Agency which was urging urban renewal. The Agency position was that if 25 percent of a neighborhood was considered substandard, the best thing to do was raze the entire area and build anew. Using $2.5 million in federal funds, the southwest section of Washington was the first to undergo demolition. As the land was confiscated, little help was given to relocate evicted families. By 1955, half of the 553 acres was cleared, and by 1961 construction started on row houses and high-rise apartment buildings.[1] Much of the construction was left to the tastes of private developers.

Fort McNair was not part of the reconstruction. Also, a few federal facilities were spared such as the Bureau of Engraving and Printing, Agriculture buildings, and those of Department of Health, Education, and Welfare. The government took over some of the cleared areas for Housing and Urban Development; Departments of Transportation, Energy, and Education; Environmental Protection Agency; and the US Information Agency.[2]

*Professor Denver Fugate gave an account of barracks life in 1951. As a corporal, he served with the 35th Antiaircraft Brigade whose job was to identify aircraft overflying the area and report findings to the Air Force Early Warning System. His 503d AAA Operational Detachment of 30 men was commanded by Major Montrone. Quartered in #52, the units part of the barracks consisted of one large squadroom for unmarried men; a cadre room for two NCOs with an adjoining shower and latrine with wash basins and toilets. The end toilet had the letters "VD" painted on the floor. Bunks and lockers lined the walls, with other rows in the middle of the bay. Footlockers containing personal gear stood at the foot of the old hospital-type bunks -- not the narrow, folding army cot. The commanding officer and married officers lived off post, as did married NCOs.

Corporal Fugate remembered a nearby restaurant on 4th Street nicknamed "The Greasy Spoon" where beer sold for ten cents a bottle. Post Headquarters was in building #48 where "Red the Barber" vowed he only knew how to do close-cropped GI cuts, but he never fulfilled his threats. [Red is Laverne Sullivan who has worked at McNair in the plumbing shop for 45 years still gives free haircuts at the Soldiers' and Airmens' Home.] A Service Club was in the north end of #48, where "donut dollies" arranged recreation for soldiers (i.e., tours to Triton Beach, Maryland). Other favorite haunts were the Blue Mirror, the Windsor Room, Club Kavakas, and Hains Point for picnics.

The officers' quarters were scheduled for updating in 1953 when 30 window air conditioners were requisitioned (two per house). However, when it came time for installation, *Brigadier General H B Powell recalled the RHIP (rank hath its privileges) rule was invoked. The air conditioners were issued according to the number of stars worn by the quarters occupant.

A news item reported the retirement of "two of the best-liked generals to have ever walked the Capital scene."

> Flanked by top Government officials, 5-star Gen. Omar Bradley, retiring chairman of the Joint Chiefs of Staff, and 4-star Gen. J Lawton Collins, retiring Chief of Staff of the Army, watched with mixed feelings, no doubt, the climax of their brilliant careers...on the parade green at Fort McNair.[3]

In 1957 disaster struck the fort in the form of the "Dutch Elm Disease." The stately 60-year-old trees were cut down and replaced with Chinese Pagodas, Sugar Maples, European Lindens, London Planes, and Red Horse Chesnuts. These strains were selected for their ornamental value, cleanliness, and low susceptibility to disease.[4]

*Captain Roy Thurman (retired as Lieutenant General) was aide de camp for General Williston ("Willie") B Palmer when he lived in #8 in 1956-57. Since the general was a bachelor and had more room than he used, he invited his aide to occupy the third floor and allowed to him to use the main floor of the quarters when the general was away. Contemporaries remember attending Roy's formal dinners where his friends would come "dressed to the nines" to enjoy the ambiance of the lovely house.

Willie had a brother, Charlie D (Charlie Dog) Palmer, who also attained general officer rank while still a bachelor. When Charlie was a Lieutenant General he decided to marry. His brother was furious, telling him that "if the Army'd wanted him to have a wife they'd have issued one," and assuring him that he "was ruining his career." This assumption was contrary to the axiom that the best bargain to be found was an Army officer and his wife. The officer didn't cost much, and his wife came free.

It was also told that Williston eventually met an interesting lady. He took a few days leave and boarded a train to the southwestern state where she lived, intending to propose. When he went to her house and knocked on her door, there was no answer. Willie got back on the train and returned to Washington, DC, and that was the end of that.

At the end of the decade, the Paddock Engineering Company began work on a $75,000 swimming pool to be completed by May 1959 on the site of a children's playground. ICAF would be built later on the site of the former pool.[5]

Retired *Lieutenant General M S Carter moved from quarters at Fort Myer located adjacent to the Arlington Cemetery chapel to #14 at Fort McNair in 1962. They fully appreciated the peaceful atmosphere of McNair after listening to drum rolls of funeral processions five days a week, and wedding bells on weekends.

*Patricia (Pachler) Medina vacationed with her parents when Major General F T Pachler lived in #12 from August 1962 to July 1963 and recalled her parents had sand bags in many areas of the quarters because of the Cuban Missile Crisis.

Their family was followed in #12 by *Major General Sidney C Wooten from August 1963 to July 1967. As the young son of Major W P Wooten, Corps of Engineers, Sid lived in #9 in 1915-16, and again when his father was a Colonel they lived in #15 from 1922 to 1925:

> During his high school days, there were some horses and mules belonging to the Engineers stabled in the building now used as the Post Theater. He has a vivid memory of the day his horse ran away with him. He had just made the turn at the point behind the college to go back to the stables when his horse got in a hurry to get home. He plowed through the new #7 green of the golf course. Father and I were much embarrassed by that event.[6]

In April 1965, the Federal Bureau of Investigation (FBI), arrested Sergeant R L Johnson, 43, a courier at Fort McNair, for supplying secrets to Soviet agents, both here and abroad, for the past 11 years. He had been recruited in Paris and operated in Berlin as well as at Fort Bliss, Texas and Washington, DC.[7]

Typical of the rival relationship between Army and Navy personnel are pranks played just before the big annual football game between the two military academies.

Several Army officers decided it was high time Navy personnel...met with the backbone of Army tradition. [The day of the Army/Navy football game] the officers rented a mule from a stable in Largo, Maryland, and caped the animal with a "Go Army - Beat Navy" blanket. With a "head him up and move him out" from Captain Paul F Vader, and an occasional "charge" from the bugle of Captain Jose Badillo, the small band of Army "backers" paraded the mule around the post with the help of volunteer "mule skinner" SP-4 Joe Keller, a cook at McNair's mess hall.

The destination of the party was the quarters of Rear Admiral Jack J Appleby on "General's Row." He is a graduate of the Naval Academy.[8]

The MDW Annual Report for 1966 recorded hosting local youngsters (ages 6-16) in "Operation Step Up" which included a tour of the post and various facilities capped by a swim in the pool and a movie. The 1967 Annual Report stated the Officers' Club was renovated, as was the Post Theater. The Army-Air Force Motion Picture Service approved $8,499 for the restoration.

*Wesley C Franklin, Major General, USA Ret, expected to move from Arlington Hall Station directly into #4 at McNair in July 1967. However, the previous occupant was fighting mandatory retirement and this took several months to settle. Therefore, the Franklins spent the summer in the basement of the old penitentiary building, #20, in an "unlovely" four-room apartment, complete with leaky floors, mice, and other creatures, and berift of air-conditioning.

Having had their authorized government move, when #4 finally became available, the Franklins had to move themselves across the parade ground, each family member carrying various pieces of household goods and luggage to the new house under cover of darkness. They later laughed about being ashamed to be seen hauling their possessions on foot.

Once, on his way home from the Pentagon, General Franklin was accosted by the Post Commander, Colonel W A McDaniel, who informed him his family would be evicted from the post if their two German shepherds didn't cease menacing post personnel. After further discussion in the Tavern Room of the Club, and promising to keep the hounds leashed, they continued to live on post in peace. Colonel McDaniel is remembered by residents for erecting a sign at a crosswalk near the bandstand warning motorists to stop at this authorized "Squirrel Crossing."

Major renovations took place at Fort McNair in 1968 according to *The Pentagram News*. Both the Commissary and PX were painted and redecorated. The six-lane bowling alley was reconditioned, and sauna and shower facilities were installed in the gym. Four greens on the 9-hole golf course were completely rebuilt with underground watering and drainage systems. The tennis courts were resurfaced and the indoor rifle and pistol range in the basement of #48 was redone.[9]

General Frank S Besson, Jr lived in #9 from January 1965 to October 1970. During his 38 years of military service, he was a general officer for more than 25 years after being promoted to brigadier general in 1945 -- the youngest general in the AGF. He is credited with organizing the US Army Material Command (AMC) in 1962 whose mission was to equip the Army and provide resources to keep equipment operational. (Besson first lived on post in #9 in 1916-17 until his 1st Lieutenant father went overseas with the First Division.) His memoirs contain this story:

> For several years, my brother and I hadn't had a lot of close parental supervision, not that Grandma Besson didn't supervise, but it had been a long time since she had handled little boys. We were kind of known as the Katz and Jammer kids; we always seemed to be getting into trouble.
>
> Shortly after we arrived in 1916, somebody on the post was having a birthday party and we weren't invited....So, as the little boys were walking down the street to the party, we would grab them and shove them down the coal chute into the basement...
>
> There were stories that when it rained we would hide behind the trees, then run out and jump in the puddles and splash the white uniforms of the officers going by. I suppose some of those things were true.

On 4 April 1968, Martin Luther King was assassinated in Memphis, Tennessee. The first notice of his death was broadcast at 8:15 PM, and almost immediately, thousands of frustrated, angry blacks filled the city's streets. Violence erupted at 14th and U Streets and rapidly spread. Police and firefighters were unable to stop or contain the arson and looting. By midnight, President Johnson ordered the flag lowered to half-mast (the first time a black had been so honored) and the following afternoon he reluctantly called in National Guard and US Army troops.[10]

MDW commander Major General Charles S O'Malley, Jr commanded a Task Force of 11,600 federal troops required to subdue three days of rioting.[11] Many people were victims of fires which swept the city's ghetto areas. The death toll reached 13; there were 1,037 injuries (seven soldiers); 5,414 arrests; and 828 fires.[12] Over

1,000 buildings were damaged, and millions of dollars of property was destroyed. The long-term consequences of the DC riots proved even more disastrous. During the next few years, 118,000 residents, 15 percent of the population, left the city. The destroyed and burned-out sectors stood many years as a silent testimonial of the senseless violence.[13]

The unrest in the nation over the war in Southeast Asia caused the Pentagon and other military installations in Washington to close their doors to public traffic in 1972. At Fort McNair, the Military Police at the gate had to tell motorists, bicyclists, strollers, and local residents accustomed to using the amenities that they could no longer enter the post for security reasons. The high brick walls that separated the fort from the city became more than symbolic barriers.[14]

Family quarters provided for 14 General/Flag officers of the Department of Defense, and 1 State Department faculty member of NWC; 24 field and company grade officers (major to lieutenants); and 12 noncommissioned officers. The average population of the post was 900 military, 600 civilian, and 150 dependents.

*Major General and Mrs R R Williams were nicely settled in #4 in August 1969 when he was nominated for Lieutenant General. As a result of the promotion, General William Westmoreland directed them to move to Fort Myer. His wife Jean had to make the move alone since her husband was ordered to accompany Westmoreland to Europe; she vowed never to forgive "Westy."

This also happened to *General and Mrs Alexander Haig, Jr who lived in #8 from March until August of 1973 when he assumed the position of Vice Chief of Staff to the US Army. They welcomed the assignment and hoped to return to the Army family after 3-1/2 years as Deputy National Security Advisor to the President. Mrs Haig was delighted with the dignified setting of the Fort McNair quarters. It seemed to them they had barely unpacked when General Haig was recalled to the White House to serve as President Nixon's Chief of Staff. "Quarters #8 is a product of the sentimental dialectic for the Haigs -- joy followed by the disappointment of a sudden departure."

*Lieutenant General and Mrs Frederick J Clarke occupied #5 from 1970 to 1973 and regularly invited Engineer wives to their quarters while their husbands were in Southeast Asia.

While commanding AMC, *General and Mrs Henry A Miley, Jr occupied #9 from 1970 until his retirement in 1975 while he commanded Army Materiel Command. His neighbors, Lieutenant General W W Vaughan, Lieutenant General Bill DePuy, and General Bruce Palmer organized a tennis foursome which played on the lighted courts from 6:00 to 7:00 AM no matter what the season.

During the Watergate affair, just before President Nixon resigned, the presidential yacht *Sequoia* frequently sailed in the channel behind the quarters. The Mileys always assumed the President was aboard when Secret Service personnel took up positions on the seawall and warned them to stay inside. A Coast Guard boat always accompanied the yacht.

*Lieutenant General and Mrs Vaughan had the pleasure of living in #11 for seven years (1971 to 1978) where, as Commanding General of AMC, they entertained distinguished guests from many foreign countries as well as US dignitaries. At a dinner party they gave for the Assistant Secretary of the Army:

> I recounted the fact that the only woman ever hanged in the United States was executed at McNair. The woman was Mary Surratt, hanged for her part in the assassination of President Lincoln. Rumor had it that her ghost still haunted the building where she was imprisoned before being led to the scaffolding erected by the tennis courts.
>
> About an hour after all the guests had departed, a knock came on the front door. There stood the disappointed Secretary who reported he had spent an hour and a half roaming around the execution site but found no sign of Mary's ghost.

Workers reporting for duty in the early morning hours of 17 Nov 1970 stared incredulously at a 20-foot cabin cruiser parked amid the cars and trucks in the parking lot. The boat fulfilled the dream of the Fort McNair Sea Explorer Scouts known as "Ship." In support of the scouting program, Major General Roland M Glezer, commanding MDW, and his executive officer, Captain John B Ramsaur who served as skipper of Ship, learned the converted skeg sailboat was available from the Coast Guard Training Center in Cape May, New Jersey. Ship members took all winter to give the boat a complete overhaul for weekend trips and a 10-day cruise in the Chesapeake Bay the next summer.[15]

*General John R Deane, Jr verified their occupation of #13 and #9 in the mid-1970s. While living there, Mrs Deane received a phone call saying her husband would be killed if he didn't leave $10,000 under a brick by the recreation center in a park in Capitol Heights. When the threat was reported to the Provost Marshal, he in turn alerted the FBI. General Deane accompanied the FBI on a wild goose chase to the park. Since no contact was made, a tap was put on the home telephone.

A few days later, President Kennedy's sister-in-law phoned the general. Nonplussed by a call from this well-known lady whom he had never met, General Deane forgot to turn off the recorder. It seems a mutual friend had told her the general was a good tennis player and she called to invite him to join a group playing tennis at their home -- a pleasure he had to refuse.

After the FBI picked up the recorder and tapes, the general remembered the Kennedy-related phone call which wasn't public domain, and should have been erased. When he encountered a lot of trouble trying to find the tape to erase the private conversation, he thought: "If the FBI can't find their own property, how will they ever find the bad guys?"

When General *Donald R Keith attended ICAF in 1967, they often thought how nice it would be to occupy the gracious old quarters. Only a short time later, they were fortunate enough to live there from 1977 to 1984 in #1 and #7.

*General Fred and Arline Weyand lived in quarters at Fort McNair on two separate tours: in #3 from 1962 to 1964, and again in #8 in 1973-74. The second tour was cut short by the death of General Creighton Abrams -- a tragic loss for the Army and a sad time for his successor as Chief of Staff of the US Army. Neighbors recalled that Fred liked to entertain guests with professional renditions on his saxaphone.

*General W T Kerwin, Jr and his wife lived in #8 when their daughter was married in the Post Chapel in 1978 and the reception was held in their quarters. "Dutch" and "B" recalled playing golf every New Year's Day -- weather notwithstanding. On a late summer night a round of golf took about an hour; in the snow it was a bit more of a challenge.

*Lieutenant General John A Kjellstrom and his wife Dorothy lived in #1 from 1974 to 1977. They recalled the last days of the Nixon era when the yacht Sequoia was docked in the Washington Channel and entertaining friends on the 4th of July with an unobstructed view of the fireworks at the Washington Monument.

The east brick wall between Fort McNair and the tempo buildings almost collapsed in December 1973. The wall is built on the old James Creek bed which is covered with landfill.[16]

The end of American participation in the Southeast Asian War in 1973, followed by the collapse of South Vietnam in April 1975, ended an era of protest and discontent in Washington and the nation as a whole. It also brought about officer resignations and a universal loss of morale among servicemen. Some with an investment in retirement elected to remain on duty, but dedicated officers were seriously disillusioned and unfairly maligned. No bands welcomed them home, no ceremonies said thanks for obeying and serving the Commander-in-Chief. Draft dodgers were granted amnesty and allowed to return without taint after amusing themselves in Sweden and Canada.

Veterans were labeled as napalm-blasting baby burners, Agent Orange disseminators, and dope addicts. The rug was pulled out from under the South Vietnamese, Cambodians, and Laotians, despite US promises of support "to the last Southeast Asian." Americans ordered to remain in Vietnam or Thailand to lend credence to free world backing had nothing but egg on their faces.

Nobody turned off the light at the end of the tunnel because no light was left burning.

Most officers who retire as colonels after 30-years service should be considered successful men. They went more places, did more things, managed more money, and controlled more men and resources than most of their civilian contemporaries would ever envision.

...The same success ethic that makes an executive want to head a corporation, an athlete to win gold medals, an author to write a bestseller, a politician to be President, makes an officer aspire to be a general.[17]

CHAPTER XIII: *The Last Quarter Century*

NATIONAL DEFENSE UNIVERSITY

In 1976, the Department of Defense established an umbrella designation called the National Defense University (NDU) to direct the programs of the National War College and the Industrial College of the Armed Forces. The move reduced administrative costs, provided for exchange of faculty expertise and educational resources, and facilitated interaction among students and faculty.

The ground floor of Eisenhower Hall was modified at a cost of $175,000 that year, and new art was obtained for the hallways. The size of classes continued to increase. In 1980, ICAF graduated 218 students (174 military) and NWC graduated 160 students (120 military).

In 1981, the Armed Forces Staff College (AFSC) in Norfolk, Virginia was added to NDU. The mission of this school is to prepare mid-career officers for joint and combined staff duty. Norfolk was originally selected because World War II facilities were available and it was near Washington, DC. AFSC maintains a library in Normandy Hall which includes 82,000 cataloged books and reports, 1,200 periodical and serial titles, 35,000 classified documents, and 10,000 microfilm and microfiche items. No improvements have been made since 1971 although a new gym and chapel are scheduled for 1992. On-post housing is available for about 250 students. (photo 42)

In 1982, the Institute of Higher Defense Studies and the Department of Defense Computer Institute became a part of NDU. Also, a National Defense University Foundation was organized in to provide private sector support through grants and donations.

In 1984, the Institute for National Strategic Studies incorporated four previous research centers: a Strategic Concepts Development Center (which analyzes existing strategic concepts and suggests alternatives to the Secretary of Defense and Chairman of JCS); a Strategic Capabilities Assessment Center (which analyzes national security resources, linkage with the economic resource base, defense strategy, and future security environments); the Research Directorate (which publishes outstanding research on national security and supports the senior Fellows independent study); and a War Gaming and Simulation Center (which conducts relevant joint war games, politico-military simulations, and computer modeling). The War Games room moved into the space under the esplanade of Roosevelt Hall with a staff of 14 and space for 100 game players. It has an

auditorium which holds 66 students, equipped with mini-computer and audio-visual capabilities. The NDU Foundation loaned 250 micro computers to support Information Resources Management and to be used by the students as word processors for computer based electives. This same year an International Fellows Program developed which invites a number of senior foreign officers to attend the university.[1]

In March 1990 a fourth college was added to NDU, the Information Resources Management College (IRMC), with 15 faculty members and 30 civilian employees. This college replaced the DoD Computer Institute and provides information resources management education to Department of Defense executives. As many as 3,400 students attend each year. Emphasis is placed on high level participants.

The Panel on Military Education of the 100th Congress reported that the NWC faculty consisted of eight military and seven civilian doctorates, thirteen military and four civilian master's degrees, and two civilian bachelor's degrees. The ICAF faculty of 43 contained 15 civilian and one military doctorates, and one civilian and 23 military master's degrees.[2] The faculties of the three colleges remained relatively stable totaling 130 military and civilians. The missions assigned the NDU have caused operating personnel to increase 79 percent, from 270 in 1976 to 484 in 1991.

The following officers have served as President of NDU:

1977-81   Lieutenant General Robert G Gard, Jr, USA
1982-83   Rear Admiral R E Narmi, USN
1983   Lieutenant General John S Pustay, USAF
1984-86   Lieutenant General Richard D Lawrence, USA
1987-89   Lieutenant General B C Hosmer USA
1990-91   Vice Admiral J A Baldwin, USN

LIFE ON POST, 1975-1991

Quarters #5 was home to *Lieutenant General Howard H Cooksey and wife Althea from 1975 until his retirement in 1977. When he was still a lieutenant, General Cooksey promised his wife he would try to become eligible to live in one of those beautiful homes someday; he said (aside from liking his chosen profession) becoming a general was the least he could do to accommodate his wife's desire to live in quarters at Fort McNair.

As Commandant of ICAF, *Major General Theodore Antonelli and wife Margaret occupied #12 from 1975 to 1978. They appreciated the dignified residence as a setting to entertain not only distinguished visitors and lecturers, but also to host receptions for the students and faculty.

The Annual Historical Report for 1977 stated there were no changes in organization, mission, or function, but other significant events had taken place. The 23d Civilian Aides to the Secretary of the Army Conference had 79 delegates, and the 19th two-week Defense Strategy Seminar (hosted by the President of NDU) was attended by over 400 reserve and active duty personnel. The Summer Youth Program invited youngsters to tour the post, and public band concerts were offered.

Maintenance of the facilities included waterproofing basements on the north end of the post, major interior and exterior renovations and redecorating of the Officers' Open Mess, sandblasting and painting of quarters #20 and #22, and construction of a tunnel to allow gravity flow of sewage into the DC collection system.

August 1977 to June 1979 seemed like only yesterday to *Major General Kenneth E Dohleman and wife Anne who lived in #3 from 1977 to 1979. His letter stated:

> I recall the struggle to justify the funding required to maintain the quarters in any semblance of decent condition. During the early years of the Carter Administration, the Army budget was tightly constrained. A case in point was the need to refurbish (nay replace) the rotten and falling decorative trim above the porticos. The opinion of the Department of the Army was "removal would be cheaper and permanent."The Post Engineer and I felt that the decorative trim was integral to the ambiance of the historic Fort, so we dug in our heels.

Major projects completed during 1978 included construction of a new rear entrance to MDW Headquarters (#32), construction of a handicapped ramp at the Officers' Club (#60), replacement of three fuel storage tanks supporting the central heating plant (#34), and replacing tiles and shelving in the Commissary (#35). The porches and exterior woodwork of the bachelor officers' quarters (#54) were repaired, and the west seawall was regrouted. The fuel storage tanks were replaced again in 1993 when the type of fuel was changed.

*Major General Elton J Delaune, Jr and his wife Grace recall their occupancy of #14 from 1978 to 1982, the 4th of July parties, the rescue of unskilled sailors who crashed into the channel seawall, and the parades and retreat ceremonies.

When General and *Mrs "Fritz" Kroesen occupied #8 in 1978-79, they always decorated a huge Christmas tree in the foyer and set up a Lionel train track to operate around it. During their occupancy, the second floor hallway had a lovely mural wallpaper which the Engineers framed with molding. Quarters #8 underwent the demise of three pets who are buried in a nearby stand of pines: Dusty Dog Palmer, Wolfgang Kroesen, and Dundee I Thurman.

*Major General Robert L Kirwan and his wife Emilia were assigned #12 at Fort McNair from 1978 until 1983. Their blind 17-year-old cocker spaniel disappeared in the channel when let out for her morning ritual.

The annual conferences, seminars, youth programs and concerts continued as usual in 1979. The post engineers resurfaced streets; replaced major steam, gas, and sewer lines; repaired the exteriors of quarters #1-#15; and renovated the interior of MDW Headquarters (#32). Yards and Grounds removed 24 dead trees and planted 128 new ones. The Post Chaplain reported there had been 12 weddings, two baptisms, and 179 funerals.

Lieutenant General and *Mrs J H Merryman lived in #9 from 1981 to 1984. Jane told of the birds dragging their fish dinner up on the ice crust when the channel froze. While living at Fort McNair, Jane did extensive research to record past occupants of the 15 houses, which she generously shared to add to this publication.

Serving in retirement as Superintendent of the Maine Maritime Academy, *Rear Admiral Sayre A Schwarztrauber enumerated their memories when they lived in #13 from 1981 until 1983:

-- Holiday parades
-- Daily Bugle calls
-- Watching Vice President Bush jogging with an entourage of Secret Service agents
-- Lighting the fort Christmas Tree
-- Tales of Mary Surratt's ghost
-- Secure feeling of a self-contained community
  [after coming home from Madrid where their quarters were fired upon by Basque dissidents.]

During my tenure as Commandant of IADC, Argentina invaded the Falklands and it almost caused the Inter-American Defense College to suspend activities. Also, the Iranian hostages were released just before our arrival, and the Honorable Bruce Laingen moved into #15 as Ambassador to the National Defense University. The yellow ribbons came down from the trees in 1981.

*Lieutenant General E D Peixotto lived in #1 from 1981 to 1984 and marveled at the "sea of tranquility" he returned to after a hectic day at the Pentagon.

Retired *General John A Wickham, Jr, stated that the year he and Lois resided in #8, 1982-83, it was the best place they lived during his service. The historic location, beautiful view (despite the noise of National Airport) made an indelible impression.

Elements of MDW were called upon to aid in the rescue and recovery of victims of the Air Florida plane crash into the 14th Street Potomac bridge on 13 January 1982.

The ghost of Mary Surratt again became the subject of an article in *Inter/Change* which reported that Major and Mrs Tonelli were told that Mary, her husband, and her daughter's spirits inhabited quarters #20 -- the courtroom where the conspirators were sentenced to be hanged. They lived in #20-2 from 1979 to 1981, and during their occupancy a ball on their pool table abruptly stopped just before entering the pocket, yet when the next player went to take his turn, the ball flew into the pocket before a shot was taken. Another time a flower pot on a locked window sill flew 7 feet across the room and broke, and the window was found open. A repair man who derided the story of ghosts was hit in the head by a 2 x 4 while working alone in the basement. Polaroid pictures in the vacant third floor apartment contained strange images. Once the kitchen clock was found lying in pieces on the table, and the final straw was when the bedroom on the third floor inexplicably burst into flames.[4]

Twenty-four demonstrators opposing US policies in Central America staged a sit-down strike in front of the entrance to Fort McNair on the morning of 23 August 1983. Sixty protesters marched in front of the Fort chanting "block the troops, stop the war," and carrying posters that said, "Quarantine is an act of war" and "Stop Reagan's illegal secret war in Nicaragua." Members participating in the one-hour disruption of business of the Military District of Washington were the Religious Task Force, the Sisters of Mercy, the Washington Committee Against Registration and the Draft, the Progressive Student Network, and the US Anti-Imperialist League.[5]

Fort McNair was briefly named "Great Lakes Naval Training Center." When Paramount Pictures was shooting a movie based on James Michener's novel *Space*, they erected a fake front gate sign and cordoned off a portion of the post before deciding cost overruns would cause Fort McNair to be scratched as a filming site.[6]

In 1985, the post suffered a serious flood with water inundating the NWC parking lot. The building had to be sandbagged to keep the basement from filling with water. Along General's Row, the water overflowed the seawall and almost reached the back doors of the quarters. That year also saw an updating of the Gymnasium with installation of Nautilus exercise equipment.[7]

*Lieutenant General Herbert R Temple, Jr and his wife Pat occupied Quarters #1 at Fort McNair from 1986 to 1990. As Chief of the National Guard Bureau, with responsibility for 456 Army and Air Force elements with units located in every state, Puerto Rico, the Virgin Islands, and Guam during the height of the Cold War, they delighted in entertaining dignitaries and sharing the history of the elegant quarters.

In April 1986, Fort McNair acquired the area occupied by the tempo buildings east of the Fort. This increased the reservation to 113 acres, and prepared the way for demolition of the tempos and clearing the land for the erection of Marshall Hall.

A 1987 headline proclaimed "McNair Navy Launched." The subject was a hand-built, outboard raft to be used to inspect and keep McNair's 100-year old seawalls in repair. Flying US and Corps of Engineer's flags, the *USS McNair* was lifted into the channel by a backhoe without traditional champagne ceremonies. Designed by Carlyle Hawkins of Roads and Grounds, Bill Maneeley of the electric shop helped build the $500 craft which surprisingly was certified by the Coast Guard. The raft was 10 x 6 feet, powered by a seven-and-a-half horsepower outboard engine, resting atop two pontoons.[8]

Events of 1989 included reopening of the Commissary after extensive repair. The 3d Infantry Old Guard, along with A Company quartered at Fort McNair, performed a phenomenal 8,189 individual actions which included 4,273 funerals, 35 official welcoming ceremonies for foreign dignitaries, 121 cordons, 55 parades, 2,386 wreath ceremonies, 33 pageants, and 33 details. The Army Band gave 88 performances, the Chorus 343, the Strings section 122, the Herald Trumpets 98, the Blues group 39, and the Bugler 3,890.[9]

*Lieutenant General H D Graves recalled living in #5 from 1989 to 1991. As Assistant to the Chairman of the Joint Chiefs of Staff, the general spent much time away negotiating with the Soviet Union and with "Desert Storm" allies.

The appearance of Greenleaf's Point has changed little during the last part of this century, however, change is inevitable. It suddenly dawned on developers that the only area left for expansion in the capital was the strip of land bordering the Anacostia River between Fort McNair and the Navy Yard. When Tempo C was torn down, the government sold eight acres to a private developer who attempted to have it rezoned for highrise office and apartment buildings. The Army managed to stave off construction on the grounds that the security of the military installation would be compromised.[10]

At the same time, the marina was upgraded. Harbor facilities were first developed here in 1913 as the Corinthian Boat Club.

> Today it is considered a major commercial boating facility with 170 wet slips, of which 145 are usable for berthing boats ranging in length from 17 to 40 feet. Limited dry land storage is also available for 30 boats. The facilities consist of three fixed docks and one floating timber pier. A concrete wall retains the on-shore portion of the marina, an area which contains a small office, an engine repair shop, parking for 50 cars, a comfort station, a 20-ton marine railway, and a concrete launching ramp.[11]

Since 1985 a plan had been on hold for the construction of a 223,000 square foot building to support the National Defense University, only awaiting congressional approval of the $31.5 million it would cost. The temporary buildings were bulldozed and clearing of

the debris started in 1988. Construction of an Academic Operations Center for NDU was started on 3 August 1989. BeCon Services Corporation of Leesburg, Virginia was awarded the contract, overseen by the Baltimore District Army Corps of Engineers. Karl Ermanis was the principal designer for the architectural firm of Ellerbe Becket of Minneapolis. Some features of the center included a:

> 4,500 square foot multi-purpose conference area and a 180 person dining facility. Also incorporated were special protection for rare books, computer rooms, closed circuit television, an extensive computer network, and security and audio-visual systems.[12]

The ultra-modern edifice grew atop steel and concrete pilings sunk deep into the former marshland. Its immense size, in stark contrast to the neoclassical Roosevelt Hall and boxlike Eisenhower Hall, is overwhelming. However, the building has a fragile look due to use of lots of glass and a variety of construction materials. Benjamin Forgey described the architectural features as follows:

> ...the main facade of the new building is asymmetrical, one wing being much longer than the other due to the shape of the site and the location of the entrance... [It is] quite beautiful [and] vaguely military in appearance, with drain spouts centered in the crenellated openings of the armory-like piers...
> Ermanis's entrance is a whomping, unapologetic, exaggerated abstraction of columns, pediment and void ...so, this principal public facade is a job well done. Behind it, the building asserts its unwieldy size...it wanders, it sprawls...there's too much of it.
> ...the most important architectural move was to provide a dramatic, skylit longitudinal "Main Street" [in the long axis of the ground floor]...that ties things together somewhat and establishes a much-needed public interior space.
> The library...is a two-level affair distinguished by a free-standing pavilion...like Oswald Mathias Ungers' "house within a house."[13] (photo 43)

The new center was named for General George C Marshall, Chief of Staff of the Army in World War II, designer of the $13 billion dollar European relief plan which followed, Secretary of State and Defense (sponsors of NDU), and winner of the Nobel Peace Prize in 1953. Of the five men who achieved the grade of five-star general, Marshall was the only non-West Pointer. A graduate of Virginia Military Institute, he described the course at the Command and General Staff

map exercise where he made 100, a classmate who scored 95 was in 47th place -- the competition was that rough.

Before World War I, Marshall established a reputation as a tactician on maneuvers in the Philippines. He served as Black Jack Pershing's aide for six years in the 1920s, having reverted to the grade of captain. He did not become a general until 1936. In 1938 he became head of the War Plans Division, and a year later was promoted over the heads of 34 senior officers to full general and Chief of Staff of the Army. In 1944 he was named General of the Army, with a five-star rank.[14]

He retired to a four-acre estate in Leesburg, Virginia -- the only home the Marshalls ever owned. Mrs Marshall once said to her husband that "army wives were like tails on kites -- they had no control over where they went and always tagged along behind." Marshall replied: "How high do you think a kite would fly without its tail?"[15]

President George Bush dedicated the NDU Academic Operations Center, Marshall Hall, at Fort McNair on 28 September 1991:

> Navy Vice Admiral J A Baldwin was host of the ceremony. Guests included Barbara Bush, Marshall's stepdaughter Molly B Winn, Chairman of the Joint Chiefs of Staff Gen Colin Powell, National Security Advisor, Gen Brent Scowcroft, Vice Chief of Staff Gen Dennis Reimer, Ambassador Edward J Perkins, and Judge William S Sessions.[16]

The combined libraries of ICAF and NWC forming the National Defense University library contain more than 500,000 bound volumes, pamphlets, and periodicals; 105,000 documents; 50,000 classified documents and 1,200 periodical subscriptions. The emphases of the collection concern history, social sciences, management, military art and science. There is a Government Document section as well as a reference and bibliography collection. The Special Collections, Archives, and History Branch contains personal papers, rare books, academic history materials, student papers, historical photographs, maps, prints, and artifacts. The manuscript section has personal papers of:

General Maxwell Taylor	33 linear feet
General Lyman Lemnitzer	75 " "
General A J Goodpaster	30 " "
General P D Adams	1.5 " "
Admiral A W Radford	200 volumes
Hoffman Nickerson (WWII military historian)	600 "
General F S Besson, Jr	
Major General S L McClellan (Vietnam)	
Dr R L Powell (China)	

Bernard Baruch
J Carlton Ward, Jr
General H A Gerhardt
General R H del Mar
Col J W Easton,
Classics on the art of war:
    Vegetius, Marshal de Saxe, Machiavelli.

The Library contains 50,000 square feet of space using free-standing mobile shelving on a foundation designed to withstand dense storage weight. Rare books and manuscripts are kept in "a stabilized environment where temperature and humidity are ideal for conservation....The windows are special glass developed to filter out harmful rays of the sun."[19] The Special Collections section, a large carpeted room framed by back-lighted display cases, beautifully hand-crafted, is used for social occasions, lectures, and ceremonies. Handsome glass enclosed tables display memorabilia of General Maxwell Taylor.

A link is maintained to the On-Line Computer Library Center at Dublin, OH giving faculty, students, and researchers access to both commercial and Federal data bases. Marshall Hall also accommodates a computer institute, administrative offices, classrooms, laboratories, conference rooms, and a printing plant.

CHAPTER XIV: *Epilogue*

Colonel Harry Summers reported in early April 1992 on a conference held in Culpeper, Virginia to discuss the US defense policy in the post-Cold War environment with the public clamoring for decreased taxation and a drastically reduced defense budget. The subject was discussed by conferees from the NDU, AWC, and the American Security Council Foundation. In his newspaper editorial he asked: "What's a Military Good for Anyway?" and answered thusly: "We need to maintain an adequate military force in peacetime [for] deterrence, assurance, and war-fighting."[1]

This maxim has been recognized forever, but once an enemy is defeated -- despite knowing conflict will never cease -- nations lay down their arms which are totally obsolete by the time a new fray looms. To keep greedy and avaricious enemies from our doorstep, they must must be absolutely certain that we will protect our territory with our lives. Further, since no man (nor nation) can exist alone, to maintain the status quo and hopefully to progress and prosper, neighbors must feel at ease about our intentions and convictions. Can we be depended upon? Will we live, let live, and deal fairly? Will we help someone in trouble? Do we covet their space? Can we be trusted or should we be feared?

Finally, unless a reputation for being on the winning team is maintained, the temptation to test weak spots exists. A healthy military is essential; a reliable defense force must be well-trained and well-led. Educational standards can never become outdated or substandard, nor can weapons of war.

The military draft ended in 1972; since that time the armed forces have relied upon volunteers. In 1989 the Army had 800,000 active soldiers with 850,000 in the National Guard and Reserves. The Navy had 590,000 active sailors with 200,000 Reserves. The Marines consisted of 190,000 members and 50,000 Reserves, and the Air Force had 600,000 active personnel with 275,000 in the Air National Guard and Reserves. There were 251,000 women serving on active duty, almost fully integrated, but still barred from combat.

When the threat of communism dissolved, the clamor to cut the defense budget began. As military/industrial spending diminishes, jobs disappear and the economy falters. One nourishes the other. As the economy falters, the face of Fort Lesley J McNair will remain much the same unless funds are found for items on a "wish list." A new Physical Fitness Center north of Marshall Hall is scheduled to be completed in late 1994. If this takes place, the present gym may be renovated for a post chapel. Another proposed change is conversion of part of the the commissary sales area combined with the vacant movie theater to form a mini-mall. A convenience store would maintain different operational hours from the commissary. Eventually the barber shop, beauty salon, laundry and dry cleaners, and credit union would be located there.[2]

A recent independent survey of the historic quarters indicated they would need substantial maintenance to remain livable, functional, and safe. Other facilities will need protection from the elements and replacement of wornout items.[3]

Whatever the future brings, Military District #5 has served our country well, and paid tribute to Pierre L'Enfant's foresight. Although the installation no longer serves as a sentinel to alert the capital of a physical invasion force, it does stand guard by preparing professional military and civil leaders to protect and perpetuate the security our forefathers sought to establish for this great nation.

ENDNOTES

CHAPTER I

1. F Gutheim, *The Potomac*, New York, Rinehart & Co: 1949, 28. **2.** S Gervasi, "Going for Good Vibes, *Washington Post*, 7 Sep 1990, B-5. **3.** S M Huddleston, "Sunny Southwest," Columbia Historical Society, V 26, 150. **4.** J Smith, *The Travels, Adventures and Observations of Captain John Smith in Europe, Asia, Afrecke, and America*, republished in Richmond at Franklin Press: 1819, 118. **5.** P L Barbour, *The Three Worlds of Captain John Smith*, Boston, Houghton Mifflin Co: 1964, 24. **6.** Gutheim, 31. **7.** C B Todd, *The Story of Washington*, New York, Putnam & Sons: 1889, 18. **8.** W W Ristow, "Augustine Herrman's Map of Virginia and Maryland," *Library of Congress Quarterly Journal of Current Acquisitions*, 17, 4 August 1960, 221-26. **9.** W J O'Brien, "The Washington Arsenal," *Army Ordnance*, V 14 no 91, July-August 1934, 32-7. **10.** American State Papers, *Military Affairs*, V 1, 175. **11.** *The Washington Post*, 14 Oct 1883, M L King Library, Washingtoniana Section. **12.** K C Summers, "...Explore," *The Washington Post*, Weekend, 13 Jan 1978, 5. **13.** Colonel J E Raymond, untitled, unpublished 128 page manuscript on the history of Fort L J McNair, 1951, 6-7. Hereafter referred to as Raymond, ms. **14.** A C Clark, *Greenleaf & Law in the Federal City*, Washington, W F Roberts Press: 1901. **15.** H P Caemmerer, *A Manual on the Origin and Development of Washington*, Washington, DC: US GPO, 1939, 51. In Sep 1846, President Polk declared that 36 sq miles of land ceded by Virginia to become part of the District of Columbia would be given back to the state because the US didn't need it, and besides, all public buildings had been erected on the Maryland side of the river. The constitutionality was questioned, but at that time a private individual was legally estopped from raising the question, and it would require the consent of Virginia to again declare it a part of the District. **16.** Todd, 23. **17.** L Van Dyne, "Uncle Sam's Neighborhood," *Washingtonian*, November 1991, 77-79. **18.** R E Dupuy, *The Compact History of the USA*, 2d ed, New York, Hawthorne Books: 1973, 39. **19.** "HMS Rose," brochure handout when the ship docked in Washington DC in June 1990. **20.** Todd, 34. **21.** "L'Enfant," Columbia Historical Society, V 2, 118. **22.** Columbia Historical Society, V 26, 180; and V 13, 122. **23.** SP-5 M D Vaughn, "?1791?" *The Passing Review*, Feb 1969, 5. **24.** An undated bit of newsprint in the M L King Library, Washingtoniana Section, Washington DC. **25.** Ibid. **26.** US, War Department, Surgeon General's Office, "Description of Military Posts and Stations, Washington, DC, US GPO: 1875, 524.

CHAPTER II

1. O'Brien, 32. 2. G S Hunsberger, "Architectural Career of George Hadfield," Columbia Historical Society, V 51, 9 Oct 1951, 46-65. 3. *Intelligencer*, 2 Nov 1810, Washingtoniana Room, M L King Library, Washington, DC. 4. SP-5 M D Vaughn, "A Post with a Past," unpublished rework of an unpublished manuscript by Colonel W A McDaniel, Post Commander 1966 to 1969. 5. *Legislative & Executive Document of Congress of the US*, 1st Sess, 17th Cong, 1780-1823. Washington, Galess & Seaton: 1834. 6. J M Goode, *Capital Losses*, Washington DC, Smithsonian Institute Press: 1979, 161. 7. US, Congress, House, "Establishment of a Foundry, and the Sale of Arms to the States," 10th Cong, 1st Sess, V 1, no 71, 19 Nov 1807, 215-16. 8. Ibid. 9. NA, RG 156, Entry 17, Letters Received, Box 1, 1792-1810. 10. *American State Papers*, V 1, 215-16. 11. Townsend, M, *US Curious Facts, Historical, Geographical, Political*, Boston, Rockwood and Churchill: 1890, 341. 12. NA, RG 156, Entry 21, Letters Received, Bx 2. 13. NA, RG 156, Entry 3, Letters Sent, Bk 1, 217. 14. Ibid. 15. J R Arnold, "Battle of Bladensburg," *Columbia Historical Society*, V 37-8, 145-68. 16. O'Brien, 34. 17. NA, RG 156, Entry 5, Letters to the Secretary of War, Bk 1, 71. 18. "Octagon House," *The Washington Times*, 22 May 1991, B6. 19. NA, RG 156, Entry 5, Bk 3, 215. 20. Ibid, 246. 21. "Damage Repaired. Restoration of Government Works on Greenleaf's Point," *The Evening Star*, Washington, DC, 9 Jan 1902. Page unknown. Washingtoniana room in M L King Library, Washington, DC. 22. F Downey, *Sound of the Guns*, New York, David McKay Co Inc: 1955, 71-72. 23. Ibid. 24. Ibid. 25. NA, RG 156 Entry 21, Letters Received, Bk 3, 127, 167, 253. 26. Ibid, Entry 3, Letters Sent, Bk 5, 28 Sep 1819. 27. Ibid, Entry 21, Letters Received, Bx 19, File N. 28. NA, RG 156, Entry 21, Box 24. 29. Ibid, Bk 9, 244, 256, 296. 30. Ibid, Bk 8, 126, 147, 155, 229. 31. Ibid. 32. NA, RG 156, Entry 21, 165.

CHAPTER III

1. B "Perley" Poore, *Perley's Reminiscences of 60 Years in the National Metropolis*, 2 Vs, Philadelphia, Hubbard Brothers: 1886, 522. 2. F A Lord, *Civil War Collector's Encyclopedia*, New York, Castle Books/Stackpole Books: 1963-65, 15. 3. NA, RG-156, Entry 21, Bk 13, 115, 324, 334-5, 418; Bk 14, 93. 4. Ibid, Bk 13, 74, 115, 362. 5. Ibid, 394. 6. Ibid, 293, 371. 7. NA, RG-156, Entry 3, Bk 17, 214. 8. NA, RG-156, Entry 21, Bk 17, 107. 9. Ibid, Bk 20, 69, 224. 10. Ibid, Bk 21, 210. 11. Ibid, Bk 23, 2, 89, 189, 266. 12. NA, RG-156, Entry 21, Bk 11, 38, 77, 367, 395. 13. NA, RG 92, Bx 1210. 14. NA, RG 156, Entry 21, Bk 26, 60, 187. 15. W Elliot, *The Washington Guide*, Washington City, Franck Taylor: 1837, 45. 16. NA, RG-156, Entry 3, Bk 29, 123-130. 17. Ibid, 249, 298, 387. Bk 30, 148. 18. Untitled news article in the M L King Library, Washington, DC, Washingtoniana Room. 19. "Near

Centenarian Turns Memories Light on Past," *Washington Star*, 1 Jan 1936. **20.** Captain A Mordecai, *Report of Experiments on Gunpowder Made at Washington arsenal in 1843-44*, Washington DC, J & G S Gideon: 1845. Plate I, II, IV. **21.** NA, RG 156, Entry 5, Bk 9, 77-79. **22.** Ibid, 184-88. **23.** Downey, 119-20. **24.** NA, J33, 979. **25.** NA, RG 156, Entry 17Bx 30, File B.

CHAPTER IV

1. NA, RG 48, Box 456, "Abstract," 1-10. **2.** Raymond, ms, 13. **3.** NA, RG 156, Entry 3, Bk 16. 214. **4.** NA, RG 48, Penitentiary, V 1, Bx 464. **5.** S Dalsheim, "The US Penitentiary of the District of Columbia," Paper read 19 May 1953 at a meeting of the Columbia Historical Society, Washington DC, 135-143. **6.** NA, RG 48, V 2, 468. **7.** Ibid, V 1, 475. **8.** Raymond, ms, 24. **9.** NA, RG 156, Entry 5, Bk 13, 492. **10.** News item in Vertical Files, Washingtoniana Room, M L King Library, Washington DC, no author, date, publication. **11.** Dalsheim, 142. **12.** *Columbian Magazine*, April, 1911. **13.** M Johnson, "Haunting Ft McNair," *The Pentagram*, Oct 1976, 11.

CHAPTER V

1. C Bohn, *Handbook of Washington*, Washington, Casimer: 1856. 54-7; Mordecai, Plates I, II, III. **2.** "Home Front August 1861--Affairs at the Arsenal," no author, date or publication. In Washingtoniana room, M L King library, Washington DC. **3.** NA, RG 156, Entry 17, V 28. **4.** R V Bruce, *Lincoln and the Tools of War*, Chicago, Univ of IL Press: 1989, 92. **5.** Proctor, 10. **6.** Townsend, 373. **7.** NA, RG 156, Entry 21, Bk 32. **8.** O'Brien, 36. **9.** R P Weinert Jr and Colonel R Arthur, *Defender of the Chesapeake*, Shippenberg, PA, White Mane Co: 1989, 172. **10.** "Improvements Taking Place at Arsenal Grounds. The Graves of the Assassins," no author, date, nor publication. In Washingtoniana room, M L King Library, Washington DC. **11.** Raymond, unpublished ms, 89d. **12.** Bruce, 298. **13.** Raymond, ms, 89d, 89e. **14.** US, War Department, QM General's Office, *Outline of US Military Posts and Stations in the Year 1871*, US GPO: 1872. **15.** *US Army Register*, Washington DC, US GPO, various years. **16.** *The Washington Post*, 10 Nov 1904, Washingtoniana Room, M L King Library, Washington DC. **17.** NA, RG 156, Entry 32, Bk 42. 93.

CHAPTER VI

1. J L Abrahamson, *America Arms for a New Century: The Making of a Great Military Power*, New York, Free Press: 1981, 146. **2.** NA, RG 94, Bx 46, 310-11. **3.** NA, RG 92, Bx 1210. **4.** News item in Washingtoniana Room, M L King Library, Washington DC. No author, date, publication. **5.** NA, RG 91, Bx 1210. **6.** Abrahamson, 180. **7.** T F Rodenbough, *Arms of the United States 1789-1896*, New York, Maynard Merrill: 1890, 29. **8.** G W Cullum, *Biographical Register of the Officers and Graduates of the United States Military Academy*, Boston and New York, Houghton Mifflin & Co, 9 Vols, 1901-1950. **9.** NA, RG 92, Box 1211, onion-skin plan; RG 94, Box 60. **10.** D R Keim, *Washington and Its Environs*, B F Owing: 1887. **11** NA, RG 94, Box 111. **12.** US, Congress, House and Senate, 51st Cong, 2d sess, 2 Dec 1890. **13.** NA, RG 94, AGO File, Box 60, Box 111. **14.** Goode, 415-16. **15.** NA M-727 Artillery Returns to 1901, #78, Drawer 7.

CHAPTER VII

1. C C Hathaway, "Concerning the Officer," *Outlook*, V 126, 22 Sep 1920, 158-60. **2.** *Encyclopedia Americana*, Int'l Ed, Danbury, CN, Grolier: 1986. **3.** NA, RG 98, Box 3. **4.** M E Gates, "Loose Board Discloses Rich Past of 'Model Arsenal'," *Pentagram*, 25 Oct 1990, 22. **5.** NA, RG 393, Box 7. **6.** NA RG 77 Box 1023, Doc 43700-3. **7.** Surgeon General's Report of 1903, 525. **8.** C C Moore, *The Life and Times of Charles F McKim*, New York, Houghton Mifflin Co: 1929, 201-02. **9.** F A Gutheim and W E Washburn, *The Federal City: Plans and Realities*, Washington, Smithsonian Institute Press: 1976, 12. **10.** Universal Restoration Inc., "Interim Report. Condition of the Guastavino Dome," Washington DC, National Register of Historic Places, 1974. **11.** A K Foster, "The Conflict Between the Engineers and Architects over Control of Washington Barracks, 1902," American Studies, George Washington University: 1986. **12.** NA, RG 77, Bx 964, Doc 41246-1. **13.** NA, RG, Bx 2369, Doc 97132. **14.** P Begler, *Washington in Focus*, Alexandria, VA, Vandimere Press: 1988, 74. **15.** NA, RG 92, Bx 2369, Doc 40317. **16.** Begler, 81. **17.** NA M-690 Engineer Battalion Returns 1901-1916, #76, Drawer 1. **18.** "The Army Post," *Scribners*, Aug 1912, 250-61. **19.** "Wrecking the United States Army," *Scientific American*, V 127, Jul 1922, 14-15.

CHAPTER VIII

In this chapter, all data stating costs and contractors between the years 1920 and 1943 came from National Archives, Suitland, Maryland, RG 77, Entry 391, Completion Reports for Washington Barracks and the Army War College.
1. "Reconstruction of Washington Barracks, District of Columbia," *Report of the Chief of Engineers, US Army*, Appendix AAA 23, Washington DC: US GPO 1902, 3866. **2.** E M Armes, "US Arsenal," *The Washington Post*, 10 Nov 1901, p unk. News item in Washingtoniana Room, M L King Library, Washington, DC. **3.** Letter to BG G L Gillespie, Chief of Engineers from Captain John Sewell, Chief of Construction, date unknown. **4.** B Goddard, *A Short Guide to the Guns at Fort McNair*, Washington DC, MDW Visual Aids, 1964. **5.** US, Surgeon General's

Endnotes to Chapter VIII (continued)

Office, 1905. **6.** NA, RG 92, Bx 4925, Doc 277017. **7.** Ibid, Bx 6933, Doc 303466. **8.** Ibid, Bx 2918, Doc 152063, blueprint. **9.** NA, RG 94, Bx 60, "Memo of 26 Apr 1882 from General Sherman to the War Department regarding a new guardhouse." **10.** NA, M-690, Roll 10. **11.** NNRR-M, RG 92, Box 275. **12.** T Mani, "You Can Go Home Again," *The Pentagram*, 5 Sep 1991, 22. **13.** NA, RG 92, Bx 6983, Doc 303466. **14.** Col J E Raymond, letter to Major G M Chandler re quarters 2-B, 5 Jan 1955, 4. **15.** US, War Department, Surgeon General's Office, 1875, 80; letter dated 26 February 1944 from Major G M Chandler, Historian, AWC regarding history of #20, then called building #2-B. **16.** G Friedman, "Ghost Stories," *Washingtonian*, Oct 1984, p unknown. **17.** NA, RG 92, Bx 7755, Doc 382884. **18.** NA, RG 77, Sheets 17, 26, 69; RG 92 Bx 1212. **19.** Raymond, letter to Maj G M Chandler, 5 Jan 1955, 4. **20.** Ibid. **21.** NA, RG 92, Bx 6422, Doc 255037. **22.** NA, RG 156, Bk 29, 249-98, 387. **23.** Friedman. **24.** NA, RG 92, Bx 2929, Doc 152063. **25.** Ibid, Bx 4925, Doc 217017. **26.** Ibid, Bx 6422, Doc 255037. **27.** Raymond, ms, 102. **28.** NA, RG 92, Bx 7624, Doc 368980. **29.** NNRR-M, RG 92, Box 274. **30.** NA, RG 92, Box 1211. **31.** Annual Historical Report 1969. **32.** NA, RG 92, Bx 4925, Doc 217071. **33.** NA, RG 92, Bx 6422, Doc 255037. **34.** NA, RG 92, Bx 4925, Doc 217017; US, Surgeon General's Report, 1871. **35.** NA, RG 92, Bx 1023, Doc 47300-146. **36.** Ibid, Bx 6422, Doc 255037. **37.** Cameron Station Archives' memo in Library of the Office of Military History, Washington DC, no author, no date. **38.** NA, RG 92, Bx 6983, Doc 303466. **39.** K C Summers, 5. **40.** NA, RG 77, Bx 1023, Doc 47300-146. **41.** NA, RG 92, Bx 6983, Doc 303466. **42.** NA, RG 77, Bx 1223, Doc 43700-32. **43.** NA, RG 92, Bx 4925, Docs 217071, 217017. **44.** Goddard, 4. **45.** NA, RG 92, Bx 4246, Doc 200436. **46.** Ibid, Bx 6983, Doc 303466. **47.** NA, RG 77, Bx 1023, Docs 47300-146. **48.** "Military Exposition and Carnival," Official Program, 30 Sep to 1 Oct 1927, *Washington Daily News*, 16 Jul 1940. **49.** Goddard, 16. **50.** NA, RG 92, Entry 225, Bx 1211. **51.** Ibid, Box 1210-1211. **52.** Ibid, Bx 713, Doc 61939. **53.** NA, RG 92, Bx 713, Doc 61939. **54.** *Washington Post*, 10 Nov 1904. News item in Washingtoniana Room, M L King Library, Washington, DC. **55.** NA, RG 98, Bx 2. **56.** "Swimming Pool Project Begins," *Passing Review*, V 9, no 14, 21 Nov 1958, 3. **57.** NA, RG 92, Bx 1211. **58.** Ibid, Bx 6993, Doc 303466. **59.** S L Fazakerley, "Shack Faces Demolition Monday," *Pentagram*, 15 Aug 1991, 11. **60.** NA, RG 98, Bx 2. **61.** M A Coppings, "Do Ghosts Walk on Ft McNair?" *MDW Post*, Aug 1977, 11. **62.** NA, RG 77, Bx 1023, Doc 47300-146; US, Surgeon General's Report. **63.** R J Spiller, ed, *Dictionary of American Military Bibliography*, Westport CN, Greenwood Press: 1984. **64.** Goddard, 14. **65.** NA, RG 92, Bx 3789, Doc 183956; Bx 1023, Doc 47300-146. **66.** NA, RG 98, Bx 3, 26 May 1902. **67.** S Lemke, Special Collections Librarian, NDU, Mar 1991. **68.** NA, RG 92, Bx 4925, Doc 217017.

CHAPTER IX

1. Ball, H P, *Of Responsible Command: A History of the US Army War College*, Carlisle Barracks, PA, Alumni Association of the US Army War College: 1984. 2. Universal Restoration Inc., "Interim Report." 3. B Levey, "Goodbye to Pigeons, Hello to Crows," *The Washington Star*, 22 Oct 1985. 4. Letter to Lieutenant Colonel G Ahern, AWC, dated 3 Mar 1919, signed W W K. 5. "The New War College," *Army Navy Journal*, V 46, 5 September 1908. 6. V Cummings, "The Past Made an Open Book. The War College Library," *Washington Star*, 17 May 1936, 15. 7. "150th Anniversary," *Wilson's Library Bulletin*, Dec 1944, 19:282. 8. C C Baldwin, *Stanford White*, New York, DeCapo Paperback, Plenum Publishing Co: 1976, 2, 306. 9. NA, RG 92, Doc 56750. 10. NA, RG 393, Box 8. 11. Raymond, ms, 104-05. 12. "Fifty Years Ago," *The Washington Star*, 21 Nov 1954, A-24. 13. "Bomb Scare Hero Retires," The Washington Star, 1 January 1931, 4. 14. Raymond, ms, 110-11. 15. Goddard, 9. 16. NA, Microfilm 1369. 17. B F Cooling, "To Preserve the Peace," *Washington History*, V 1, no 1, Spring 1989, 71-86. 18. Ibid. 19. Abrahamson, 65-7. 20. Ibid, 84. 21. Cooling, "To Preserve the Peace," 80. 22. G S Pappas, *Prudens Futuri: US Army War College, 1901-1967*, Carlisle, PA, US Alumni Association of the AWC: 1967, 20. 23. Cooling, "To Preserve the Peace," 86. 24. Pappas, 85. 25. E E Farman, "Reminiscences of Colonel E E Farman," MID, War College Building, Washington, DC, 1947. 26. B W Bidwell, *History of the Military Intelligence Division*, Department of the Army General Staff: 1775-1941, Frederick, MD, University Publications of America: 1986, 117. 27. H O Yardley, *The American Black Chamber*, New York, Blue Ribbon Books: 1931, 38. 28. *Historical Sketch of the Signal Corps (1860-1941)*, Fort Monmouth, NJ, US Eastern Signal Corps School: 1942, 110-11. 29. Ball

CHAPTER X

1. NNRR-M, RG 92, SBB Doc 12-201. 2. NNRR-M, RG 92, Fort Humphreys Box. 3. Begler, 75, 86. 4. Ibid, 5. Ball, 223. 6. Ibid, 229-30. 7. Raymond, ms, 114-15. 8. NNRR-M, RG 92, Fort Humphreys Box. 9. Ball, 242-43. 10. "War Office Seeks to Get Rid of 21 Million Old Draft Files," *The Sunday Star*, Washington, DC, 6 Jul 1941, Part One. 11. W L Lange, ed, "Selective Service System," *An Encyclopedia of World History*, 5th ed, Boston, Houghton Mifflin: 1972. 12. Raymond, ms, 116. 13. Ibid, 117. 14. Ibid, 118. 15. Ibid. 16. Ibid. 17. Begler, 95. 18. Ibid, 110-11. 19. "Historic Army War College Becomes Fort Lesley J McNair," *The Washington Star*, 15 January 1948. 20. CWO E J Kahn Jr, "McNair, Educator of the Army," *The Infantry Journal*, Jan 1950. 21. Pappas, 55. 22. Raymond, ms, 126-7.

CHAPTER XI

1. M Mylander, *The Generals*, New York, Dial Press: 1974, 55. 2. "Who's in the Army Now?" *Fortune*, Sep 1935, 39. 3. Mylander, 63. 4. Pappas, 140. 5. Annual Historical Report, NWC, 1946. 6. NWC Historical Landmark brochure. 7. Annual Historical Report, NWC, 1974. 8. Annual Historical Reports, NWC. 9. S Kimbel, "Last of WWI Tempo Buildings Erected on Mall Demolished," *The Pentagram News*, Jul 23, 1970. 10. Annual Historical Report, ICAF, 1946. 11. "New Building To Be Erected for ICAF," *The Passing Review*, V 9, no 14, 1. 12. "ICAF Tempo Building Burns," *The Washington Star*, 31 Aug 1960. 13. Annual Historical Reports, ICAF. 14. "Opening of IADC, OAS School, Lends Hemispheric Air to Fort McNair," *The Passing Review*, V 13, 21 Sep 1962, 3. 15. "Defense College Welcomes First Students October 9," *The Passing Review*, 2 Oct 1962, 1. 16. "Colonel Matlock Takes Command of 3d Infantry," *Fort Myer Post*, V 9, no 9, 11 Feb 1958, 2. 17. "Traditional Horse-Drawn Caissons To Be Replaced by Motor Vehicles," *The Fort Myer Post*, V 8, no 8, 8 Feb 1957, 1; "Caissons Will Stay," *The Fort Myer Post*, V 8, no 10, 21 Feb 1957, 1. 18. "HQ Co, MDW Moves to Fort McNair," *The Fort Myer Post*, V 7, no 27, 21 Jun 1957, 1. 19. MDW Historical Background handout, nd. 20. "Shoulder Patch Has Unique Background," *The Fort Myer Post*, 5 May 1957, 3. 21. G Sheftick, "Plans Call for Enlarged MDW," *Pentagram*, 18 Jun 1992, 3.

CHAPTER XII

1. Goode, 150-51. 2. L Van Dyne, 193. 3. Betty Beale, "Bradley and Collins Feted at Reception," *The Washington Star*, 14 Aug 1953, Society News section. 4. "Elm Epidemic! Post Counters with Tree Planting Program," *Passing Review*, 27 Nov 1957, 2. 5. "Swimming Pool Project Begins," 1. 6. "General Recalls Early Days at Fort McNair," *The Passing Review*, V 14, no 8, 18 Aug 1964, 1. 7. E A Lolito, "Area Pair Seized as Red Spies. Fort McNair GI Seized as Red Spy," *The Washington Post*, 6 Apr 1965, A-10. 8. "McNair Mule Weighs Anchor for Army," The Passing Review, 7 Dec 1966, 3. 9. "Fort McNair Today," *The Pentagram News*, 21 Nov 1968, 8. 10. Begler, 128. 11. *TF Insider*, V 1, no 1, 8 Apr 1968, 1. 12. *TF Insider*, V 1, no 2, 9 Apr 1968, 1. 13. Begler, 129. 14. Mylander, 16. 15. F Hunt, "McNair 'Ship' Gets Its own Boat," *The Pentagram News*, 14 Nov 1971, 16. 16. "Landmarks Need Frequent Repair," *The Pentagram News*, 6 Dec 1973, 3. 17. Mylander, 83.

CHAPTER XIII

1. The foregoing information is included in a 30-page DoD booklet entitled "National Defense University," published by NDU in Dec 1989. Other data were found in MDW Annual Historical Reports. 2. US, Congress, House. Committee on Armed Services, "Report of the Panel on Military Education of the one Hundredth Congress, 101th Cong. 1st Sess. no 4, USGPO Washington, 21 Apr 1989. 3. S W Kelly, "'Just Cause' Paintings," *Pentagram*, 20 Jun 1991, 6. 4. J Dolenga, "Ghosts Haunt Quarters at Fort McNair," *Inter/Change*, 2 Aug 1982, 4-6. 5. C Murphy, "24 Arrested in Protest at Ft McNair," *The Washington Post*, 23 Aug 1983. 6. "Great Lakes," *Pentagram*, 19 Jul 1984, 20. 7. "It's a New Workout in McNair Gym," *Pentagram News*, 16 Jan 1986, 36. 8. J Garamone, "McNair Navy Launched," *Pentagram*, 1 Oct 1987, 3. 9. Annual Historical Report, MDW. 10. D M Thomas, "Army Opposes Planned Highrise," *Pentagram*, 10 Mar 1988, 3; J Knight, "The Renaissance of Buzzard Point," *The Washington Post*, 16 Oct 1989, 1, 5, 30-32. 11. US, Department of the Interior, NPS, "Environmental Assessment: Two Marinas, Buzzard Point," Jul 1987, 3. 12. "Building Plans Underway at NDU," *Pentagram*, 10 Aug 1989, 3. 13. B Forgey, "Marching in Step at Fort McNair," *The Washington Post*, 16 Nov 1991, D-1, D-7. 14. E F Puryear, *Nineteen Stars: A Study in Military Character and Leadership*, Washington DC, Coiner Publications, LTD: 1971, 152, 219, 250, 280; J Purnell, "Heck of a Mess," *The Washington Times*, 6 Jun 1991, 1. 15. K T Marshall, *Together: Annals of an Army Wife*, New York, Tupper & Love, Inc: 1946, 34, 52, 86, 137, 146, 147. 16. Lieutenant K Jabs, "Bush Dedicates Marshall Hall as NDU's Academic Center," *Pentagram*, 3 Oct 1991, 2.

CHAPTER XIV

1. H Summers, "What's a Military for Anyway?" *The Washington Times*, 10 Apr 1992, F-4. 2. Gibson, 4. 3. STV/Lyon, "Master Plan Update for MDW/Fort Myer/Fort McNair," Nov 1991, IV-27-28.

APPENDIX A

POST COMMANDERS 1791 - 1991

COL H BURBANK   1791-1801
Col Burbank was the first officer to Command Military District #5 at Greenleaf's Point. Listed in Heitman Register as commandant of a battery of artillery from 1791 to 1798; from 1798 to 1802 as a lieutenant colonel, he commanded a Corps of Artillerists and Engineers; as a colonel he was commandant of the 1st Regiment of Artillery from 1802 to 1814.

Rank	Initials	Name	Dates
MR	H	ROGERS (Military Storekeeper)	1803 - 1806
1L	T S	PERKINS	AUG 1812 - AUG 1813
CPT	E	TYLER	APR 1813 - APR 1814
MR	A J	VILLARD (in charge of repair)	MAY 1813 - JUN 1818
2LT	T T	STEPHENSON	JUL 1815 - MAR 1817
CPT	N	BADEN	MAY 1817 - JUL 1817
CPT	J S	NELSON	JUL 1817 - APR 1821
1LT	J	SIMONSON	APR 1821 - APR 1823
1LT	W E	WILLIAMS	APR 1823 - DEC 1824
MAJ	W	WADE	DEC 1825 - JUL 1826
2LT	W H	BELL	JUL 1826 - DEC 1826
1LT	J	SYMINGTON	DEC 1826 - APR 1833
CPT	A	MORDECAI	APR 1833 - OCT 1833
CPT	R	BACHE	OCT 1833 - JUN 1835
LT	J B	SCOTT	JUN 1835 - SEP 1836
CPT	G D	RAMSAY	SEP 1836 - SEP 1838
CPT	W H	BELL	SEP 1838 - APR 1840
1LT	R H	WHITLEY	APR 1840 - OCT 1840
1LT	L A	WALLACH	OCT 1840 - NOV 1840
CPT	J	SYMINGTON	NOV 1840 - NOV 1844
CPT	A	MORDECAI	OCT 1844 - OCT 1854
MAJ	W H	BELL	OCT 1854 - JUN 1858
MAG	G D	RAMSAY	JUN 1858 - JUN 1861
LTC	G D	RAMSAY	JUL 1861 - SEP 1863
LTC	J G	BENTON	OCT 1863 - JUN 1866
MG	G D	RAMSAY	JUN 1866 - JAN 1870
MAJ	J R	EDIE	FEB 1879 - JUN 1870
COL	F D	CALLENDER	JUL 1870 - SEP 1875
LTC	J	McNUTT	NOV 1875 - MAY 1878
CPT	F	WHYTE	MAY 1878 - JUN 1878
CPT	G W	McKEE (CO ORD)	JUL 1878 - MAR 1880
CPT	J	BRECKENRIDGE (CO ARTY)	JAN 1878 - JAN 1881

LTC	J M	WHITTEMORE	JUN 1880 -	APR 1881
COL	R B	AYRES	APR 1881 -	MAY 1885
COL	H G	GIBSON	MAY 1885 -	MAY 1891
COL	L L	LIVINGSTON	JUN 1891 -	MAY 1893
COL	H W	CLOSSON	MAY 1893 -	APR 1896
MAJ	J B	RAWLES	MAY 1896 -	SEP 1896
COL	F L	GUENTHER	OCT 1896 -	APR 1899
MAJ	G C	GREENOUGH	JUN 1899 -	AUG 1901

Artillery units left when the post became the Engineer School.

US ARMY ENGINEER SCHOOL COMMANDERS

MAJ	W M	BLACK	OCT 1901 -	APR 1903
MAJ	E	BURR	APR 1903 -	MAY 1906
LTC	W C	LANGFITT	JUN 1906 -	OCT 1906
MAJ	E E	WINSLOW	NOV 1906 -	AUG 1907
LTC	W C	LANGFITT	JAN 1908 -	AUG 1908
MAJ	R R	RAYMOND	SEP 1908 -	1911
MAJ	W J	BARDEN	1911 -	1912
MAJ	W D	CONNOR	1912 -	1916
COL	M M	PATRICK	1916 -	1917
COL	H	JERVEY	1917 -	
MAJ	J N	HODGES	1917 -	
COL	W W	HARTS	1917 -	
BG	F B	ABBOT	1917 -	1919

AWC COMMANDERS

MG	J W	McANDREW	1919	1921
BG	E I	BROWN	1921	1921
BG	E F	McGLACHLIN JR	1921	1923
MG	H E	ELY	1923	1927
MG	W D	CONNOR	1927	1932
MG	G S	SIMONDS	1932	1935
MG	M	CRAIG	1935	1935
BG	W S	GRANT	1935	1937
MG	J L	DeWITT	1937	1939
BG	P B	PEYTON	1939	1940

POST COMMANDERS

LTC	E A	WILLIAMS		1940 -	JUN 1941
LTC	T F	BRESNAHAN	JUL	1941 -	1942
COL	G I	SMITH		1943 -	
COL	W N	TODD JR		1943 -	1945
COL	L S	Berry		1945 -	
COL	C H	OWENS		1946 -	1948
COL	E C	NORMAN		1948 -	1950
COL	J E	RAYMON		1950 -	1951
COL	H R	JACKSON		1951 -	1953
COL	J D	MOSS		1953 -	1954
COL	G W	BIBBS		1954 -	1956
COL	R H	WILTAMUTH		1956 -	
COL	A G	STONE		1956 -	1957
COL	G C	DUEHRING		1957 -	1960
LTC	L S	McLEAN		1960 -	
COL	G J	McGOWAN		1960 -	1961
COL	H E	TOWNSEND		1960 -	1965
COL	J J	MOORE		1965 -	1966
COL	W A	McDANIEL		1966 -	1969
COL	R L	INMAN		1969 -	1971
COL	F J	RAMOS		1971 -	1972
COL	J E	McDANIELS		1972 -	1976
COL	W H	EATON		1976 -	1979
COL	C G	BARENS		1979 -	1981
COL	C L	ALTON		1981 -	1986
COL	J W	BAGNERISE Jr		1986 -	1989
COL	D E	HARBACH		1989 -	1991
COL	B P	COOPER	OCT	1991 -	

APPENDIX B

FORMER OCCUPANTS OF OFFICERS' QUARTERS

LAST NAME	INITIAL	RANK	QTRS	YR IN	YR OUT
ABRAMS Jr - V/CS	C W	GEN	8	1964	1967
ABRAMSON	I J	MAJ	20-3	1967	1967
ACREE II	G W	COL	21-1	1982	1985
ADAMS	E M	1LT	3	1907	1908
ADAMSON - MDW	J B	MG	3	1972	1973
ADDAMS - NWC	J F	RADM	5	1986	1989
ALEXANDER	R G	2LT	11	1910	1913
ALGER	J D	LTG	1	1967	1970
ALLEN - USN	J B	CPT	21-2	1980	1982
ALTON - CO	C L	COL	16	1981	1986
AMMON - NWC	W B	RADM	6	1959	1960
ANDERSON	J R	GEN	3	1961	1962
ANDERSON - AWC	J W	MAJ	12	1927	1932
ANDREWS	J R	COL	18-4	1971	1974
ANTONELLI - ICAF	T	MG	12	1975	1978
APPLEBY	J J	RADM	12	1966	1968
ARDERY	E D	1LT	13	1911	1913
ARNOLD	W H	MG	2	1948	1951
ARTER - MDW	R	MG	3	1979	1983
ASHFORD	B K	CPT	6	1905	1909
ATCHINSON	D A	CPT	20-2	1969	1970
AULT	J W	MAJ	21-1	1968	1969
AURAND	H S	MAJ	4	1933	1937
AYERS	H B	COL	19	1970	1972
BAGNERISE - CO	J W	COL	21-1	1986	1989
BALDWIN JR	J A	VADM	12	1989	1991
BALLANTYNE 3 - MDW	J L	MG	2	1983	1986
BALLENTYNE 3 - IADC	J L	LTG	2	1986	1989
BARDEN	W J	CPT	10	1905	1908
BARDEN	W J	MAJ	8	1911	1913
BARNES	M B	HON	15	1948	1949
BARNETT	J W	LTC	10	1937	1940
BARRENS	C G	COL	16	1979	1981
BARR	D G	MG	12	1946	1947
BARROW - NWC	J	RADM	5	1978	1980
BARTH	H C	MAJ	10	1909	1911

Appendix B: Former Occupants of Officers' Quarters

LAST NAME	INITIAL	RANK	QTRS	YR IN	YR OUT
BAUER	E R	COL	19	1973	1974
BAYNE - NWC	M G	VADM	7	1973	1977
BEATTY Jr	G S	MG	4	1972	1975
BEAULAC	W L	AMB	15	1961	1962
BECK	R M	LTC	5	1931	1935
BECKER - SURG/G	Q H	LTG	11	1985	1988
BELL	D B	RADM	14	1968	1970
BELL	J G	1LT	3	1910	1913
BENDRICK	F	MAJ	21-1	1967	1968
BENEDICT - CER/EV	C F	CPT	20-1	1986	1987
BENSON	J D	COL	17	1975	1978
BENSON	J D	COL	18-4	1974	1975
BERGER	S D	AMB	15	1964	1965
BERRY	R W	MG	6	1956	1958
BERTMAN	M	1LT	13	1916	
BESSON	F S	1LT	5	1916	1917
BESSON Jr	F S	GEN	2	1962	1965
BESSON Jr - AMC	F S	GEN	9	1965	1970
BIBBS	G W	COL	16	1954	1956
BIRNEY Jr	U	LTC	10	1925	
BOETCHERS	L H	GEN	3	1960	1961
BOGGS	F C	CPT	4	1905	1907
BOICE	W M	MAJ	19	1974	1974
BOLLING	A R	BG	3	1940	1943
BOLLING - INTEL	A R	MG	6	1948	1952
BOLTE	C L	MAJ	1	1940	1940
BOLTE	C L	MAJ	21-1	1937	1940
BOLTE	C L	MG	4	1948	1952
BONHAM	F G	MAJ	20-3	1935	1937
BONHAM	G	MAJ	21-1	1935	1935
BONHAM	P G	MAJ	6	1937	1939
BONHET	W J	1LT	20-3	1966	1966
BRADSHAW	A	MG	5	1948	1952
BRATTON - COE	J K	LTG	4	1980	1984
BREZ	D	MAJ	19	1991	
BRINSON	N M	1LT	17	1932	1936
BROOK	M	1LT	11	1905	1907
BROWN	E I	CPT	10	1905	1906
BROWN	H A	MAJ	13	1913	1915
BROWN	H A	MAJ	13	1908	1910
BROWN	L	CPT	14	1907	1909
BROWN	P	COL	11	1919	
BROWN	W G	AMB	15	1962	1964
BROWN - v/CS	A E	GEN	8	1987	1989

Appendix B: Former Occupants of Officers' Quarters 215

LAST NAME	INITIAL	RANK	QTRS	YR IN	YR OUT
BRUMMITT	M J	CPT	18-1	1971	1973
BRYANT - TOG	T	CPT	20-5	1988	1990
BUCK	B B	MAJ	12	1909	1910
BUCK	C D	MAJ	6	1914	1917
BUCKNER	S B	MAJ	1	1929	1932
BULL - AWC	H R	LTG	9	1950	1952
BURR	E	MAJ	8	1905	1906
BUSBY	C M		15	1930	1931
BUTT	H C	LTC	20-2	1965	1967
CABOT	J M	AMB	15	1965	1966
CANINE	R J	MG	14	1951	1952
CANNON	R M	MG	15	1957	1957
CARAWAY	P W	BG	1	1953	1955
CARLETON	G	MAJ	4	1909	1910
CARRINGTON	G	LTC	4	1938	1939
CARTER - CIA	M S	LTG	14	1962	1965
CASAUS	J F	MAJ	20-4	1965	1969
CASTLEMAN	P A	1LT	20-1	1979	1980
CATE	W D	1LT	18-2	1977	1978
CHANDLER		RADM	13	1987	1989
CHAPIN	S	HON	15	1959	1960
CHESAREK	F J	GEN	10	1967	1970
CHIARAVALLE	P	WO1	18-2	1975	1977
CHRISTIANSON	J G	LTC	10	1941	1945
CLARK	M	BG	11	1940	1942
CLARK - ICAF	S	RADM	1	1957	1959
CLARKE	F J	LTG	5	1970	1973
COLLINS	J L	LTG	7	1945	1947
COLLINS	J L	MAJ	3	1938	1941
COLLINS	J L	GEN	8	1947	1956
COLLINS - G5	E T	COL	5	1919	1920
CONAWAY - NGB	J B	LTG	1	1990	
CONGER	A W	COL	1	1919	
CONNELL	J P	CPT	20-4	1971	1972
CONNOR	W D	MAJ	9	1911	1913
CONNOR - AWC	W D	MG	8	1927	1932
CONNORS	J T	1LT	20-2	1974	1975
CONOLLY II	R C	RADM	13	1979	1981
COOKSEY	H H	LTG	5	1975	1977
COOPER - CO	B P	COL	16	1991	
COOPER - NWC	A J	COL	11	1935	1936
COUTHEN	S	CW2	18-3	1979	1980
COWPER	H W	1LT	12	1905	1908
CRAIG	M	BG	13	1919	1920

Appendix B: Former Occupants of Officers' Quarters

LAST NAME	INITIAL	RANK	QTRS	YR IN	YR OUT
CRAIG - AWC	M	MG	8	1935	1935
CRAIG - USAF NWC	H A	LTG	9	1953	1955
CREER	W E	MG	14	1967	1968
CRITCHFIELD	J B	MAJ	18-2	1978	1981
CROSEY	H B	LTC	3	1922	
CRUZ	A	CPT	20-5	1980	1982
CURRY - MDW	J R	MG	2	1980	1983
DALEY	E L	1LT	13	1910	1911
DALTON	R A	COL	21-2	1969	1971
DALTON	R L	COL	18-3	1969	1969
D'AMBROSIO	E J	MG	13	1975	1979
DAVIS	J J	LTG	5	1966	1970
DAVIS	L I	LTG	6	1967	1968
DAVISON - MDW	F E	MG	3	1973	1974
DE PUY	W E	LTG	10	1971	1973
DEANE Jr	J R	MG	13	1972	1975
DEANE Jr - AMC	J R	GEN	9	1975	1977
DECKER - V/CS	G H	GEN	8	1959	1962
Del MAR	R H	MG	5	1965	1966
Del MAR	R H	MG	4	1963	1965
DELAUNE Jr	E	MG	14	1978	1982
DENYS	A J	1LT	18-4	1977	1979
DEUTERMANN	H T	RADM	2	1957	1959
DEVERS - AGF	J	GEN	8	1945	1946
DeWITT	C H	CPT	18-3	1974	1976
DeWITT	J J	MAJ	15	1919	1921
DeWITT - AWC	J J	MG	8	1937	1939
DeWITT Jr	C H	CPT	18-2	1973	1974
DIXON	D C	CPT	20-3	1966	1966
DIXON	D C	CPT	18-4	1966	1967
DOCTOR Jr - IG	H	LTG	3	1987	1989
DODD		LTC	3	1932	1936
DOHLEMAN - MDW	K E	MG	3	1977	1979
DOMINY	C E	LTG	7	1992	
DONAHUE	D	LTC	17	1985	1989
DONALDSON		CPT	20-5	1969	1970
DONOHEW	J N	MG	3	1966	1967
DOWNING	F B	1LT	15	1910	1912
DOYLE	D K	LTG	14	1984	1986
DROCKINIS	J P	1LT	20-5	1977	1980
DUEHRING	G C	COL	10	1957	1960
DUNCAN	C L	CPT	15	1913	1914
DURBROW	E	HON	15	1949	1950
EARLE	J H	CPT	3	1915	1917

Appendix B: Former Occupants of Officers' Quarters

LAST NAME	INITIAL	RANK	QTRS	YR IN	YR OUT
EATON	W H	COL	16	1976	1979
EBERLE	G L	GEN	2	1951	1954
ECKLBARGER	D E	MAJ	21-1	1972	1973
EINSELN	A	MAJ	20-2	1967	1968
ELLIOTT	M A	CPT	7	1911	1913
ELLIS	C W	LTC	16	1963	1965
ELY - AWC	H E	MG	8	1923	1927
EMBICK	S D	COL	12	1921	1923
EMERSON	T H	CPT	15	1916	
ENDRESS	W F	1LT	1	1908	1909
ENEMARK	W A	MG	2	1968	1972
ENGINEER HOLD			20-5	1983	1984
ENGINEER HOLD			20-1	1981	1981
ENGINEER HOLD			20-4	1983	1984
ENGINEER HOLD			20-2	1983	1984
ENGINEER HOLD			20-1	1983	1984
ENNIS - AWC	W P	LTG	2	1960	1962
ERICKSON	H	LTC	14	1919	1922
ERVIN	H E	CPT	18-2	1966	1968
FARR	R R	MAJ	20-1	1967	1967
FARREN	K	CPT	18-2	1981	1983
FINLEY	M R	CPT	21-1	1964	
FIRE VACANT			20-5	1967	1967
FISCHER	M G		11	1961	1962
FISHER	R P	1SGT	18-4	1921	1928
FISHER - ICAF	W P	MG	1	1963	1964
FORSYTHE	G I	LTG	4	1970	1972
FRANKLIN	W C	BG	20-1	1967	1967
FRANKLIN	W C	MG	4	1967	1969
FREAKLEY	B	CPT	18-4	1979	1983
FREEHOFF	W M	MAJ	15	1934	1937
FREITAG - COMPT	M	LTG	5	1991	
FREY	D J	MAJ	20-4	1977	1980
FRIES	A A	MAJ	9	1913	1916
FRIES	A A	CPT	4	1910	1912
FRYER	J C	MG	13	1992	
FULLER	M D	LTG	2	1977	1977
FULMER	J J	LTC	1	1927	1929
GAGNEY	B J	1LT	20-3	1988	1989
GAGNEY - HHC TOG	B J	1LT	20-4	1989	1990
GALLMAN	W J	HON	15	1951	1952
GAMBLE	C	COL	1	1941	1943
GARD Jr	R G	LTG	7	1977	1981
GARNER - CO A	C H	1LT	20-5	1985	1988

Appendix B: Former Occupants of Officers' Quarters

LAST NAME	INITIAL	RANK	QTRS	YR IN	YR OUT
GASKIN - NDU	P	COL	21-2	1989	
GEFELL	J G	COL	18-4	1971	1971
GERHARDT	H A	MG	13	1961	1962
GIBBINS	H	LTC	1	1922	
GIBSON	E J	GEN	1	1965	1967
GIBSON	P W	LTC	2	1932	1936
GILLETTE		CPT	20-5	1966	1967
GLASSFORD	P D	LTC	4	1922	
GOLF SHACK			17	1991	
GOODPASTER - NWC	A J	LTG	7	1967	1968
GOODRICH	D M	MG	3	1989	1991
GORDON	W W	MAJ	7	1935	1939
GOWEN	J B	COL	7	1920	1921
GOWEN	J B	COL	12	1919	1920
GOWEN	J B	COL	21-2	1922	1922
GRAHAM	R D	CPT	18-1	1973	1974
GRANT	W S	BG	9	1935	1936
GRANT	W S	LTC	14	1926	1927
GRANT	W S	LTC	12	1923	1925
GRANT - AWC	W S	MG	8	1936	1937
GRANT III	U S	1LT	5	1905	1907
GRANT III	U S	1LT	4	1907	1908
GRAVES	A J	CPT	18-1	1975	1977
GRAVES - JCS	H D	MG	5	1989	1991
GREELEY - ICAF	L J	BG	15	1952	1953
GRIFFITH - IG	R H	LTG	4	1991	
GRISWOLD - NWC	F H	LTG	9	1961	1964
GRUENTHER	A M	MG	14	1946	1947
GRUNERT	G	MAJ	20-1	1921	1926
GRUNERT	G	LTC	7	1932	1935
GUSTIN	E Y	SGT	18-1	1929	1936
GUTHRIE - AMC	J R	GEN	9	1977	1981
HAIG - V/CS	A M	GEN	8	1973	1973
HAINES Jr	R E	LTG	1	1967	1967
HAINES Jr - V/CS	R E	GEN	8	1967	1968
HALL	C L	2LT	1	1909	1912
HAMAKER	B B	2LT	20-3	1966	1967
HAMBY	J	1LT	20-2	1988	1990
HANLETT - V/CS	B	GEN	8	1962	1964
HANNUM	W T	1LT	13	1905	1907
HARBACH	D V	COL	21-1	1989	1991
HARDIN Jr	H F	LTG	6	1979	1982
HARDING	J R	MG	2	1992	
HARDY	J S	LTG	7	1968	1970

Appendix B: Former Occupants of Officers' Quarters 219

LAST NAME	INITIAL	RANK	QTRS	YR IN	YR OUT
HARDY	J S	LTG	19	1968	1968
HARKINS	P D	BG	1	1950	1952
HARRINGTON		LTC	2	1939	1940
HARRINGTON	F C	2LT	2	1912	1914
HARROLD - NWC	T L	LTG	9	1958	1961
HART	W L	1LT	12	1908	1909
HART Jr	H	1LT	20-4	1980	1983
HART Jr	H	CPT	18-4	1983	1984
HATCH - COE	H J	LTG	9	1988	1990
HAZAM	M J	COL	19	1972	1973
HEIBERG III - COE	E R	LTG	9	1986	1988
HEINTZELMAN	S	COL	1	1919	
HENNESSEY	J J	LTG	5	1973	1974
HENRY Jr	J B	MG	3	1967	1969
HERKNESS	L C	1LT	11	1913	1916
HERR		LTC	2	1929	1932
HESTER	M E	CPT	20-3	1985	1986
HETRICK	H S	1LT	2	1910	1912
HICKERSON	J D	HON	15	1954	1955
HICKEY III	E I	CPT	20-3	1990	1992
HILBERT - MDW	D C	MG	14	1986	1990
HILL	H	VADM	9	1947	1949
HILMES - INFSYS	J B	LTG	10	1989	
HINNRICHS	J M	LTG	4	1960	1962
HITT - SigC	P	COL	11	1922	
HODGES	J N	CPT	12	1916	
HODGES - IADC	P H	MG	13	1985	1987
HODGINS	S F	COL	21-2	1964	1964
HOFFMAN - ENGR	J R	LTC	19	1980	1983
HOFFORD	R	CPT	21-2	1982	1984
HOLCOMBE	W H	2LT	13	1915	1916
HOLCOMBE	W H	1LT	11	1916	1917
HOLLIS	R P	MG	7	1956	1957
HONEYCUTT - AWC	F W	LTC	14	1931	1935
HOSMER	B D	LTG	12	1986	1989
HOUSEMAN	E M	MG	5	1959	1961
HOWZE - ENGR	J	MAJ	19	1988	1991
HULL	J E		7	1952	
HUMPHREY	E H	COL	9	1933	1938
INGRAM Jr	O B	CPT	19	1974	1974
INMAN	R L	COL	16	1969	1970
JACKSON	H R	COL	10	1952	1953
JACKSON	H R	COL	16	1951	1952
JACKSON	P W	RADM	14	1970	1972

Appendix B: Former Occupants of Officers' Quarters

LAST NAME	INITIAL	RANK	QTRS	YR IN	YR OUT
JACOBSON	W R	LTC	18-2	1974	1975
JERVEY	J P	CPT	10	1907	1908
JEWETT	H C	CPT	3	1913	1915
JEWETT	H C	CPT	5	1915	1916
JOHNSON - INTEL	C L	MG	14	1966	1967
JONES	J W	AMB	15	1969	1971
JONES	R	CPT	20-5	1972	1973
JONES III	L	MAJ	21-1	1969	1972
JORDAN	L W	CPT	7	1913	1915
JORDAN	R A	CPT	20-5	1984	1985
JOULWAN	G A	MAJ	21-1	1973	1974
JOYNER	E D	CPT	18-3	1969	1972
KALERGIS	J G	LTG	10	1973	1974
KEENAN	G E	LTC	20-2	1977	1979
KEITH - AMC	D R	GEN	7	1981	1984
KEITH - RD&A	D R	LTG	10	1977	1981
KELLEY	D R	LTC	17	1973	1975
KELLY - NWC	J E	LTG	6	1968	1970
KENDALL	B E	MG	12	1968	1970
KENNAN	G F	HON	15	1947	1948
KERWIN Jr	W T	GEN	5	1974	1975
KERWIN Jr - V/CS	W T	GEN	8	1975	1978
KILBOURNE	C E	COL	13	1920	1924
KIND	P A	LTG	12	1992	
KING	C	LTC	3	1919	1921
KING	E L	BG	9	1922	1924
KINGMAN	J J	CPT	14	1914	1916
KIRWAN	R L	MG	12	1978	1983
KITCHIN	D	LTC	18-3	1978	1979
KJELLSTROM	J A	LTG	10	1974	1977
KOESTER	F J	CPT	7	1905	1911
KOPEC	J L	CPT	20-2	1975	1977
KROESEN - V/CS	F	GEN	8	1978	1979
KRUEGER	W	LTC	15	1921	1922
KUBISCH	J B	AMB	15	1977	1979
KUCHEMAN	H B	MG	12	1972	1972
KUHN	J E	BG	8	1917	
LaFATE	K	1LT	20-5	1982	1983
LAINGEN - NDU	L B	AMB	15	1981	1986
LAMPERT	J B	LTG	13	1966	1969
LANDON	T H	BG	13	1946	1948
LANGFITT	W C	MAJ	9	1905	1906
LANGFITT	W C	LTC	8	1906	1910
LaROCQUE	G R	RADM	3	1969	1972

Appendix B: Former Occupants of Officers' Quarters 221

LAST NAME	INITIAL	RANK	QTRS	YR IN	YR OUT
LASSETTER Jr	R	MG	14	1965	1966
LAWRENCE - NDU	R D	LTG	12	1983	1986
LEACH	J H	LTC	21-1	1964	1967
LeBLANC	M	LTC	17	1966	1968
LEDFORD - SURG/G	F F	LTG	11	1988	1991
LEE	F	VADM	10	1964	1965
LEE	R M	MG	14	1972	1974
LEE - NWC	F	VADM	6	1965	1967
LEMNITZER	L L	MG	3	1954	
LEMNITZER	L L	MG	1	1948	1949
LEMNITZER - V/CS	L L	GEN	8	1957	1959
LEONHART	W	AMB	15	1971	1977
LEWIS	T E		17	1942	
LIGHTNER Jr	E A	AMB	15	1966	1969
LINEWEAVER	W P	1LT	20-5	1970	1971
LOBDELL - USAF NWC	H	MG	14	1976	1978
LOEFFKE	B	MG	2	1989	
LOMBARD	R T	COL	21-2	1975	1980
LOMBARDO - EOD	M F	CPT	20-4	1990	
LOPEMAN	R G	CPT	18-4	1969	1971
LOYSEN	G J	CPT	20-4	1969	1970
LYLES Jr	R H	MAJ	18-1	1966	1967
LYSTAD		1LT	17	1929	1932
MACKLIN	D K	WO1	18-3	1981	1982
MacLAUGHLIN	V J	MG	12	1965	1966
MAHONEY	M S	CPT	18-4	1967	1968
MAILLET	E	COL	21-1	1978	1982
MALLAMO	J P	1LT	20-5	1976	1977
MALONY	H J	COL	5	1938	1940
MANLOVE	R	CPT	20-1	1973	1974
MAPLES	H N	LTG	2	1974	1976
MARKHAM	E M	CPT	3	1905	1907
MARKS	E H	1LT	1	1913	1914
McANDREW - AWC	J W	MG	8	1919	1921
McAULIFF	A C	MG	13	1952	
McCAFFREY	B R	LTG	6	1992	
McCAFFREY	W J	LTG	2	1972	1973
McCARDELL	J E	RADM	13	1983	1985
McCLENDON	E H	MAJ	18-2	1969	1971
McCLENDON	E H	MAJ	18-4	1968	1969
McCLURE	R	MAJ	1	1938	1940
McCLURE - ADJ	R A	LTC	17	1936	1938
McCONNELL	J B	WO1	18-1	1977	1983
McDANIEL	W A	COL	18-3	1966	1966

Appendix B: Former Occupants of Officers' Quarters

LAST NAME	INITIAL	RANK	QTRS	YR IN	YR OUT
McDANIEL - CO	W A	COL	16	1966	1969
McDANIELS - CO	J E	COL	16	1972	1976
McDONALD	L P	MAJ	19	1969	1970
McGLAUGHLIN - AWC	E F	MG	8	1921	1923
McGOUGH III	E A	MG	12	1972	1975
McGOWAN - AWC	G J	BG	10	1960	1961
McGRORY Jr	J C	CPT	20-4	1970	1972
McLAIN	J	COL	16	1956	1957
McLAIN	R S		3	1946	1952
McNAIR - CG-AGF	L J	LTG	8	1941	1944
McNARNEY	J T	MAJ	20-1	1935	1937
McPHERSON - NWC	J B	LTG	7	1970	1973
MELBYE	J	MAJ	19	1966	1967
MERRILL HHH 3d	W G	1LT	20-2	1985	1987
MERRITT - JCS	J N	GEN	3	1983	1985
MERRYMAN - RD&A	J H	LTG	9	1981	1984
MERTZ JR - ENGR	W M	LTC	19	1983	1986
MEYER	R D	MG	10	1965	1967
MEYER	R L	CPT	20-4	1984	1986
MICHAELIS	J H	MG	3	1956	1959
MILEY Jr - AMC	H A	GEN	9	1970	1975
MILLAWAY	R J	CW2	18-3	1977	1978
MILLER - NDU	R H	AMB	15	1986	1989
MINDRUM	G G	CPT	20-3	1965	1966
MINEZ	P	CPT	20-1	1981	1983
MISER - MTMC	J L	CPT	20-5	1991	
MITCHELL	W A	1LT	1	1905	1906
MITTEMYER - SURG/G	B	TG	11	1982	1985
MOELLERING - JCS	J H	LTG	3	1985	1987
MONTEMAYOR	E A	MAJ	20-2	1968	1969
MOORE	J J C	COL	16	1965	1966
MOORE	R C	1LT	2	1907	1908
MOORE - DIC	W D	COL	16	1990	1991
MORGAN	P A	PT	18-2	1971	1973
MORRIS	J W	MG	4	1975	1980
MORRIS	S J	CPT	6	1909	1910
MORRIS Jr	H H	MAJ	4	1930	1933
MOSS	J D	COL	16	1953	1954
MUELLER Jr	E M	CPT	20-2		1963
MUNDY - ICAF	G W	LTG	7	1957	1959
MURPHY - NWC	J S	MG	14	1975	1976
MYER	R D	LTG	4	1965	1967
NATHAN	A P	LTC	19	1956	1957
NAYLOR	W K	COL	1	1920	

Appendix B: Former Occupants of Officers' Quarters 223

LAST NAME	INITIAL	RANK	QTRS	YR IN	YR OUT
NIBLO	U	BG	15	1955	1956
NICHOLAS	R U	1LT	1	1916	
NOAH - COMPT	M W	LTG	10	1984	1988
NOLAN	D E	BG	10	1919	
NORMAN	E C	COL	16	1948	1950
NORRIS	C R	COL	21-1	1974	1978
NORTH	E	2LT	12	1911	1914
NOVAK	J R	CAPT	18-2	1966	1966
OBERBECK	A W	LTG	1	1970	1972
O'CONNELL	J D	LTG	11	1959	
O'DONNELL	K W	LCDR	19	1975	1977
OLIVER	BUGS		3	1942	
OLIVER	L E	1LT	2	1916	
OLIVER	L E	MG	4	1945	1947
ONO - DSPER	A K	LTG	4	1987	1990
OSBORNE	D	CPT	20-1	1989	
OSBORNE	J R	MAJ	20-1	1964	1967
OSTROWSKI	P	1LT	20-2	1987	1988
OTWELL	C H	CPT	14	1909	1914
OWENS	C H	COL	16	1946	1948
PACHLER - NWC	F T	MG	12	1962	1963
PALMER Jr - V/CS	B	GEN	8	1968	1973
PALMER - V/CS	W B	GEN	8	1956	1957
PALMER Jr	B	LTG	7	1968	1968
PARKER	E D	LTG	7	1989	
PARKER	J B	CW3	18-3	1976	1977
PARKER - HHC	J	CPT	20-1	1987	1989
PARKS	F L	MG	10	1946	1948
PATCH	J D	COL	6	1942	1943
PATCH	J D	LTC	4	1939	1940
PATRICK	M M	COL	8	1916	1917
PATRICK - ICAF		RADM	1	1959	1962
PAUL - G4	W S	BG	15	1940	1942
PEIXOTTO	E D	LTG	10	1981	1984
PETERSON	V L	CPT	14	1916	
PEWETT	R H	LCDR	20-4	1972	1973
PEYTON - AWC	P B	MG	8	1939	1940
PHILLIPS - NWC	R H	VADM	6	1961	1962
PHIPPS	M A	1LT	18-4	1982	1983
PIERCE	C C		13	1907	1908
PIERCE	R K	MG	12	1970	1972
PLANA	A T	2LT	18-3	1983	1984
PLANA	A T	1LT	20-1	1984	1986
POINT	W H	CPT	7	1916	

LAST NAME	INITIAL	RANK	QTRS	YR IN	YR OUT
POLONIS	W G	LTG	6	1991	1992
POWELL	H B	BG	4	1952	1953
POWELL	R G	2LT	11	1908	1910
POWELL - NSA	C L	LTG	7	1987	1987
PRILLAMAN	R	LTG	14	1982	1984
PUTNAM	E L	MAJ	19	1968	1969
QUANDER	F A	2LT	20-4	1973	1975
QUILL - ICAF	J B	MG	5	1961	1962
RALSTON	R R	1LT	15	1906	1908
RAMOS	F J	COL	16	1971	1972
RAND	L B	CPT	10	1911	1912
RAYMOND	J E	MAJ	20-1	1937	1939
RAYMOND	J E	COL	16	1950	1951
RAYMOND	R R	MAJ	8	1910	1911
RAYMOND	R R	MAJ	9	1908	1910
REHKOPF	N B	LTC	13	1924	1928
REHKOPF	N B	COL	9	1939	1940
REIMER - V/CS	D J	GEN	8	1991	
REINECKE	P S	1LT	10	1914	1915
REYNA	L	1LT	20-1	1974	1978
REYNOLDS	C R	CPT	6	1911	1914
RICASSI - V/CS	R W	GEN	8	1989	1990
RIDLEY	C S	1LT	4	1908	1909
RIGGS		LTC	10	1934	1937
RIPPER	J K	COL	21-2	1964	
ROBINS	T M	1LT	15	1908	1910
ROBINS	T M	CPT	5	1913	1915
RODGERS - DCA	T	LTG	4	1990	1991
ROSE	W H	1LT	11	1907	1908
ROSE	W H	1LT	15	1905	1906
ROSE	W H	MAJ	10	1908	1909
ROSE - ICAF	R E	VADM	10	1961	1964
ROSTOW	E V	Mr	21-2	1984	1989
ROWNY	E L	LTG	6	1973	1979
RUFFNER		MG	14	1961	1962
RUSIN	J D	CPT	20-5	1973	1976
SACKTON	F J	MG	2	1965	1967
SALTER Jr	A T	CPT	18-1	1968	1969
SARLES	T B	CPT	20-2	1981	1983
SARLES	T B	CPT	20-1	1980	1981
SAUNDERS	G E	LTC	18-1	1969	1971
SCHLEY	J L	1LT	2	1906	1907
SCHMID - Chap	W L	LTC	20-2	1991	
SCHMID - Chap	W L	LTC	17	1989	1991

Appendix B: Former Occupants of Officers' Quarters 225

LAST NAME	INITIAL	RANK	QTRS	YR IN	YR OUT
SCHMIDTMAN - CO	M C	COL	16	1986	1990
SCHOLLIAN		2LT	20-5	1967	1967
SCHOMBURG - ICAF	A	LTG	13	1962	1965
SCHOMBURG - ICAF	A	LTG	7	1965	1967
SCHULTZ	R S	LTC	17	1968	1973
SCHWARZTRAUBER	S A	RADM	13	1981	1984
SCHWEITZER	R L	LTG	6	1983	1986
SCOTT	S L	MG	6	1940	
SEALS	C L	LTC	18-3	1966	1966
SHELLNUT	T C	1LT	20-5	1965	1966
SHIELDS	J F	CPT	20-3	1984	1985
SHORT	J W	MAJ	20-2	1972	1974
SHORT, JR	A E	LTG	3	1991	
SICILIA	B K	1LT	18-3	1966	1966
SIMONDS	G S	LTC	5	1920	1921
SIMONDS	G S	COL	10	1922	1924
SIMONDS - POSTCO	G S	MG	8	1932	1935
SIMONS			9	1921	1922
SIMPSON	W H	LTC	12	1936	1940
SIMSON	B W	BG	8	1944	1945
SMITH	C S	CPT	14	1905	1907
SMITH	F	MSG	17-A	1929	1936
SMITH	J	MAJ	17	1981	1983
SMITH	J V	RADM	6	1970	1973
SMITH - AWC	W		9	1919	1920
SMITH - USAF NWC	P M	MG	5	1983	1986
SMITH, JR	J E	RADM	11	1991	
SONTAG	P D	LTC	19	1977	1978
SPALDING	M E	MAJ	4	1919	1922
SPRINGMAN - EOD	M D	CPT	20-4	1986	1989
STADLER - NWC	G P	MG	13	1989	1991
STADTLER - NDU	W E	AMB	15	1989	1991
STARBIRD	A D	LTG	11	1963	1971
STEARNS	M	AMB	15	1979	1981
STEELE	W S	GEN	3	1965	1966
STEELE - ICAF	W S	MG	1	1964	1965
STEWART	G H	LTC	7	1922	1923
STILWELL - AGF	J W	LTG	8	1945	1945
STOKEY	W P	CPT	15	1914	1916
STOLBRON	C J	1LT	12	1910	1911
STOUGHTON - ICAF	T R	MG	5	1962	1964
STREETER - MDW	R	MG	14	1990	1993
STRITTMATTER	L E	MAJ	20-4	1969	1969
STRITTMATTER	L E	MAJ	20-1	1969	1972

LAST NAME	INITIAL	RANK	QTRS	YR IN	YR OUT
STRONG Jr	F S	1LT	12	1914	1915
STRUBE	R C	WO4	18-2	1968	1969
SUELLENTUE	D M	LTC	17	1983	1985
SULLIVAN - V/CS	G	LTG	8	1990	1991
SULTAN	D I	2LT	5	1910	1913
SUMNER Jr	G	MG	1	1975	1978
SURUT - NWC	L E	MG	5	1980	1983
SUTHERLAND Jr	W A	ADM	6	1962	1964
SUVER	W G	2LT	20-3	1986	1988
SWEENEY	W C	LTC	5	1921	
TALLEY	E J	LTC	16	1962	1963
TAYLOR	M C	COL	21-2	1963	1964
TAYLOR	M D	GEN	5	1952	
TAYLOR	M D	GEN	7	1961	1962
TAYLOR	M D	MG	13	1948	
TEMPLE Jr - NGB	H R	LTG	1	1986	1990
THOMAS	C	LTC	1	1934	1937
THOMAS	J E	CPT	20-4	1975	1977
THOMPSON - AMC	R H	GEN	7	1984	1986
THURMAN - V/CS	M R	GEN	8	1983	1987
TIMBERMAN	T S	BG	2	1948	1951
TODD	D C	CPT	18-1	1965	1966
TOLMAN	A L	2LT	20-1	1972	1973
TONELLI	G E	MAJ	20-2	1979	1981
TORYANSKI	M E	CPT	20-2	1984	1985
TOWNSEND	E C	MG	2	1967	1968
TOWNSEND	H E	COL	16	1961	1962
TRAHAN	E	COL	21-2	1965	1969
TRUESDELL	K	MAJ	14	1935	1937
TRUMPS - CER/EV	T H	CPT	20-1	1986	1986
TRUSCOTT III	L K	LTG	8	1946	1947
TUBB	A H	MAJ	21-2	1971	1973
TYLER	M C	1LT	5	1907	1910
UNGER	F T	LTG	13	1969	1970
VADER	P	CPT	18-4	1965	1966
VANAMAN	A W	MG	11	1948	1952
VAN NATTA		GEN	4	1962	1963
VAUGHAN	W W	LTG	11	1971	1978
VESSEY Jr - V/CS	J W	GEN	8	1979	1982
VESTAL	S C	LTC	2	1922	
VILLARD	H S	HON	15	1956	1957
WADHAMS - MedC	S H	COL	6	1919	1919
WAGLEY	P C	LTC	20-2	1963	1964
WAGNER Jr - AMC	L C	GEN	7	1987	1989

Appendix B: Former Occupants of Officers' Quarters

LAST NAME	INITIAL	RANK	QTRS	YR IN	YR OUT
WAGNER Jr - RD&A	L C	LTG	4	1984	1987
WAILES	E T	AMB	15	1958	1959
WALKER	F L	MAJ	6	1934	1937
WALKER	H H	AMB	15	1992	
WALKER	M		7	1919	1920
WALKER - G4	W G	COL	15	1942	
WALKER Jr - NGB	E H	LTG	1	1982	1986
WARD - G3	F	COL	6	1943	1944
WASIELEWSKI	J S	LTC	19	1978	1980
WEAVER	J K	MAJ	18-3	1955	1969
WEBB Jr - DSPER	W L	MG	11	1978	1982
WEBER	L E	MG	1	1978	1982
WEEKS		LTC	3	1920	1921
WEINSTEIN - DCSI	S T	LTG	10	1988	1989
WEISKOPF	J D	CPT	18-3	1972	1974
WEISSINGER II	W T	LTC	13	1933	1937
WEST - MDW	R L	LTG	2	1977	1980
WEYAND	F C	GEN	3	1962	1964
WEYAND - V/CS	F C	GEN	8	1973	1974
WEYLAND	O P	MG	14	1948	1950
WHEELER - AMC	A G	MG	6	1986	1991
WICHMANOWSKI	W F	COL	17	1978	1981
WICKHAM - V/CS	G A	GEN	8	1982	1983
WIGFALL	B J	CPT	18-4	1975	1977
WIGMORE	H L	CPT	15	1912	1913
WIGMORE	H L	CPT	3	1908	1909
WILBY	F B	1LT	10	1912	1914
WILBY	F B	1LT	2	1908	1909
WILKINS	V C	COL	21-2	1973	1975
WILLHOUSE - ENGR	D	LTC	19	1986	1988
WILLIAMS	A E	LTG	9	1991	
WILLIAMS	C W	1LT	5	1917	
WILLIAMS	R R	MG	4	1969	1970
WILLING	W	CPT	4	1912	1917
WILSON	D	LTG	19	1967	1968
WILSON Jr - ICAF	A T	MG	1	1962	1963
WIMER	D J	CPT	20-3	1967	1967
WIMER	D J	CPT	20-1	1967	1969
WINSLOW	E E	MAJ	9	1907	1908
WISSINGER	T R	CPT	18-1	1967	1968
WOOD	S	GEN	7	1962	1965
WOODS	P F	LCDR	20-2	1970	1972
WOODWARD - IG	G H	LTG	2	1973	1973
WOOLDRIDGE - NWC	E T	VADM	9	1956	1958

Appendix B: Former Occupants of Officers' Quarters

LAST NAME	INITIAL	RANK	QTRS	YR IN	YR OUT
WOOLWINE	W J	LTG	1	1972	1975
WOOTEN	S C	MG	12	1963	1965
WOOTEN	W P	COL	15	1922	1925
WOOTEN	W P	MAJ	8	1914	1916
YERKS - MDW	R G	MG	3	1975	1977
YOUNG	J E	CPT	11	1917	
YOUNGBERG	G A	CPT	3	1909	1910
ZAIS	M	LTG	13	1970	1972
ZITZMAN	K F	BG	5	1957	1959

YEARLY LISTING OF QUARTERS OCCUPANTS (OFFICERS)

LAST NAME	INITIAL	RANK	QTRS	YR IN	YR OUT
MITCHELL	W A	1LT	1	1905	1906
ENDRESS	W F	1LT	1	1908	1909
HALL	C L	2LT	1	1909	1912
MARKS	E H	1LT	1	1913	1914
NICHOLAS	R U	1LT	1	1916	
HEINTZELMAN	S	COL	1	1919	
CONGER	A W	COL	1	1919	
NAYLOR	W K	COL	1	1920	
GIBBINS	H	LTC	1	1922	
FULMER	J J	LTC	1	1927	1929
BUCKNER	S B	MAJ	1	1929	1932
THOMAS	C	LTC	1	1934	1937
McCLURE	R	MAJ	1	1938	1940
BOLTE	C L	MAJ	1	1940	1940
GAMBLE	C	COL	1	1941	1943
LEMNITZER	L L	MG	1	1948	1949
HARKINS	P D	BG	1	1950	1952
CARAWAY	P W	BG	1	1953	1955
CLARK - ICAF	S	RADM	1	1957	1959
PATRICK - ICAF		RADM	1	1959	1962
WILSON Jr - ICAF	A T	MG	1	1962	1963
FISHER - ICAF	W P	MG	1	1963	1964
STEELE - ICAF	W S	MG	1	1964	1965
GIBSON	E J	GEN	1	1965	1967
HAINES Jr	R E	LTG	1	1967	1967
ALGER	J D	LTG	1	1967	1970
OBERBECK	A W	LTG	1	1970	1972
WOOLWINE	W J	LTG	1	1972	1975
SUMNER Jr	G	MG	1	1975	1978
WEBER	L E	MG	1	1978	1982
WALKER Jr - NGB	E H	LTG	1	1982	1986
TEMPLE Jr - NGB	H R	LTG	1	1986	1990
CONAWAY - NGB	J B	LTG	1	1990	
SCHLEY	J L	1LT	2	1906	1907
MOORE	R C	1LT	2	1907	1908
WILBY	F B	1LT	2	1908	1909
HETRICK	H S	1LT	2	1910	1912
HARRINGTON	F C	2LT	2	1912	1914
OLIVER	L E	1LT	2	1916	
VESTAL	S C	LTC	2	1922	

LAST NAME	INITIAL	RANK	QTRS	YR IN	YR OUT
HERR		LTC	2	1929	1932
GIBSON	P W	LTC	2	1932	1936
HARRINGTON		LTC	2	1939	1940
ARNOLD	W H	MG	2	1948	1951
EBERLE	G L	GEN	2	1951	1954
DEUTERMANN	H T	RADM	2	1957	1959
ENNIS - AWC	W P	LTG	2	1960	1962
BESSON Jr	F S	GEN	2	1962	1965
SACKTON	F J	MG	2	1965	1967
TOWNSEND	E C	MG	2	1967	1968
ENEMARK	W A	MG	2	1968	1972
McCAFFREY	W J	LTG	2	1972	1973
WOODWARD - IG	G H	LTG	2	1973	1973
MAPLES	H N	LTG	2	1974	1976
FULLER	M D	LTG	2	1977	1977
WEST - MDW	R L	LTG	2	1977	1980
CURRY - MDW	J R	MG	2	1980	1983
BALLANTYNE3 - MDW	J L	MG	2	1983	1986
BALLENTYNE3 - IADC	J L	LTG	2	1986	1989
LOEFFKE	B	MG	2	1989	
HARDING	J R	MG	2	1992	
MARKHAM	E M	CPT	3	1905	1907
ADAMS	E M	1LT	3	1907	1908
WIGMORE	H L	CPT	3	1908	1909
YOUNGBERG	G A	CPT	3	1909	1910
BELL	J G	1LT	3	1910	1913
JEWETT	H C	CPT	3	1913	1915
EARLE	J H	CPT	3	1915	1917
KING	C	LTC	3	1919	1921
WEEKS		LTC	3	1920	1921
CROSEY	H B	LTC	3	1922	
DODD		LTC	3	1932	1936
COLLINS	J L	MAJ	3	1938	1941
BOLLING	A R	BG	3	1940	1943
OLIVER	BUGS		3	1942	
McLAIN	R S		3	1946	1952
LEMNITZER	L L	MG	3	1954	
MICHAELIS	J H	MG	3	1956	1959
BOETCHERS	L H	GEN	3	1960	1961
ANDERSON	J R	GEN	3	1961	1962
WEYAND	F C	GEN	3	1962	1964
STEELE	W S	GEN	3	1965	1966
DONOHEW	J N	MG	3	1966	1967

Appendix B: Yearly Listing of Quarters Occupants (Officers) 231

LAST NAME	INITIAL	RANK	QTRS	YR IN	YR OUT
HENRY Jr	J B	MG	3	1967	1969
LaROCQUE	G R	RADM	3	1969	1972
ADAMSON - MDW	J B	MG	3	1972	1973
DAVISON - MDW	F E	MG	3	1973	1974
YERKS - MDW	R G	MG	3	1975	1977
DOHLEMAN - MDW	K E	MG	3	1977	1979
ARTER - MDW	R	MG	3	1979	1983
MERRITT - JCS	J N	GEN	3	1983	1985
MOELLERING - JCS	J H	LTG	3	1985	1987
DOCTOR Jr - IG	H	LTG	3	1987	1989
GOODRICH	D M	MG	3	1989	1991
SHORT, JR	A E	LTG	3	1991	
BOGGS	F C	CPT	4	1905	1907
GRANT III	U S	1LT	4	1907	1908
RIDLEY	C S	1LT	4	1908	1909
CARLETON	G	MAJ	4	1909	1910
FRIES	A A	CPT	4	1910	1912
WILLING	W	CPT	4	1912	1917
SPALDING	M E	MAJ	4	1919	1922
GLASSFORD	P D	LTC	4	1922	
MORRIS Jr	H H	MAJ	4	1930	1933
AURAND	H S	MAJ	4	1933	1937
CARRINGTON	G	LTC	4	1938	1939
PATCH	J D	LTC	4	1939	1940
OLIVER	L E	MG	4	1945	1947
BOLTE	C L	MG	4	1948	1952
POWELL	H B	BG	4	1952	1953
HINNRICHS	J M	LTG	4	1960	1962
VAN NATTA		GEN	4	1962	1963
Del MAR	R H	MG	4	1963	1965
MYER	R D	LTG	4	1965	1967
FRANKLIN	W C	MG	4	1967	1969
WILLIAMS	R R	MG	4	1969	1970
FORSYTHE	G I	LTG	4	1970	1972
BEATTY Jr	G S	MG	4	1972	1975
MORRIS	J W	MG	4	1975	1980
BRATTON - COE	J K	LTG	4	1980	1984
WAGNER Jr - RD&A	L C	LTG	4	1984	1987
ONO - DSPER	A K	LTG	4	1987	1990
RODGERS - DCA	T	LTG	4	1990	1991
GRIFFITH - IG	R H	LTG	4	1991	
GRANT III	U S	1LT	5	1905	1907
TYLER	M C	1LT	5	1907	1910
SULTAN	D I	2LT	5	1910	1913

LAST NAME	INITIAL	RANK	QTRS	YR IN	YR OUT
ROBINS	T M	CPT	5	1913	1915
JEWETT	H C	CPT	5	1915	1916
BESSON	F S	1LT	5	1916	1917
WILLIAMS	C W	1LT	5	1917	
COLLINS - G5	E T	COL	5	1919	1920
SIMONDS	G S	LTC	5	1920	1921
SWEENEY	W C	LTC	5	1921	
BECK	R M	LTC	5	1931	1935
MALONY	H J	COL	5	1938	1940
BRADSHAW	A	MG	5	1948	1952
TAYLOR	M D	GEN	5	1952	
ZITZMAN	K F	BG	5	1957	1959
HOUSEMAN	E M	MG	5	1959	1961
QUILL - ICAF	J B	MG	5	1961	1962
STOUGHTON - ICAF	T R	MG	5	1962	1964
Del MAR	R H	MG	5	1965	1966
DAVIS	J J	LTG	5	1966	1970
CLARKE	F J	LTG	5	1970	1973
HENNESSEY	J J	LTG	5	1973	1974
KERWIN Jr	W T	GEN	5	1974	1975
COOKSEY	H H	LTG	5	1975	1977
BARROW - NWC	J	RADM	5	1978	1980
SURUT - NWC	L E	MG	5	1980	1983
SMITH USAF - NWC	P M	MG	5	1983	1986
ADDAMS - NWC	J F	RADM	5	1986	1989
GRAVES - JCS	H D	MG	5	1989	1991
FREITAG - COMPT	M	LTG	5	1991	
ASHFORD	B K	CPT	6	1905	1909
MORRIS	S J	CPT	6	1909	1910
REYNOLDS	C R	CPT	6	1911	1914
BUCK	C D	MAJ	6	1914	1917
WADHAMS - MedC	S H	COL	6	1919	1919
WALKER	F L	MAJ	6	1934	1937
BONHAM	P G	MAJ	6	1937	1939
SCOTT	S L	MG	6	1940	
PATCH	J D	COL	6	1942	1943
WARD - G3	F	COL	6	1943	1944
BOLLING - INTEL	A R	MG	6	1948	1952
BERRY	R W	MG	6	1956	1958
AMMON - NWC	W B	RADM	6	1959	1960
PHILLIPS - NWC	R H	VADM	6	1961	1962
SUTHERLAND Jr	W A	ADM	6	1962	1964
LEE - NWC	F	VADM	6	1965	1967

Appendix B: Yearly Listing of Quarters Occupants (Officers)

LAST NAME	INITIAL	RANK	QTRS	YR IN	YR OUT
DAVIS	L I	LTG	6	1967	1968
KELLY - NWC	J E	LTG	6	1968	1970
SMITH	J V	RADM	6	1970	1973
ROWNY	E L	LTG	6	1973	1979
HARDIN Jr	H F	LTG	6	1979	1982
SCHWEITZER	R L	LTG	6	1983	1986
WHEELER - AMC	A G	MG	6	1986	1991
POLONIS	W G	LTG	6	1991	1992
McCAFFREY	B R	LTG	6	1992	
KOESTER	F J	CPT	7	1905	1911
ELLIOTT	M A	CPT	7	1911	1913
JORDAN	L W	CPT	7	1913	1915
POINT	W H	CPT	7	1916	
WALKER	M		7	1919	1920
GOWEN	J B	COL	7	1920	1921
STEWART	G H	LTC	7	1922	1923
GRUNERT	G	LTC	7	1932	1935
GORDON	W W	MAJ	7	1935	1939
COLLINS	J L	LTG	7	1945	1947
HULL	J E		7	1952	
HOLLIS	R P	MG	7	1956	1957
MUNDY - ICAF	G W	LTG	7	1957	1959
TAYLOR	M D	GEN	7	1961	1962
WOOD	S	GEN	7	1962	1965
SCHOMBURG - ICAF	A	LTG	7	1965	1967
GOODPASTER - NWC	A J	LTG	7	1967	1968
PALMER Jr	B	LTG	7	1968	1968
HARDY	J S	LTG	7	1968	1970
McPHERSON - NWC	J B	LTG	7	1970	1973
BAYNE - NWC	M G	VADM	7	1973	1977
GARD Jr	R G	LTG	7	1977	1981
KEITH - AMC	D R	GEN	7	1981	1984
THOMPSON - AMC	R H	GEN	7	1984	1986
POWELL - NSA	C L	LTG	7	1987	1987
WAGNER Jr - AMC	L C	GEN	7	1987	1989
PARKER	E D	LTG	7	1989	
DOMINY	C E	LTG	7	1992	
BURR	E	MAJ	8	1905	1906
LANGFITT	W C	LTC	8	1906	1910
RAYMOND	R R	MAJ	8	1910	1911
BARDEN	W J	MAJ	8	1911	1913
WOOTEN	W P	MAJ	8	1914	1916
PATRICK	M M	COL	8	1916	1917

Appendix B: Yearly Listing of Quarters Occupants (Officers)

LAST NAME	INITIAL	RANK	QTRS	YR IN	YR OUT
KUHN	J E	BG	8	1917	
McANDREW - AWC	J W	MG	8	1919	1921
McGLAUGHLIN - AWC	E F	MG	8	1921	1923
ELY - AWC	H E	MG	8	1923	1927
CONNOR - AWC	W D	MG	8	1927	1932
SIMONDS - POSTCO	G S	MG	8	1932	1935
CRAIG - AWC	M	MG	8	1935	1935
GRANT - AWC	W S	MG	8	1936	1937
DeWITT - AWC	J J	MG	8	1937	1939
PEYTON - AWC	P B	MG	8	1939	1940
McNAIR CG-AGF	L J	LTG	8	1941	1944
SIMSON	B W	BG	8	1944	1945
STILWELL - AGF	J W	LTG	8	1945	1945
DEVERS - AGF	J	GEN	8	1945	1946
TRUSCOTT III	L K	LTG	8	1946	1947
COLLINS	J L	GEN	8	1947	1956
PALMER - V/CS	W B	GEN	8	1956	1957
LEMNITZER - V/CS	L L	GEN	8	1957	1959
DECKER - V/CS	G H	GEN	8	1959	1962
HANLETT - V/CS	B	GEN	8	1962	1964
ABRAMS Jr - V/CS	C W	GEN	8	1964	1967
HAINES Jr - V/CS	R E	GEN	8	1967	1968
PALMER Jr - V/CS	B	GEN	8	1968	1973
HAIG - V/CS	A M	GEN	8	1973	1973
WEYAND - V/CS	F C	GEN	8	1973	1974
KERWIN Jr - V/CS	W T	GEN	8	1975	1978
KROESEN - V/CS	F	GEN	8	1978	1979
VESSEY Jr - V/CS	J W	GEN	8	1979	1982
WICKHAM - V/CS	G A	GEN	8	1982	1983
THURMAN - V/CS	M R	GEN	8	1983	1987
BROWN - V/CS	A E	GEN	8	1987	1989
RICASSI - V/CS	R W	GEN	8	1989	1990
SULLIVAN - V/CS	G	LTG	8	1990	1991
REIMER - V/CS	D J	GEN	8	1991	
LANGFITT	W C	MAJ	9	1905	1906
WINSLOW	E E	MAJ	9	1907	1908
RAYMOND	R R	MAJ	9	1908	1910
CONNOR	W D	MAJ	9	1911	1913
FRIES	A A	MAJ	9	1913	1916
SMITH - AWC	W		9	1919	1920
SIMONS			9	1921	1922
KING	E L	BG	9	1922	1924
HUMPHREY	E H	COL	9	1933	1938

Appendix B: Yearly Listing of Quarters Occupants (Officers)

LAST NAME	INITIAL	RANK	QTRS	YR IN	YR OUT
GRANT	W S	BG	9	1935	1936
REHKOPF	N B	COL	9	1939	1940
HILL	H	VADM	9	1947	1949
BULL - AWC	H R	LTG	9	1950	1952
CRAIG - USAF NWC	H A	LTG	9	1953	1955
WOOLDRIDGE - NWC	E T	VADM	9	1956	1958
HARROLD - NWC	T L	LTG	9	1958	1961
GRISWOLD - NWC	F H	LTG	9	1961	1964
BESSON Jr - AMC	F S	GEN	9	1965	1970
MILEY Jr - AMC	H A	GEN	9	1970	1975
DEANE Jr - AMC	J R	GEN	9	1975	1977
GUTHRIE - AMC	J R	GEN	9	1977	1981
MERRYMAN - RD&A	J H	LTG	9	1981	1984
HEIBERG III - COE	E R	LTG	9	1986	1988
HATCH - COE	H J	LTG	9	1988	1990
WILLIAMS	A E	LTG	9	1991	
BROWN	E I	CPT	10	1905	1906
BARDEN	W J	CPT	10	1905	1908
JERVEY	J P	CPT	10	1907	1908
ROSE	W H	MAJ	10	1908	1909
BARTH	H C	MAJ	10	1909	1911
RAND	L B	CPT	10	1911	1912
WILBY	F B	1LT	10	1912	1914
REINEKE	P S	1LT	10	1914	1915
NOLAN	D E	BG	10	1919	
BIRNEY Jr	U	LTC	10	1921	1922
SIMONDS	G S	COL	10	1922	1924
RIGGS		LTC	10	1934	1937
BARNETT	J W	LTC	10	1937	1940
CHRISTIANSON	J G	LTC	10	1941	1945
PARKS	F L	MG	10	1946	1948
JACKSON	H R	COL	10	1952	1953
DUEHRING	G C	COL	10	1957	1960
McGOWAN - AWC	G J	BG	10	1960	1961
ROSE - ICAF	R E	VADM	10	1961	1964
LEE	F	VADM	10	1964	1965
MEYER	R D	MG	10	1965	1967
CHESAREK	F J	GEN	10	1967	1970
DE PUY	W E	LTG	10	1971	1973
KALERGIS	J G	LTG	10	1973	1974
KJELLSTROM	J A	LTG	10	1974	1977
KEITH - RD&A	D R	LTG	10	1977	1981
PEIXOTTO	E D	LTG	10	1981	1984

Appendix B: Yearly Listing of Quarters Occupants (Officers)

LAST NAME	INITIAL	RANK	QTRS	YR IN	YR OUT
NOAH - COMPT	M W	LTG	10	1984	1988
WEINSTEIN - DCSI	S T	LTG	10	1988	1989
HILMES - INFSYS	J B	LTG	10	1989	1992
BROOK	M	1LT	11	1905	1907
ROSE	W H	1LT	11	1907	1908
POWELL	R G	2LT	11	1908	1910
ALEXANDER	R G	2LT	11	1910	1913
HERKNESS	L C	1LT	11	1913	1916
HOLCOMBE	W H	1LT	11	1916	1917
YOUNG	J E	CPT	11	1917	
BROWN	P	COL	11	1919	
HITT - SigC	P	COL	11	1922	
COOPER - NWC	A J	COL	11	1935	1936
CLARK	M	BG	11	1940	1942
VANAMAN	A W	MG	11	1948	1952
O'CONNELL	J D	LTG	11	1959	
FISCHER		MG	11	1961	1962
STARBIRD	A D	LTG	11	1963	1971
VAUGHAN	W W	LTG	11	1971	1978
WEBB Jr - DSPER	W L	MG	11	1978	1982
MITTEMYER - SURG/G	B	LTG	11	1982	1985
BECKER - SURG/G	Q H	LTG	11	1985	1988
LEDFORD - SURG/G	F F	LTG	11	1988	1991
SMITH Jr	J E	RADM	11	1991	
COWPER	H W	1LT	12	1905	1908
HART	W L	1LT	12	1908	1909
BUCK	B B	MAJ	12	1909	1910
STOLBRON	C J	1LT	12	1910	1911
NORTH	E	2LT	12	1911	1914
STRONG Jr	F S	1LT	12	1914	1915
HODGES	J N	CPT	12	1916	
GOWEN	J B	COL	12	1919	1920
EMBICK	S D	COL	12	1921	1923
GRANT	W S	LTC	12	1923	1925
ANDERSON - AWC	J W	MAJ	12	1927	1932
SIMPSON	W H	LTC	12	1936	1940
BARR	D G	MG	12	1946	1947
PACHLER - NWC	F T	MG	12	1962	1963
WOOTEN	S C	MG	12	1963	1965
MacLAUGHLIN	V J	MG	12	1965	1966
APPLEBY	J J	RADM	12	1966	1968
KENDALL	B E	MG	12	1968	1970
PIERCE	R K	MG	12	1970	1972
KUCHEMAN	H B	MG	12	1972	1972

Appendix B: Yearly Listing of Quarters Occupants (Officers)

LAST NAME	INITIAL	RANK	QTRS	YR IN	YR OUT
McGOUGH III	E A	MG	12	1972	1975
ANTONELLI - ICAF	T	MG	12	1975	1978
KIRWAN	R L	MG	12	1978	1983
LAWRENCE - NDU	R D	LTG	12	1983	1986
HOSMER	B D	LTG	12	1986	1989
BALDWIN Jr	J A	VADM	12	1989	1991
KIND	P A	LTG	12	1992	
HANNUM	W T	1LT	13	1905	1907
PIERCE	C C		13	1907	1908
BROWN	H A	MAJ	13	1908	1910
DALEY	E L	1LT	13	1910	1911
ARDERY	E D	1LT	13	1911	1913
BROWN	H A	MAJ	13	1913	1915
HOLCOMBE	W H	2LT	13	1915	1916
BERTMAN	M	1LT	13	1916	
CRAIG	M	BG	13	1919	1920
KILBOURNE	C E	COL	13	1920	1924
REHKOPF	N B	LTC	13	1924	1928
WEISSINGER II	W T	LTC	13	1933	1937
LANDON	T H	BG	13	1946	1948
TAYLOR	M D	MG	13	1948	
McAULIFF	A C	MG	13	1952	
GERHARDT	H A	MG	13	1961	1962
SCHOMBURG - ICAF	A	LTG	13	1962	1965
LAMPERT	J B	LTG	13	1966	1969
UNGER	F T	LTG	13	1969	1970
ZAIS	M	LTG	13	1970	1972
DEANE Jr	J R	MG	13	1972	1975
D'AMBROSIO	E J	MG	13	1975	1979
CONOLLY II	R C	RADM	13	1979	1981
SCHWARZTRAUBER	S A	RADM	13	1981	1984
McCARDELL	J E	RADM	13	1983	1985
HODGES - IADC	P H	MG	13	1985	1987
CHANDLER		RADM	13	1987	1989
STADLER - NWC	G P	MG	13	1989	1991
FRYER	J C	MG	13	1992	
SMITH	C S	CPT	14	1905	1907
BROWN	L	CPT	14	1907	1909
OTWELL	C H	CPT	14	1909	1914
KINGMAN	J J	CPT	14	1914	1916
PETERSON	V L	CPT	14	1916	
ERICKSON	H	LTC	14	1919	1922
GRANT	W S	LTC	14	1926	1927
HONEYCUTT - AWC	F W	LTC	14	1931	1935

Appendix B: Yearly Listing of Quarters Occupants (Officers)

LAST NAME	INITIAL	RANK	QTRS	YR IN	YR OUT
TRUESDELL	K	MAJ	14	1935	1937
GRUENTHER	A M	MG	14	1946	1947
WEYLAND	O P	MG	14	1948	1950
CANINE	R J	MG	14	1951	1952
RUFFNER		MG	14	1961	1962
CARTER - CIA	M S	LTG	14	1962	1965
LASSETTER Jr	R	MG	14	1965	1966
JOHNSON - INTEL	C L	MG	14	1966	1967
CREER	W E	MG	14	1967	1968
BELL	D B	RADM	14	1968	1970
JACKSON	P W	RADM	14	1970	1972
LEE	R M	MG	14	1972	1974
MURPHY - NWC	J S	MG	14	1975	1976
LOBDELL - USAF NWC	H	MG	14	1976	1978
DELAUNE Jr	E	MG	14	1978	1982
PRILLAMAN	R	LTG	14	1982	1984
DOYLE	D K	LTG	14	1984	1986
HILBERT - MDW	D C	MG	14	1986	1990
STREETER - MDW	R	MG	14	1990	1993
ROSE	W H	1LT	15	1905	1906
RALSTON	R R	1LT	15	1906	1908
ROBINS	T M	1LT	15	1908	1910
DOWNING	F B	1LT	15	1910	1912
WIGMORE	H L	CPT	15	1912	1913
DUNCAN	C L	CPT	15	1913	1914
STOKEY	W P	CPT	15	1914	1916
EMERSON	T H	CPT	15	1916	
DeWITT	J J	MAJ	15	1919	1921
KRUEGER	W	LTC	15	1921	1922
WOOTEN	W P	COL	15	1922	1925
BUSBY	C M		15	1930	1931
FREEHOFF	W M	MAJ	15	1934	1937
PAUL - G4	W S	BG	15	1940	1942
WALKER - G4	W G	COL	15	1942	
KENNAN	G F	HON	15	1947	1948
BARNES	M B	HON	15	1948	1949
DURBROW	E	HON	15	1949	1950
GALLMAN	W J	HON	15	1951	1952
GREELEY - ICAF	L J	BG	15	1952	1953
HICKERSON	J D	HON	15	1954	1955
NIBLO	U	BG	15	1955	1956
VILLARD	H S	HON	15	1956	1957
CANNON	R M	MG	15	1957	1957
	E T	AMB	15	1958	1959

Appendix B: Yearly Listing of Quarters Occupants (Officers)

LAST NAME	INITIAL	RANK	QTRS	YR IN	YR OUT
CHAPIN	S	HON	15	1959	1960
BEAULAC	W L	AMB	15	1961	1962
BROWN	W G	AMB	15	1962	1964
BERGER	S D	AMB	15	1964	1965
CABOT	J M	AMB	15	1965	1966
LIGHTNER Jr	E A	AMB	15	1966	1969
JONES	J W	AMB	15	1969	1971
LEONHART	W	AMB	15	1971	1977
KUBISCH	J B	AMB	15	1977	1979
STEARNS	M	AMB	15	1979	1981
LAINGEN - NDU	L B	AMB	15	1981	1986
MILLER - NDU	R H	AMB	15	1986	1989
STADTLER - NDU	W E	AMB	15	1989	1991
WALKER	H H	AMB	15	1992	
OWENS	C H	COL	16	1946	1948
NORMAN	E C	COL	16	1948	1950
RAYMOND	J E	COL	16	1950	1951
JACKSON	H R	COL	16	1951	1952
MOSS	J D	COL	16	1953	1954
BIBBS	G W	COL	16	1954	1956
McLAIN	J	COL	16	1956	1957
TOWNSEND	H E	COL	16	1961	1962
TALLEY	E J	LTC	16	1962	1963
ELLIS	C W	LTC	16	1963	1965
MOORE	J J C	COL	16	1965	1966
McDANIEL - CO	W A	COL	16	1966	1969
INMAN	R L	COL	16	1969	1970
RAMOS	F J	COL	16	1971	1972
McDANIELS - CO	J E	COL	16	1972	1976
EATON	W H	COL	16	1976	1979
BARRENS	C G	COL	16	1979	1981
ALTON - CO	C L	COL	16	1981	1986
SCHMIDTMAN - CO	M C	COL	16	1986	1990
MOORE - DIC	W D	COL	16	1990	1991
COOPER - CO	B P	COL	16	1991	
LYSTAD		1LT	17	1929	1932
BRINSON	N M	1LT	17	1932	1936
McCLURE - ADJ	R A	LTC	17	1936	1938
LEWIS	T E		17	1942	
LeBLANC	M	LTC	17	1966	1968
SCHULTZ	R S	LTC	17	1968	1973
KELLEY	D R	LTC	17	1973	1975
BENSON	J D	COL	17	1975	1978
WICHMANOWSKI	W F	COL	17	1978	1981

Appendix B: Yearly Listing of Quarters Occupants (Officers)

LAST NAME	INITIAL	RANK	QTRS	YR IN	YR OUT
SMITH	J	MAJ	17	1981	1983
SUELLENTUE	D M	LTC	17	1983	1985
DONAHUE	D	LTC	17	1985	1989
SCHMID - Chap	W L	LTC	17	1989	1991
GOLF SHACK			17	1991	
SMITH	F	MSG	17-A	1929	1936
GUSTIN	E Y	SGT	18-1	1929	1936
TODD	D C	CPT	18-1	1965	1966
LYLES Jr	R H	MAJ	18-1	1966	1967
WISSINGER	T R	CPT	18-1	1967	1968
SALTER Jr	A T	CPT	18-1	1968	1969
SAUNDERS	G E	LTC	18-1	1969	1971
BRUMMITT	M J	CPT	18-1	1971	1973
GRAHAM	R D	CPT	18-1	1973	1974
GRAVES	A J	CPT	18-1	1975	1977
McCONNELL	J B	WO1	18-1	1977	1983
NOVAK	J R	CAPT	18-2	1966	1966
ERVIN	H E	CPT	18-2	1966	1968
STRUBE	R C	WO4	18-2	1968	1969
McCLENDON	E H	MAJ	18-2	1969	1971
MORGAN	P A	CPT	18-2	1971	1973
DEWITT Jr	C H	CPT	18-2	1973	1974
JACOBSON	W R	LTC	18-2	1974	1975
CHIARAVALLE	P	WO1	18-2	1975	1977
CATE	W D	1LT	18-2	1977	1978
CRITCHFIELD	J B	MAJ	18-2	1978	1981
FARREN	K	CPT	18-2	1981	1983
WEAVER	J K	MAJ	18-3	1955	1969
SICILIA	B K	1LT	18-3	1966	1966
McDANIEL	W A	COL	18-3	1966	1966
SEALS	C L	LTC	18-3	1966	1966
DALTON	R L	COL	18-3	1969	1969
JOYNER	E D	CPT	18-3	1969	1972
WEISKOPF	J D	CPT	18-3	1972	1974
DeWITT	C H	CPT	18-3	1974	1976
PARKER	J B	CW3	18-3	1976	1977
MILLAWAY	R J	CW2	18-3	1977	1978
KITCHIN	D	LTC	18-3	1978	1979
COUTHEN	S	CW2	18-3	1979	1980
MACKLIN	D K	WO1	18-3	1981	1982
PLANA	A T	2LT	18-3	1983	1984
FISHER	R P	1SGT	18-4	1921	1928
VADER	P	CPT	18-4	1965	1966
DIXON	D C	CPT	18-4	1966	1967

Appendix B: Yearly Listing of Quarters Occupants (Officers)

LAST NAME	INITIAL	RANK	QTRS	YR IN	YR OUT
MAHONEY	M S	CPT	18-4	1967	1968
McCLENDON	E H	MAJ	18-4	1968	1969
LOPEMAN	R G	CPT	18-4	1969	1971
GEFELL	J G	COL	18-4	1971	1971
ANDREWS	J R	COL	18-4	1971	1974
BENSON	J D	COL	18-4	1974	1975
WIGFALL	B J	CPT	18-4	1975	1977
DENYS	A J	1LT	18-4	1977	1979
FREAKLEY	B	CPT	18-4	1979	1983
PHIPPS	M A	1LT	18-4	1982	1983
HART Jr	H	CPT	18-4	1983	1984
NATHAN	A P	LTC	19	1956	1957
MELBYE	J	MAJ	19	1966	1967
WILSON	D	LTG	19	1967	1968
HARDY	J S	LTG	19	1968	1968
PUTNAM	E L	MAJ	19	1968	1969
McDONALD	L P	MAJ	19	1969	1970
AYERS	H B	COL	19	1970	1972
HAZAM	M J	COL	19	1972	1973
BAUER	E R	COL	19	1973	1974
INGRAM Jr	O B	CPT	19	1974	1974
BOICE	W M	MAJ	19	1974	1974
O'DONNELL	K W	LCDR	19	1975	1977
SONTAG	P D	LTC	19	1977	1978
WASIELEWSKI	J S	LTC	19	1978	1980
HOFFMAN - ENGR	J R	LTC	19	1980	1983
MERTZ Jr - ENGR	W M	LTC	19	1983	1986
WILLHOUSE - ENGR	D	LTC	19	1986	1988
HOWZE - ENGR	J	MAJ	19	1988	1991
BREZ	D	MAJ	19	1991	
GRUNERT	G	MAJ	20-1	1921	1926
McNARNEY	J T	MAJ	20-1	1935	1937
RAYMOND	J E	MAJ	20-1	1937	1939
OSBORNE	J R	MAJ	20-1	1964	1967
FARR	R R	MAJ	20-1	1967	1967
FRANKLIN	W C	BG	20-1	1967	1967
WIMER	D J	CPT	20-1	1967	1969
STRITTMATTER	L E	MAJ	20-1	1969	1972
TOLMAN	A L	2LT	20-1	1972	1973
MANLOVE	R	CPT	20-1	1973	1974
REYNA	L	1LT	20-1	1974	1978
CASTLEMAN	P A	1LT	20-1	1979	1980
SARLES	T B	CPT	20-1	1980	1981
ENGINEER HOLD			20-1	1981	1981

Appendix B: Yearly Listing of Quarters Occupants (Officers)

LAST NAME	INITIAL	RANK	QTRS	YR IN	YR OUT
MINEZ	P	CPT	20-1	1981	1983
ENGINEER HOLD			20-1	1983	1984
PLANA	A T	1LT	20-1	1984	1986
TRUMPS - CER/EV	T H	CPT	20-1	1986	1986
BENEDICT - CER/EV	C F	CPT	20-1	1986	1987
PARKER - HHC	J	CPT	20-1	1987	1989
OSBORNE	D	CPT	20-1	1989	
MUELLER Jr	E M	CPT	20-2		1963
WAGLEY	P C	LTC	20-2	1963	1964
BUTT	H C	LTC	20-2	1965	1967
EINSELN	A	MAJ	20-2	1967	1968
MONTEMAYOR	E A	MAJ	20-2	1968	1969
ATCHINSON	D A	CPT	20-2	1969	1970
WOODS	P F	LCDR	20-2	1970	1972
SHORT	J W	MAJ	20-2	1972	1974
CONNORS	J T	1LT	20-2	1974	1975
KOPEC	J L	CPT	20-2	1975	1977
KEENAN	G E	LTC	20-2	1977	1979
TONELLI	G E	MAJ	20-2	1979	1981
SARLES	T B	CPT	20-2	1981	1983
ENGINEER HOLD			20-2	1983	1984
TORYANSKI	M E	CPT	20-2	1984	1985
MERRILL HHH 3d	W G	1LT	20-2	1985	1987
OSTROWSKI	P	1LT	20-2	1987	1988
HAMBY	J	1LT	20-2	1988	1990
SCHMID - Chap	W L	LTC	20-2	1991	
BONHAM	F G	MAJ	20-3	1935	1937
MINDRUM	G G	CPT	20-3	1965	1966
BONHET	W J	1LT	20-3	1966	1966
DIXON	D C	CPT	20-3	1966	1967
HAMAKER	B B	2LT	20-3	1966	1967
ABRAMSON	I J	MAJ	20-3	1967	1967
WIMER	D J	CPT	20-3	1967	1967
SHIELDS	J F	CPT	20-3	1984	1985
HESTER	M E	CPT	20-3	1985	1986
SUVER	W G	2LT	20-3	1986	1988
GAGNEY	B J	1LT	20-3	1988	1989
HICKEY III	E I	CPT	20-3	1990	1992
CASAUS	J F	MAJ	20-4	1965	1969
STRITTMATTER	L E	MAJ	20-4	1969	1969
LOYSEN	G J	CPT	20-4	1969	1970
McGRORY Jr	J C	CPT	20-4	1970	1972
CONNELL	J P	CPT	20-4	1971	1972
PEWETT	R H	LCDR	20-4	1972	1973

Appendix B: Yearly Listing of Quarters Occupants (Officers)

LAST NAME	INITIAL	RANK	QTRS	YR IN	YR OUT
QUANDER	F A	2LT	20-4	1973	1975
THOMAS	J E	CPT	20-4	1975	1977
FREY	D J	MAJ	20-4	1977	1980
HART Jr	H	1LT	20-4	1980	1983
ENGINEER HOLD			20-4	1983	1984
MEYER	R L	CPT	20-4	1984	1986
SPRINGMAN - EOD	M D	CPT	20-4	1986	1989
GAGNEY - HHC TOG	B J	1LT	20-4	1989	1990
LOMBARDO - EOD	M F	CPT	20-4	1990	
SHELLNUT	T C	1LT	20-5	1965	1966
GILLETTE		CPT	20-5	1966	1967
SCHOLLIAN		2LT	20-5	1967	1967
FIRE VACANT			20-5	1967	1967
DONALDSON		CPT	20-5	1969	1970
LINEWEAVER	W P	1LT	20-5	1970	1971
JONES	R	CPT	20-5	1972	1973
RUSIN	J D	CPT	20-5	1973	1976
MALLAMO	J P	1LT	20-5	1976	1977
DROCKINIS	J P	1LT	20-5	1977	1980
CRUZ	A	CPT	20-5	1980	1982
LaFATE	K	1LT	20-5	1982	1983
ENGINEER HOLD			20-5	1983	1984
JORDAN	R A	CPT	20-5	1984	1985
GARNER - CO A	C H	1LT	20-5	1985	1988
BRYANT - TOG	T	CPT	20-5	1988	1990
MISER - MTMC	J L	CPT	20-5	1991	
BONHAM	F G	MAJ	21-1	1935	1935
BOLTE	C L	MAJ	21-1	1937	1940
FINLEY	M R	CPT	21-1	1964	
LEACH	J H	LTC	21-1	1964	1967
BENDRICK	F	MAJ	21-1	1967	1968
AULT	J W	MAJ	21-1	1968	1969
JONES III	L	MAJ	21-1	1969	1972
ECKLBARGER	D E	MAJ	21-1	1972	1973
JOULWAN	G A	MAJ	21-1	1973	1974
NORRIS	C R	COL	21-1	1974	1978
MAILLET	E	COL	21-1	1978	1982
ACREE II	G W	COL	21-1	1982	1985
BAGNERISE - CO	J W	COL	21-1	1986	1989
HARBACH	D V	COL	21-1	1989	1991
GOWEN	J B	COL	21-2	1922	1922
TAYLOR	M C	COL	21-2	1963	1964
RIPPER	J K	COL	21-2	1964	
HODGINS	S F	COL	21-2	1964	1964

Appendix B: Yearly Listing of Quarters Occupants (Officers)

LAST NAME	INITIAL	RANK	QTRS	YR IN	YR OUT
TRAHAN	E	COL	21-2	1965	1969
DALTON	R A	COL	21-2	1969	1971
TUBB	A H	MAJ	21-2	1971	1973
WILKINS	V C	COL	21-2	1973	1975
ALLEN	J B	CPT	21-2	1980	1982
LOMBARD	R T	COL	21-2	1975	1980
HOFFORD	R	CPT	21-2	1982	1984
ROSTOW	E V	Mr	21-2	1984	1989
GASKIN - NDU	P	COL	21-2	1989	

GLOSSARY

ADA	Alley Dwelling Authority.
AEF	American Expeditionary Force, WWI.
AFSC	Armed Forces Staff College, Norfolk, VA.
AGF	Army Ground Forces.
AGO	Adjutant General's Office.
AIC	Army Industrial College, 1924-1962.
AMC	Army Materiel Command.
BOQ	Bachelor Officers' Quarters.
BRAC	Base Realignment and Closure.
C&O	Chesapeake and Ohio.
CIA	Central Intelligence Agency.
CONARC	Continental Army Command, Fort Monroe, VA.
DC	District of Columbia.
DCS	Deputy Chief of Staff.
DEML	Detached Enlisted Men's List.
DODCI	Department of Defense Computer Institute.
FBI	Federal Bureau of Investigation.
GHQ	General Headquarters.
IADC	Inter-American Defense College, Fort McNair, DC.
ICAF	Industrial College of the Armed Forces, Fort McNair, DC.
IRMC	Information Resources Management Center, NDU.
JCEWS	Joint Command, Control, and Electronic Warfare School.
JCS	Joint Chiefs of Staff.
JCSOS	Joint and Combined Staff Officers' School, Norfolk, VA.
MDW	Military District of Washington, Fort McNair, DC.
MID	Military Intelligence Division, WWI.
MOS	Military Occupational Specialty.
MP	Military Police.
NA	National Archives.
NCO	Noncommissioned Officer.
NDU	National Defense University.
NWC	National War College, Fort McNair, DC.
OAS	Organization of American States.
OER	Officer Efficiency Rating.
OSS	Office of Strategic Services, WWII.
PITS	Personel, Intelligence, Training, Supply.
PX	Post Exchange.
RG	Record Group.
ROTC	Reserve Officers' Training Corps.
SSS	Selective Service System (Draft Board).
USO	United Service Organization.
USMA	United States Military Academy, West Point, NY.
WPA	Works Progress Administration.

BIBLIOGRAPHY

*An asterisk by a proper name indicates a personal letter or an interview with the individual in 1991-1992.

"150th Anniversary." *Wilson's Library Bulletin*. Dec 1944, 19:282.

Abrahamson, J L. *America Arms for a New Century: The Making of a Great Military Power*. New York, Free Press: 1981.

Annual Historical Report, AWC, various years.

Annual Historical Report, ICAF, various years.

Annual Historical Report, MDW, various years.

Annual Historical Report, NWC, various years.

Armes, E W. "U.S. Arsenal." *Washington Post*. 10 Nov 1901. News item in Washingtoniana Room, M L King Library, Washington, DC.

"The Army Post." *Scribners*. Aug 1912, 250-51.

Arnold, J R. "The Battle of Bladensburg." *Columbia Historical Society*. V 33-38, 145-68.

Baldwin, C C. *Stanford White*. NY, A DeCapo Paperback, Plenum Publishing Co: 1976.

Ball, H P. *Of Responsible Command. A History of the US Army War College*. Carlisle Barracks, PA: Alumni Association of the Army War College, 1984.

Barbour, P L. *The Three Worlds of Captain John Smith*. Boston, Houghton Mifflin Co: 1964.

Beale, B. "Bradley and Collins Feted at Reception." *The Washington Star*. 14 August 1953, Society News.

Begler, P. *Washington in Focus*. Alexandria, VA, Vandimere Press: 1988.

Benjamin, M. *Washington During Wartime*. New York, Macmillian Co: 1914.

Bidwell, B W. *History of the Military Intelligence Division, Department of the Army General Staff: 1775-1941*. Frederick, MD, University Publications of America: 1986. Bohn, C. Handbook of Washington. Washington DC, Casimer: 1856.

Bolte, BG (Ret) P. "Early Years at Fort McNair." *Basecamp Briefs*. Jan/Feb, 1991, 4.

"Bomb Scare Hero Retires." *The Washington Star*. 1 Jan 1931.

Bryan, W B. *A History of the National Capital*. 2 Vols. New York, McMillan: 1914.

Bruce, R V. *Lincoln and the Tools of War*. Chicago, U of IL Press: 1989.

"Building Plans Underway at NDU." *Pentagon*. 10 Aug 1989, 3.

Caemmerer, H P. "The Life of Pierre Charles L'Enfant," *Columbia Historical Society*. V 50, 323-40.

_____. *A Manual on the Origin and Development of Washington*. Washington. US GPO: 1939.

"Caissons Will Stay." *Fort Myer Post*. V 8, no 10, 21 Feb 1957, 1.

Clark, A C. *Greenleaf & Law in the Federal City*. Washington, W F Roberts Press: 1901.

"Colonel Matlock Takes Command of 3d Infantry." *Fort Myer Post*. V 9, no 9, 11 Feb 1958, 2.

"Colored Hero Ends Service as Laborer at War College." *Washington Star*. 1 Jan 1931.

Columbia Historical Society. V 26, 280; V13, 122; V50. 526.

Columbian Magazine, Apr 1911.

Cooling III, B F, and W H Owen, II. *Mr. Lincoln's Forts*. Shippenburg, PA, White Mane Publishing Co: 1988.

Cooling, B F. "To Preserve the Peace." *Washington History*. V 1, no 1, Spring 1989, 71-86.

Coppings, M A. "Do Ghosts Walk at Fort McNair?" *MDW Post*. Aug 1977, 11.

Bibliography

Cowdrey, A E. *A City for the Nation: The Army Engineers and the Building of Washington, D.C. 1790-1967*. History Division, Office of Administrative Services, Office of the Chief Engineer. Washington, GPO: 1978.

Cullum, G W. *Biographical Register of the Officers and Graduates of the United States Military Academy*. New York: Houghton Mifflin & Co: 1891-1930. V1-V9, 1901-1950.

Cummings, V. "The Past Made an Open Book. The War College Library." *The Washington Star*. 17 May 1936.

Dalsheim, S. "The US Penitentiary of the District of Columbia." Paper read 19 May 1953 at a meeting of the Columbia Historical Society.

"Damage Repaired. Restoration of Government Works on Greeleaf's Point." *The Evening Star*. Washington DC, 9 Jan 1902. News item in Washingtoniana Room, M L King Library, Washington, DC.

"Defense College Welcomes First Students October 9." *The Passing Review*. 2 Oct 1962, 2.

"Demolition Begun. Removal of Old Buildings from Arsenal Grounds. The Old Penitentiary Consigned to Oblivion." News item in Washingtoniana room, M L King Library, Washington, DC.

Depuy, R E. *The Compact History of the United States Army*. 2d ed. New York, Hawthorne Books: 1973.

Dolenga, J. "Ghosts Haunt Quarters at Fort McNair." *Inter/Change*. 2 Aug 1982, 4-6.

Downey, F. *Sound of the Guns*. New York, David McKay Co: 1955.

Duggan, E. "History of Fort McNair." *Pentagram News*. 16 Dec 1974, 8.

Elliot, W. *Washington Guide*. Washington City, Franc Taylor: 1837.

"Elm Epidemic: Post Counters with Tree Planting Program." *Passing Review*. 27 Nov 1957, 2.

Encyclopedia Americana. International Edition. Danbury, CN, Grolier: 1989.

Farman, E E. "Reminiscences of Colonel E E Farman." MID, War College Building. Washington, DC, 1917.

Fazakerley, S L. "Shack Faces Demolition Monday." *Pentagram*. 15 Aug 1991, 11.

"Fifty Years Ago in the Star." *Washington Star*, 21 Nov 1954, A-24.

Forgey, B. "Marching in Step at Fort McNair." *The Washington Post*. 16 Nov 1991, D-1, 8.

"Fort McNair Today." *The Pentagon News*. 21 Nov 1968, 8.

Foster, A K. "The Conflict Between the Engineers and Architects over Control of Washington Barracks, 1902" American Studies, GWU: 1986.

Friedman, G. "Ghost Stories." *Washingtonian*. Oct 1984.

Garamone, J. "McNair Navy Launched." *Pentagram*. 1 Oct 1987, 3.

Gates, M E. "Loose Board Discloses Rich Past of 'Model Arsenal.'" *Pentagram*. 25 Oct 1990, 22.

"General Recalls Early Days at Fort McNair." *The Passing Review*. V 14, no 8, 18 Aug 1964, 1.

Gervasi, S. "Going for Good Vibes." *The Washington Post*. 7 Sep 1990, B-5.

Gibson, S. "McNair To See Retail Facility Change." *Pentagram*. 20 Feb 1992, 4.

Goddard, B. *A Short Guide to the Guns at Fort McNair*. Washington DC, MDW Visual Aids: 1964.

Goode, J M. *Capital Losses*. Washington, Smithsonian Institute Press: 1979.

"Great Lakes." *Pentagram*. 19 Jul 1984, 20.

Gutheim, F A. *The Potomac*. New York, Rinehart & Co: 1949.

_____ and W E Washburn. *The Federal City: Plans and Realities*. Washington, Smithsonian Institute Press: 1976.

Harrison, B. *Recollections Grave and Gay*. New York, Scribners: 1911.

Hathaway, C C. "Concerning the Officer." *Outlook*. V 126, 22 Sep 1920, 158-60.

Heitman, F B. *Historical Register and Dictionary of the United States Army from its Origin 29 September 1789 to 2 March 1903*. Washington, DC, USGPO: 1903.

"Historic Army War College Becomes Fort Lesley J McNair." *The Washington Star*. 15 Jan 1948.

Historical Sketch of the Signal Corps (1860-1941). Fort Mommonth NJ, US Eastern Signal Corps School: 1942.

"HQ Company MDW Moves to Fort McNair." *The Fort Myer Post*. V 8, no 27, 21 Jun 1957, 1.

Huddleston, S M. "Sunny Southwest." *Columbia Historical Society*. V 26, 150.

Hunsberger, G S. "Architectural Career of George Hadfield." *Columbia Historical Society*. V 31, 9 Oct 1951, 46-65.

Hunt, F. "McNair 'Ship' Gets Its Own Boat." *The Pentagram News*. 14 Nov 1971, 16.

Hunter, A. *The Washington and Georgetown Directory*. Washington DC, Kirkwook and McGill Printers: 1853.

"ICAF Tempo Building Burns." *The Washington Star*. 31 Aug 1960.

"Improvement at the Washington Arsenal Grounds. The Graves of the Assassins." News item in Washingtoniana Room, M L King Library, Washington, DC.

Intelligencer. 2 Nov 1810. News item in Washingtoniana Room, M L King Library, Washington, DC.

"It's a New Workout in McNair Gym." *Pentagram News*. 16 Jan 1986, 36.

Jabs, K. "Bush Dedicates Marshall Hall as NDU's Academic Center." *Pentagram*. V 38, no 3, 3 Oct 1991, 1-3.

_____. "NDU Library Moves," MDW News Release, 27 Sep 1991.

Johnson, M. "Haunting Fort McNair," *The Pentagram*. Oct 1976, 11.

Kahn, Jr, CWO E J. "McNair, Educator of the Army." *The Infantry Journal*. Jan 1950.

Keim, DeB R. *Washington and Its Environs.* McGill and Witherow Printers: 1874.

_____. *Washington and Its Environs.* B F Owing Printers: 1879, 1887.

Kelly, S H. "'Just Cause' Paintings." *Pentagram.* 20 Jun 1991, 6.

Kimbel S. "Last of WWI Tempo Buildings Erected on the Mall Demolished." *The Pentagram News.* 23 Jul 1970, 3.

Knight, J. "The Renaissance of Buzzard Point." *The Washington Post.* 16 Oct 1989, 1, 5, 50.

"Landmarks Need Frequent Repair." *The Pentagram News.* 6 Dec 1973, 3.

Lange, W L. Ed. "SSS." *An Encyclopedia of World History.* 5th ed. Boston, Houghton Mifflin: 1972.

Legislative and Executive Document of the Congress of the United States. 1st Sess, 17th Cong, 1780-1823. Washington DC, Galess and Seaton: 1834.

"L'Enfant." *Columbia Historical Society.* V 2, 118.

Levey, B. "Goodby to Pigeons, Hello to Crows." *The Washington Star.* 22 Oct 1985.

Lolito, E A. "Area Pair Siezed as Red Spies." *The Washington Post.* 6 Apr 1965, A-10.

Lord, F A. *Civil War Collector's Encyclopedia.* New York, Castle Books/Stackpole Books: 1963-65.

Mani, T. "You Can Go Home Again." *The Pentagram.* 5 Sep 1991, 22.

Marshall, K T. *Together: Annals of an Army Wife.* New York, Tupper and Love Inc: 1946.

"McNair Mule Weighs Anchor for Army." *The Passing Review.* 7 Dec 1966, 3.

MDW Historical Background handout, no date.

"Military Exposition and Carnival." Official Program, 30 Sep - 1 Oct 1927. *Washington Daily News.* 16 Jul 1940.

Moore, C C. *The Life and Times of Charles Follet McKim.* New York, Houghton Mifflin: 1929.

Mordecai, Captain A. *Report of Experiments on Gunpowder Made at Washington Arsenal in 1843-44.* Washington, DC, J & G S Gideon: 1845.

Murphy, C. "Twenty-four Arrested in Protest at Fort McNair." *Washington Post.* 23 Aug 83.

Mylander, M. *The Generals.* New York: Dial Press, 1974.

National Defense University. NDU: 1989.

National Defense University 1991-1992 Catalog. Washington, NDU.

"Near Centenarian Turns Memories Light on Post." *Sunday Star.* Washington DC, 1 Jan 1936.

"The New War College." *Army Navy Journal.* V 46, 5 Sep 1908.

"New Building To Be Erected for ICAF." *The Passing Review.* V 9, no 14, 1.

NWC Historical Landmark brochure.

O'Brien, W J. "The Washington Arsenal." *Army Ordnance.* V 16, no 91, Jul-Aug 1935, 32-7.

"Octagon House." *The Washington Times.* Washington DC, 22 May 1991, B-6.

"Opening of IADC, OAS School, Lends Hemispheric Air to Fort McNair." *The Passing Review.* V 13, 21 Sep 1962, 3.

Pappas, G S. *Prudens Futuri. The U.S. Army War College 1901-67..* Carlisle, PA, The US Alumni Assn of the US Army War College: 1967.

Pearson, D. "Pershing's Last Drink." Scrapbook newspaper item. Date and publication unknown.

Poore, B ["Perley"]. *Perley's Reminiscences of 60 Years in the National Metropolis.* 2 Vols. Philadelphia, Hubbard Brothers: 1886.

Proctor, J C. "Story of Old Arsenal and Penitentiary." *Sunday Star,* 17 Apr 1932.

Purnell, J. "Heck of a Mess." *The Washington Times*. 6 Jun 1991, A-1, A-10.

Puryear, E F. *Nineteen Stars: A Study in Military Character and Leadership*. Washington, DC, Coiner Publications LTD: 1971.

Raymond, J E. Untitled, unpublished, 128 page manuscript on the history of Fort L J McNair, 1951. Hereafter referred to as Raymond, ms.

"Reconstruction of Washington Barracks, District of Columbia." *Report of Chief of Engineers, US Army*. Appendix AAA-23. Washington, DC, US GPO: 1902, 3866.

Ristow, W W "Augustine Herrman's Map of Virginia and Maryland." Washington, DC: *Library of Congress Quarterly Journal of Current Acquisitions*. V 17, Aug 1960, 221-26.

Rodenbaugh, T F. *Army of the United States, 1789-1896*. New York, Maynard, Merrill: 1896.

Sheftick, G. "Plans Call for Enlarged MDW." *Pentagram*. 18 Jun 1992, 3

"Shoulder Patch Has Unique Background." *The Fort Myer Post*. 5 May 1957, 3.

Smith, Captain John. *The Travels, Adventures and Observations of Captain John Smith in Europe, Asia, Afrecke, and America*. Republished in Richmond at Franklin Press in 1819.

Spiller, R J, ed. *Dictionary of American Military Biography*. Westport, CN, Greenwood Press: 1984.

STV/Lyon. "Master Plan Update for MDW/Fort Myer/Fort McNair." Nov 1991.

Summers, Colonel H. "What's a Military Good for Anyway?" *The Washington Times*. 10 Apr 1992, F-4.

Summers, K C. "...Explore." *The Washington Post*. Weekend, 13 Jan 1978, 5.

"Swimming Pool Project Begins." *The Passing Review*. V 9, no 14, 21 Nov 1958, 1.

"TF Insider." V1, no 1, 8 Apr 1968, 1.

"TF Insider." V 1, no 2, 9 Apr 1968, 1.

Todd, C B. *The Story of Washington*. NY, Putnam & Sons: 1889.

Thomas, D M. "Army Opposes Planned Highrise." *Pentagram*. 10 Mar 1988, 3.

Townsend, M. *US Curious Facts, History, Geography, Politics*. Boston, Rockwood & Churchill: 1890.

"Traditional Horse-Drawn Caissons To Be Replaced by Motor Vehicles." *The Fort Myer Post*. V 8, no 8, 8 Feb 1957, 1.

"Uncle Sam's Temple of Mars." *Cincinnati Enquirer*. 13 Sep 1908. M L King Library, Washington, DC. Washingtoniana Room.

Universal Restoration, Inc. *Interim Report, Condition of the Guastavino Dome, National War College*. Washington, DC, National Register of Historic Places: 1974.

US Army Register. Washington DC, US GPO. Annual.

Van Dyne, L. "Uncle Sam's Neighborhood." *The Washingtonian*. Nov 1991, 71-8, 1934.

Vaughn, SP-5 M D. "A Post with a Past." Unpublished rework of an unpublished manuscript by Colonel W A McDaniel, Post Commander 1966 to 1969.

_____. "?1791?" *The Passing Review*. Feb 1969, 5.

"War Office Seeks to Get Rid of 21 Million Old Draft Files." *Sunday Star*. 6 Jul 1941, Part 1, 3.

The Washington Post. 14 Oct 1888. News item in Washingtoniana Room, M L King Library, Washington, DC.

The Washington Post. 10 Nov 1904. Item in Washingtoniana Room, M L King Library, Washington, DC.

Watterston, G. *A Picture of Washington*. Joseph Etter Printer: 1841.

Weinert Jr, R P and Colonel R Arthur. *Defender of the Chesapeake*. Shippensberg, PA, White Mane Co: 1989.

Who Was Who in America. V 1 (1897-1942) and Historical V (1607-1896). Chicago, A N Marquis Co: 1942.

"Who's in the Army Now?" *Fortune.* Sep 1935, 38.

"Wrecking the United States Army." *Scientific American.* V 127, 22 Jul 1922, 14-5.

Yardley, H O. *The American Black Chamber.* New York: Blue Ribbon Books, 1931.

Letters

Letter to Lieutenant Colonel Ahern, AWC, signed W W K. 3 Mar 1919.

Letter from Major G M Chandler, Historian, AWC, re building 2-B. 26 Feb 1944.

Letter to Brigadier General Gillespie, Chief of Engineers, from Captain J Sewell, Chief of Construction. Date unknown.

Letter from Colonel J E Raymond to Major G M Chandler regarding building 2-B. 5 Jan 1955.

National Archives Sources

American State Papers: Military Affairs, 7 V, Washington: 1834-1860.

NA J-33 Cost of Repairs and Erection Buildings, Cl 5, V2, 918-22.

NNSC RG 28, Records of the Postal Service, #27, F-104a, F-102, F-445.

NA RG 48 Records of Office of Secretary of the Interior: Penitentiary 3 Vols #464-68; Register of Punishments, 3 V, #475.

NNSC RG 77, Maps of Records of Office of Chief of Engineers. Territory of the District of Columbia, F-105-Flat 7 (1792); F-160 (1797); 859- (1791-93).
    Washington Barracks, #32 (1827).
    Canal, #70, Atlas, 1803; #32-(1827).
    Washington Arsenal #48 (Plan of Post); #50 (1863-64); #54 (1855); #57-A (1881); #60 (Plat of Post Manuscript-1883).
    Washington Barracks, (1847).
    Canals, by Graham (1852).
    Washington Barracks, by Meigs (1853).
    #54-60 Boschke Map of 1857-1859; F-119; F-69.
    Fortifications of DC, Drawer 127 Sh 6a (1861).
    Washington, DC, Atlas 11007 #38 (1865).

Bibliography

Other Maps Consulted

John Smith Map of 1612.
Map of Carrollsburg, 1770.
Moore and Jones Map of 1802.
Herrman Map of Washington 1801-02 (1931).
Plats of the Washington Arsenal, 1815, 1823, 1855.
Van Deever Map of 1851.

NNRR-M RG 77, Records of Office of the Chief of Engineers. Entry 391, Completion Report, 1920, Washington Barracks; Completion Reports, Army War College, 1917-1943.

NNRR-M RG 92, Records of Office of Quartermaster General. SBB, Doc 12-201; Fort Humphreys Bx.

NA RG 92, #10 1900 linen trace w/key to 41 bldgs.
#14-23 1904-05 facades of Post Hospital.
Bx 1212 Arsenal, 1885, Fishpond & Buildings.
Bx 1213 Blueprint of Washington Barracks.
#1 1910 Grounds.
#10 linen trace seawall 1910, Army War college.
Bx 1210-12, 1215-16.
Bx 2918, 4925, 6933.
File 1800-1916, Bx 111.

NA RG 94 Records of the Office of the Adjutant General.

NA RG 98 USA Commands, Washington Barracks, Bk 2-3.

NA RG 156, Records of the Office of the Chief of Ordnance. Entry 3, Letters Sent, Bks 1-30; Entry 5, Letters to Secretary of War, Bks 1-16; Entry 17, Letters to the Chief of Ordnance; Entry 17, Letters Received 1792 to 1810, Bx 1; Entry 21, Letters Received Bks 1-29, 40-60. Entry 21, Bx 2, 19, 24, 30.

NA RG 233, AGO Reports to Congress on Penitentiary.

NA Microfilm:

M-166, BX 1369-1379 Records of the Army War College, Arsenal, Cook and Baker's School, Army General Hospital.
M-690, Engineer Battalion Returns from 1846 to 1916, #78 Dr 3.
M-727 Artillery Returns from 1876 to 1901, #78, Dr 7.
M-903 Medical History of Posts, #79, Dr 7.
M-1023, Correspondence Army War College and General Staff with the Office of the Adjutant General, #78, Dr 3.

US Government Documents

US. Congress. House. "Establishment of a Foundry and the Sale of Arms to the States." 10th Cong, 1 Sess, V 1, No 7, 19 Nov 1807.

US. Congress. House. Committee on Armed Services. "Report of the Panel on Military Education of the 100th Congress of the Committee on Armed Services." 1st Sess, no 4. Washington DC, USGPO: 21 Apr 1989.

US. Department of the Interior. US National Park Service. "Environmental Assessment: Two Marinas, Buzzard Point." July 1987.

US. War Department. Office of the Chief of Engineers. "Annual Report of Operations on the Reconstruction of Washington Barracks, DC for FY 1904 ending 30 Jun." 22 Jul 1904.

US. War Department. Office of the Quartermaster General. "Outline of Military Posts and Stations." Various years.

US. War Department. Surgeon General's Office. *Description of Military Posts and Stations.* Washington DC, US GPO. 1871, 1875, 1901, 1905.

INDEX

----, Louise 37
ABRAMS, Creighton 184
ADAMS, John 33 P D 196
ADAMSON, J B 173 175
ADDAMS, John F 165
AMES, 123
ANDERSON, Dorothy 149
ANTONELLI, Margaret 189 T 170 Theodore 189
APPLEBY, Jack J 180
ARMSTRONG, Donald 170
ARNOLD, 44 "Hap" 164 Samuel 40
ARTER, R E 175
ASTOR, John Jacob 70
ATZERODT, 53 George 40 41 99
AURAND, Family 151 Henry Jr 151 Henry S Jr 150 Maj 150
AYERS, 63 R B 116 Romeyn B 63 64
BABBITT, Lt 47
BACHE, 24 Capt 24 25 Richard 24
BADEN, 11 1st Lt 11 Lt 11 Nehemiah 11
BADILLO, Jose 180
BALDWIN, J A 189 196
BALL, H P 133
BALLANTYNE, J L 175
BALLARD, Peggy (Ward) 155
BALTIMORE, Lord 2
BANDHEITS, H H 174
BARDEN, W J 75
BARLOW, Joel 16
BARNETT, Betsy 152
BARROW, John C 165
BARRY, T W 143
BARUCH, Bernard 197
BASSFORD, Lt 47
BAYNE, Marmaduke G 165
BEAULAC, W L 169
BECKET, Ellerbe 195
BEHR, Dr 12
BELL, W H 31 47 William H 21 28
BENTON, Capt 76 James G 29 Lt Col 40 51 Major 50
BERENGER, 170
BERGER, S D 169
BERKHEIMER, Adjutant 68 W E 64
BESSON, 181 F S Jr 196 Frank S Jr 181 Grandma 181
BIRKHAM, Adjutant 68
BLACK, Maj 75 W M 75 83 120
BLAGDEN, George 9
BLISS, T H 143 Tasker 131
BOGGS, F C 75
BOLLING, 156 Alexander R Jr 155 Alexander R Jr 155 Kathryn 156 Raynal Cawthorne 156
BOLTE, Boys 151 C L Mrs 128 Charles L 103 153 David 151 Family 151 Gen 151 Mrs 103 Mrs C L 151 Phil 95 Philip 151
BOMFORD, 16 Col 31 George 13 16 Lt Col 15 18
BONHAM, Family 152 Ham 152 J B 152 JB 152
BOOTH, 41 53 John Wilkes 40
BORDEN, W C 83 121 W J 83
BRADFORD, Lt 47
BRADLEY, 150 156 Omar 150 156 178
BRADY, John B 67 Matthew 44
BRECKINRIDGE, Joseph C 62 Secretary Of War 140
BRERETON, Lt 47

BRESNAHAN, T F 152
BRITT, George H 11
BROWN, E I 143 Thomas B 51
  W G 169
BRUBAKER, Mrs Ed (Buckner)
  149
BRUCE, 55 R V 50 55
BRUCKER, Wilber M 172
BUCK, B B 83 Mr 28
BUCKLEY, Lt 18
BUCKNER, Simon Bolivar Jr
  149 William 149
BULL, Harold R 165
BULLFINCH, 55 Chas 33 Mr 15
BURBECK, H 174 Henry 8
BURR, E 83 Edward 75 83 137
  Maj 113
BUSH, Barbara 196 George
  172 196 Vice President 191
CABOT, J M 169
CALLAHAN, 12 Trooper 12
CALLENDER, 58 Franklin D 17
  58
CAMPBELL, 36
CAPRON, A 64
CARLSON, R 13
CARR, Irving J 169
CARROLL, 2 Daniel 2 5
CARTER, M S 179
CASS, Secretary Of War 24
CATES, Clifton B 153
CHAFFEE, Adna R 137
CHARLES, Mrs 37
CHASE, Adjutant 65
CHEEVER, Ezekiel 8
CHILDS, Lt 47
CHRISTIANSEN, Jane 155
  CHURCHILL, Winston 159
CLARK, 153 Governor 18 Isaac
  37 Mark 155 Mark W 152
  Warden 37
CLARKE, Frederick J 182
CLELAND, Capt 146
CLOSSON, 69 Henry W 69
CLUSS, Adolph 55 99
COCKBURN, Admiral 11

COLE, J 174
COLLINS, 153 "Lightning Joe"
  156 E T 174 Family 156 J
  Lawton 153 155 156 159
  178 Jerry 156 Joseph B 51
  Nancy 156
COLT, Col 47
COLTMAN, Robert 38
CONGREVE, William 16
CONNOR, Gen 147 148 W D 83
  143 147
CONNORS, W D 80
COOK, Peggy 99
COOKSEY, Althea 189 Gen
  189 Howard H 189
COOPER, Ella 149 Kenneth
  150 Kenny 151
COPELAND, W 22
COSTELLO, Frances 149 N A
  149
COX, A L 174
COXE, 142 A B 142
CRAIG, Howard A 165 M 143
  Malin 149
CRANCH, Judge 3
CROZIER, W 143
CUMMINGS, W W 125
CURRY, J R 175
CUSTIS, Elizabeth Parke 3
DADE, John B 37
DALTON, James E 170
DAVIS, 65 Leighton I 170
DAVISON, F E 175
DEAN, C D 170
DEANE, Gen 183 John R Jr
  183 Mrs 183
DEARBORN, Secretary Of War
  10
DELAUNE, Elton J Jr 190
  Grace 190
DELMAR, R H 197
DEPUY, Bill 182
DERRINGER, 18
DESAXE, Marshal 197
DEVERS, J I 174 Jacob L 149
  Jake 155 156

Index

DEWITT, 152 Gen 101 152 J L 143 151 155 162
DIGGER, Family 7
DIX, Dorothea Lynde 38
DOHLEMAN, Anne 190 K E 175 Kenneth E 190
DONALDSON, M T 174
DOUGHERTY, Thomas 15
DOWNEY, Fairfax 16
DROSKIN, Jim 99 Family 99
DRUM, H L 154 155
DUNCANSON, Captain 3
DUTTON, Clarence E 61
EASTERBROOK, Nancy (Stilwell) 155
EASTON, J W 197
EDDY, Manton 163
EISENHOWER, 138 150 D W 151 "Ike" 164 John 151 President 156 168
EKIN, James 41
ELIOT, Samuel 3
ELIZABETH, Queen of England 123
ELLIS, George C 137 Jonas 38 Mr 137
ELY, 147 Gen 146 H E 143 Madge 146
ERMANIS, Karl 195
EVANS, 18
EWELL, Dr 12
EXTON, Marjory (Grant) 89 92 146
FAIRFIELD, R J Jr 175
FARMAN, 142 143 E E 142 Lt 142
FARREL, D A 107
FERGUSON, Harley B 169
FILLMORE, President 40
FIRENBAUGH, C B 174
FISHER, R P 97
FITMAN, Thomas 38 Warden 38
FORGEY, Benjamin 195
FORSYTHE, Betsy (Barnett) 152 Gen 152

FOULOIS, B D 83
FOXHALL, 10 Henry 10
FRANKLIN, Family 180 Gen 180 Wesley C 180
FREDENDALL, Lloyd R 145
FREDERICK THE GREAT, 137 "Freddy" 137 138
FUGATE, Corporal 178 Denver 127 177
FUGER, 64
GAILEY, C K 175
GAILLARD, D D 138
GARD, Robert G 189
GAVAN, P 175
GAY, H R 174 Hobart R 159
GERHARDT, H A 197
GEROW, L T 162
GIBBONS, Henry 146
GIBSON, Alice 149 H G 64 65
GILLESPIE, G L 75
GILMORE, J C 138
GIVEN, Thomas 15
GLASSFORD, Guy 146 Pete 146
GLEZER, R M 175 Roland M 183
GOETHALS, G W 137 138
GOODPASTER, A J 196 Andrew J 165 Dorothy (Anderson) 149
GOODRICH, D M 170
GOWAN, Dorothy 92 J B 92
GRANT, 44 137 F D 137 Francis 146 Francis C 146 General 40 Marjory 89 92 146 Phil 151 President 83 U S 30 Ulysses S III 83 W S 89 143 150 Walter 146 Walter F 146
GRAVES, H D 193
GREELY, J M 174
GREENLEAF, 3 4 James 2 Lady 3
GRIFFIN, Nehemiah 15
GRISWOLD, Francis H 165
GRUENTHER, Alfred M 153

GRUNERTS, Family 149
GUASTAVINO, 133
GUENTHER, 69 70 F L 69
 Francis 64
GULLION, Allen 162
HADFIELD, George 9
HAGNER, Lt 47 Peter 29
HAGUE, Wesley McL 170
HAIG, Alexander Jr 182 Gen
 182 Mrs 182 Mrs Alexander
 Jr 182
HAINS, Col 128 Major 67 Peter
 C 128 Peter Conover 67
HALSEY, William F 150
HANCOCK, Winfield Scott 44
HARDY, John S 170
HARRIS, T H 174
HARRISON, William Henry 29
 William K Jr 153
HARROLD, Thomas L 165
HART, Thomas C 145
HAWKINS, Carlyle 193
HAWTHORNE, H L 64
HAZEN, 62
HENWOOD, Mr 23
HERO, Andrew 64
HEROLD, 41 53 David 41 99
HERRMAN, Augustine 2
HERSHEY, Lewis B 150
HIDDEN, Enoch 22
HILBERT, D C 175
HILL, H W 164 Harry W 159
 165
HOBBS, 106
HODGES, Courtney 150
HOFFMAN, Elzie S 116 Sylvia
 Ruth 116
HOGE, 109
HOLLIS, 170
HONEYCUTT, Francis W 149
 Jane 148
HOOVER, Herbert 147
HOPKINS, Steven 5
HOSMER, B C 189
HOURSON, 106
HUBERT, Father 146

HUMPHREY, Jimmy 146
HUMPHREYS, A A 150
HUNTER, David 41
HUSTER, Clare 159
HYMAN, G A 168
INDIAN, Powhatan 1
JACKSON, 137 President 44
JAMES, 9
JEFFERSON, Thomas 134
JERVEY, J P 83
JEWETT, H C 83
JOHNSON, 18 President 181 R
 L 179 R M 12 Thomas 5
 Vice President 40 William
 Coal 27
JONES, J W 169
JORDAN, Harry B 169
KAISER, The 166
KAUTZ, August 41
KEIM, D R 65
KEITH, Donald R 184
KELLER, Joe 180
KELLY, John E 165
KENNEDY, President 183
KENNEY, George C 150
KERWIN, "B" 184 "Dutch" 184
 W T Jr 184 W T Jr Mrs 184
KILBOURNE, Girl and Boy 146
KING, C T 107 H J 39 Martin
 Luther 181 Sylvia Ruth
 (Hoffman) 116
KINGMAN, J J 83
KIRBEY, William 37
KIRWAN, Emilia 191 Robert L
 191
KITTS, Mrs 146
KJELLSTROM, Dorothy 184
 John A 184
KNAUSS, W 106
KROESEN, Mrs "Fritz" 190
KROMER, Rosetta 149
KRUEGER, W 155
KUBISCH, J B 169
KUHN, J E 142 143
L'ENFANT, 5 7 21 24 76 Pierre
 1 200 Pierre Charles 5

Index

LAIDLEY, T T S 29
LAINGEN, Bruce 191 L B 169
LANCASTER, 65
LANGE, 156 H W 156
LANGFITT, W C 75 83
LARNED, George B 11
LATERI, C 123
LAVAL, J 17
LAW, Elizabeth Parke 3 Thomas 3
LAWRENCE, Richard D 189
LEAR, Ben 155
LEE, 137 Fitzhugh 165 Richard Bland 3 15 Robert E 30
LEMNITZER, Lyman 164 196 Lyman L 153
LEONHART, W 169
LEWIS, J T 174 John E 170 T E 154 Washington 3
LIGGETT, H 143
LIGHTNER, E A Jr 169
LINCOLN, 51 99 Martha 38 Mrs 40 President 40 49
LIVINGSTON, 69 Col 68 LaRhett L 68
LLOYD, P J 152
LOBDELL, Harrison Jr 165
LOVELESS, 120
LUEBKERT, 109
MACARTHUR, Doug 83 Douglas 83 148 149 Gen 149
MACHIAVELLI, 197
MACOMB, M M 143
MADISON, 12 Captain 2 James 10 Mrs James 12 Pres 12
MALONY, Anne 152 Jim 152 Thurman 152
MANEELEY, Bill 193
MANN, W A 138
MARCH, 64 70 Peyton C 64 70
MARCY, William 138
MARKHAM, Capt 76 E M 83
MARSHALL, 196 Gen 154 Geo 152 George C 195 Mrs 196
MARTIN, John S 97 N W Brothers 146

MASON, Capt 142 General 18
MCANDREW, 145 J W 143
MCCAIN, William A 169
MCCLELLAN, George B 50 S L 196
MCCLURE, Bob 152
MCCRAY, W H 114
MCDANIEL, Col 180 W A 180
MCGLACHLIN, E F 145 E F Jr 143
MCGOUGH, Edward A III 170
MCINERNEY, J E 170
MCKEE, Capt 62 George W 62
MCKIM, 74 107 133 136 Charles F 76
MCKINLEY, Edward B 159 170
MCMILLAN, James 76
MCNAIR, 154 Clare (Huster) 159 Douglas 159 Gen 154 155 157 159 L J 138 Lesley J 125 154 Mrs 155
MCNUTT, 61 62 John 61 Lt Col 61
MCPHERSON, John B 165
MEAD, 74 107 133
MEADS, 121
MEDINA, Patricia (Pachler) 179
MEIGS, Gen 62
MERRILL, D T 174
MERRYMAN, J H 191 J H Mrs 191 Jane 172 191
MICHENER, James 192
MICHIE, R E L 138
MILES, Francis H Jr 169
MILEY, Family 182 Henry A Jr 182 Mrs Henry A Jr 182
MILLER, L D 156 Mr 28 R H 169 Sonny 146
MILLS, P I 174
MITCHELL, Billy 83
MONTANDON, W 22
MOORE, 9
MORDECAI, 23 Alfred 23 Capt 28 30 31 47 Maj 29
MORRIS, 3
MORTON, C G 138 J 13

MOULTON, 51 "The Judge" 51 Hosea B 51
MUDD, Dr 44 Samuel 41
MUNDY, George W 170
MURPHY, James S 165
MURRAY, M 174
NAPOLEON, 30
NARMI, R E 189 Ronald E 170
NATHAN, A P 97 Mrs 97
NEEDLE, John 125
NEELY, Anne 152 Bill 152
NELSON, 16 17 18 Captain 16 17 Joseph S 15 Major 15 16
NICHOLSON, 3
NICKERSON, Hoffman 196
NIXON, President 182
NORTH, 18
NOTLEY, Thomas 2
O'LAUGHLIN, 44 Michael 40
O'MALLEY, C S Jr 175 Charles S Jr 181
ORD, J B 103
PACHLER, F T 179 Patricia 179
PADDOCK, 121
PAINE, Lewis 40 41 99
PALMER, Bruce 182 Charlie D "Charlie Dog" 179 Willie 179 Williston 179 Williston "Willie" B 178
PAPPAS, G S 133
PARKHURST, C D 74 Captain 74
PARKINGSON, 106
PARROTT, R P 95 Robert P 31
PATRICK, M M 75 Mason M 83
PATTON, Gen 97
PAYNE, 53
PEIXOTTO, E D 191
PENNINGTON, Alexander Cc M 64
PERKINS, Edward J 196 Samuel 9 11
PERSHING, Black Jack 145 196 Gen 83 145 J J 137 J J "Black Jack" 138

PETAIN, Henri 125
PEYTON, P B 143 152
PICKERING, Secretary Of War 8
POLK, President 138
POMEROY, 18
POND, Dana 145
POORE, Maj Gen 103
PORTER, Commodore 30 George Loring 44
POST, Calvin 22
POWELL, Colin 196 H B 178 R L 196
PRATT, F 22
PROCTOR, Redfield 67
PUSTAY, John S 189
RADFORD, A W 196
RALPH, John E 170
RAMSAUR, John B 183
RAMSAY, 49 50 55 Capt 28 G D 50 George D 27 49 64 Maj Gen 58
RAWLES, J B 69 Jacob B 64
RAYMOND, 154 Col 55 160 J E 101 154 J R 33 R R 75
RED THE BARBER, 178
REED, Maj 121 Walter 120 123
REHKOPF, Family 146 Nardy 152
REIMER, Dennis 196
RENO, Lt 47
REYNOLDS, 121 J S 120
RICHARDSON, R C III 142
RIDGWAY, 153 Matthew B 153
RINGGOLD, Lt 47 Samuel 29
ROBERTS, D C 174
ROBINS, T M 83
RODGERS, John 16
RODMAN, Thomas J 31 Thomas Jackson 16
ROGERS, 18 Hezekiah 9 10 Lt 47
ROOSEVELT, 148 Franklin D 148 166 President 134 136 137 Teddy 83 140 Theodore 138

Index 265

ROOT, Elihu 73 83 131 146 Secretary 136 139 Secretary Of War 131
ROSE, Rufus E 170
ROSS, 12 General 11 12 16
RUBINO, Nancy (Collins) 156
RUSK, Dean 171
RUSSELL, J T 133
RYAN, Marge 149 Marjory (Simonds) 92 149
SAINTJOHN, Mr 24 28
SCHALCH, 138 A 127
SCHERER, L C 138
SCHOFIELD, J M 67
SCHOMBURG, August 170
SCHWARZTRAUBER, Sayre A 191
SCOTT, 120 John Benjamin 25 Lieut 24 Winfield 171
SCOWCROFT, Brent 196
SEMPLE, Frederick 68
SENGSTACK, C P 38
SESSIONS, William S 196
SEWARD, 41 Secretary Of State 40
SEWELL, 136 Capt 136 Captain 76 John 136 John S 76
SHERIDAN, Philip 134
SHERMAN, 137
SHORT, Walter C 145
SHRAPNEL, Henry 16
SHUTTUCK, Mr 22
SIMONDS, Girls 146 Frances 149 G S 143 Gen 149 George S 148 Marjory 92 149
SIMONSON, First Lt 18 Lt 47
SKINNER, 106
SLOCUM, Bonnie 123
SMITH, 1 152 Captain 1 G I 152 H A 174 J V 170 John 1 Perry M 165 Walter B 152
SNEAD, 145
SPANGLER, 44 Edward 41
SPIER, W E 120
SPRATT, Pierce 37

STADLER, Gerald P 165
STADTLER, W E 169
STAKES, J A Jr 174
STAN, 18
STANNARD, J 116
STANTON, E M 39 Secretary 55 Secretary Of War 44 51
STEARNS, M 169
STEBBINS, E M 51
STEPHENSON, Thomas T 11
STILWELL, J W "Vinegar Joe" 155 Nancy 155
STIMPSON, Henry 142
STONE, C P 51
STRATEMEYER, George 153
STREETER, W F 175
STRONG, 64 Frederick 64
STUART, David 5 Gilbert 134
SULLIVAN, Laverne "Red The Barber" 178
SUMMERS, Harry 199
SURRATT, Anne 41 99 Mary 41 44 99 146 183 191 192 Mrs 40 53 99
SURUT, Lee E 165
SUVAROFF, 137
SWEENEY, Lt Gen 146
SYMINGTON, 21 23 John 21 28 Lt 22 35
TAFT, Secretary Of War 137
TAYLOE, John III 12
TAYLOR, 153 Maxwell 164 196 197 Maxwell D 153
TEMPLE, Herbert R Jr 192 Pat 192
THAW, Harry 75
THOMAS, C W 134 Dr 37 Ella (Cooper) 149
THOMPSON, C P 174 J K 138 James 2
THORNLEY, Thos 38
THURMAN, Roy 178
TODD, W N Jr 152
TOMPKINS, Charles 41
TONELLI, Maj 192 Mrs 192
TOWER, Charlemagne 137

TUCKER, Alice 149 Alice (Gibson) 149
TURNBULL, 65
TURNER, Jack 146
TYLER, 11 Captain 11 Charles H 51 Edwin 11
UNGERS, Oswald Mathias 195
UPHUES, 137
UPTON, L S 174
VADER, Paul F 180
VANAMAN, Arthur W 170
VANBUREN, President 24
VANDEMAN, 142 R H 138 142
VANDENBERG, 153 Hoyt S 152
VANHOUTEN, J D 174
VANNATTA, Thomas F 170
VANNESS, General 11
VAUGHAN, Lt Gen 183 Mrs 183 W W 182
VEGETIUS, 197
VILLA, Pancho 171
VILLARD, 11 A D 8 15 A J 11 Andrew 9 13 Mr 13 17
VILLIARD, 12 Mr 9
VILLIERS, Captain 8
VONSTERNBERG, Baron 137
VONSTEUBEN, Baron 134
WADE, Brevet Major 19 Major 21 William 16
WADSWORTH, Decius 12
WAINWRIGHT, Jonathan M 150
WALDRON, A E 83
WALKER, Jane (Christiansen) 155 Walton H 153
WALLACE, Lew 41
WALLING, W F 92
WARD, Edben 15 J Carlton Jr 197 Peggy 155 Robt M 155
WARREN, Francis E 138
WASHINGTON, 4 General 2 5 George 2 4 5 Martha 3 President 4 7 8
WATKINS, 18

WATT, Capt 41
WEISSINGER, Bill 152
WELLER, 121
WELLINGTON, 16 137
WELLS, William 40
WEST, Jane (Honeycutt) 148
WESTMORELAND, 182 Jean 182 "Westy" 182 William 182
WEYAND, Arline 184 Fred 184
WHEAT, John 3 16
WHEELER, A G 170
WHITE, 74 107 133 Henry 40 Stanford 74 136
WHITEHEAD, Frank 170
WHITNEY, 18
WHITTEMORE, James M 62
WICKHAM, 18 John A Jr 191 Lois 191
WILBY, F B 83
WILHELM II, Emperor Of Germany 137 Kaiser 137
WILLIAMS, 37 174 Benjamin 35 E A 152 Mrs R R 182 R R 182 Samuel T 153 Thomas 36 W E 18 47 Warden 35 37
WILMARTH, Mark 76
WILSON, Henry 61 President 82 140 166 Woodrow 82
WINN, Molly B 196
WINSLOW, E E 75 83
WIRZ, 53
WOOLDRIDGE, E Tyler 165
WOOLWINE, Walter J 170
WOOTEN, Maj 83 Sid 92 179 Sidney C 179 W P 75 179 William P 169
WOTHERSPOON, W W 139 143
WRIGHT, E K 174 George 28 49 Mr 28
YARDLEY, 143 H O 142
YERKS, R G 175
YOUNG, Mrs Benjamin 2 Notley 2 R N 174 S B M 138
YOUNGBERG, G A 83

www.ingramcontent.com/pod-product-compliance
Lightning Source LLC
Chambersburg PA
CBHW050133170426
43197CB00011B/1817